1991

TO: Suzy Rowden

On the occasion of my departure from this position, please
accept this as a reminder of more than three years of a
wonderful friendship and business relationship.

Good luck in your future business.
Thanks for your help.

Shami Waldman   District Manager   Southwestern USA
EL AL ISRAEL AIRLINES LTD.
1 Greenway Plaza East, Suite 722, Houston, TX 77~

STAR IN THE SKY

By Marvin G. Goldman
Illustrated by Mike Machat

WORLD TRANSPORT PRESS

Designed by Mike Machat

Edited & Produced by John Wegg

Typesetting by Al Beechick

Color Separations & Printing by Scott Piazza,
The Drawing Board

Manufactured in Hong Kong

Published by
World Transport Press, Inc.
P.O. Box 521238
Miami, Florida 33152
USA

ISBN 0-9626730-0-5

Library of Congress Catalog Card Number 90-70242

CONTENTS

DEDICATION

To the employees, past and
present, of El Al Israel Airlines.

FOREWORD

Raphael Harlev
President
El Al Israel Airlines

When Marvin Goldman originally approached me regarding his dream of producing an illustrated history of El Al, I noted that people who become involved with us usually find that their dreams come true. I am happy to see that his dream has indeed come true.

The plan for an airline called El Al originated with a group of dreamers, who in September 1948 believed that a new, fledgling nation and democracy in the Middle East required a national airline. They put their dream into the hands of fellow idealists, many of whom were immigrants from different countries with no airline experience, who converted military transports and began commercial operations ten months later. It was in July 1949 that the dream of a National Airline for the State of Israel became a commercial reality.

El Al's history since its humble beginnings in 1949 reflects a pattern of continuous advancement in the field of aviation. Early investment and development in an engineering and maintenance infrastructure has paid off over the years as El Al built a reputation for engineering excellence. Staff recruitment from all sectors of the Israeli Air Force has also contributed to El Al's stature in operations quality and efficiency.

In June 1961 El Al demonstrated the intercontinental ability of the Boeing 707. A world record was set by operating the longest nonstop commercial flight between New York and Tel Aviv covering 9,270km (5,760mi) in 9 hours and 33 minutes. Twenty-three years later El Al proved the safety and ability of twin-engine aircraft to perform nonstop trans-Atlantic flights as one of its Boeing 767s performed the first scheduled commercial trans-Atlantic flight, operating nonstop between Montreal and Tel Aviv.

El Al has entered the 1990s with major plans for expansion and development. New gateways to the capitals of Eastern European countries have been added, and our sights are set for the Far East as well. The Israel Government's plan to privatize El Al should provide the necessary capital to fund the purchase of $1.5 billion worth of new aircraft in the coming years. New aircraft, new destinations, as well as new financial resources, signify additional dreams that are becoming a reality.

Today, El Al is in the process of playing a major national role in the airlift of thousands of immigrants from the Soviet Union to Israel. During the course of *Operation Exodus*, El Al remains on standby to operate special immigrant flights at all times of the day or night. As a final note I am reminded of the saying that "history repeats itself". Even now as this book is being produced, we in El Al are re-experiencing history.

R. Harlev

PREFACE

by Noam Hartoch

EL AL: STAR IN THE SKY is not just another history of an international commercial airline. It is a unique record of how a small group of dedicated individuals joined together in troubled times to set up the first airline of the State of Israel, with few funds, a handful of converted military transport aircraft, pilots drawn from every corner of the world, and no past experience on how to run an airline at all! Add to this a key role in airlifts of entire Jewish communities from hostile countries, and the bizarre fact that the name El Al was carried on an aircraft well before the airline was established, and you really have the right background to relax and enjoy Marvin Goldman's thoroughly researched history of a magnificent airline, which today ranks as one of the most efficient in the world.

El Al came into being as a result of the War of Independence fought between the State of Israel and five hostile neighboring countries during May 1948 to January 1949. It grew directly out of the *Lahak Tovala Avirit* (LATA), or Air Transport Command, which was part of the newly born Israeli Air Force and a crucial cornerstone in winning the war. Without LATA's fleet of Douglas C-54 Skymasters, Curtiss C-46 Commandos and a Lockheed Constellation, the Air Force could never have become a fighting unit. These transports flew disassembled fighter planes and spare parts and ammunition from Czechoslovakia to Israel under unbelievable conditions, their crews knowing that without their efforts the young State's future would be doomed. Less than a year later, El Al passengers occupied the seats of several of these same aircraft, the majority of them unaware of the vital role they played in stopping Egyptian armored columns from reaching the heart of the land.

Fortunately, the war was soon over, most of the war-weary aircraft were refurbished and repainted (repainting was a very frequent job in El Al's hangars as you will notice in the book), and within two years the Israeli Star of David was flown in the sky to a dozen countries on four continents. El Al became the first airline outside the United States and Europe to inaugurate scheduled trans-Atlantic service, a marvelous achievement due chiefly to the high spirits of those who had the honor to be called "the first El Al employees".

Not all was rosy, however. The majority of air crews were still foreigners, most Israeli pilots were still serving with the Air Force, and the situation did not reverse itself until the second half of the 'fifties. Strong pressure was exerted on El Al to rely on Israel's own military aircraft overhaul facility (*Bedek*, later known as Israel Aircraft Industries), but El Al resisted and eventually developed its own superb independent maintenance capability. Then came the obvious question of how long El Al could continue to rely on second-class war surplus aircraft. In the early 'fifties turbine power started to be applied to commercial aircraft, and the whine of pure jets could be heard in the distance. For a well-established airline the answer was easy—get rid of the obsolete and buy the latest the manufacturers had to offer—but in the case of El Al this was a painful dilemma due to Israel's austerity economy. In a bold and courageous move, El Al's management signed up with Britain's Bristol Aeroplane Company to purchase the "Whispering Giant" Britannia turboprop aircraft, the first airline outside of the state-owned British Overseas Airways Corporation (BOAC) to do so. This decision finally put El Al on the map, as in 1957-58 it set new speed records across the Atlantic coupled with a new standard in comfortable quiet flight.

The joy of the Britannia was short-lived, however. By the end of 1958 Pan American placed the Boeing 707 pure jet into service, and soon the skies over the North Atlantic became crowded with 707s and Douglas DC-8s, all representing huge capital investments. For El Al, which struggled to finance the Britannias, this meant arranging even more funds to order its first 707s. Despite the hardships, El Al took the initiative again, starting 707 service in 1961. By the following year it was the proud owner of five new Boeing jetliners, and its propeller-driven Lockheed Constellations became history. In 1967 El Al sold its last Britannia and it became the first all-pure jet airline in the Middle East.

With the development of a more advanced Dash 200B version of the Boeing 747 "jumbo jet", El Al found the ideal aircraft for its long-haul routes to New York. In April 1973 it became the first airline to receive this model, and over the years it has continued to expand its successful all-Boeing fleet, including additional 747s as well as 737s, 757s and 767s. Meanwhile, El Al's routes more than doubled during the jet era, and today it serves over 35 destinations in regular scheduled service.

Researching the history of El Al is no easy task. In the early years few took the trouble of photographing its aircraft or facilities, or recording important events. It is thus with admiration that I have followed Marvin's attempts to put together every piece of information and locate any known photograph, so that as complete a story as possible of a great airline can be told. Enjoy reading through this book, savor the pictures, and every time you see an El Al jetliner at an airport somewhere around the world, reflect at the incredible way the airline has become a "star in the sky".

Noam Hartoch is a well-known historian of Israeli aviation, who has researched the subject for the past 20 years. Since 1975 he has held senior posts in the operations departments of the Israel Civil Aviation Administration and the Israel Airports Authority. Mr. Hartoch is an associate editor of BIAF—Israel Aviation & Space Magazine, *a member of the American Aviation Historical Society and the International Association of Aviation Historians (London). He has written several articles on the development of Israeli aviation and contributed to many books on the subject.*

ACKNOWLEDGMENTS

When artist Mike Machat and aviation editor John Wegg enthusiastically agreed to join me on this book, I knew I had two key ingredients for a successful project. I first met Mike and John through the World Airline Historical Society. Mike is noted as one of the world's leading aviation artists, having created the artwork for the recent histories of Delta Air Lines, Finnair, Lufthansa and Pan Am. In *El Al: Star in the Sky*, Mike not only prepared the cover artwork and aircraft profiles, he also took my text and illustrations and designed the layout of every page.

John Wegg had already developed an excellent reputation by writing the superb illustrated history of Finnair, a landmark in the field for thoroughness and accuracy. After 22 years in the commercial aviation industry, John established World Transport Press, where he is the editor of their publications, including the flagship magazine *Airliners*. John edited my manuscript and provided numerous helpful suggestions based on his detailed aviation knowledge. He also contributed to the fleet lists and supplied many of the photographs of El Al aircraft. My enduring thanks to John Wegg and Mike Machat as well as to the other principals of World Transport Press.

My interest in El Al arose out of my many trips to Israel on the airline. As symbolized by the Star of David carried to the skies on the tail of each El Al aircraft, El Al is the principal airlink to the world for the State of Israel, whose history it so closely parallels. El Al is also a "Star in the Sky" due to its efficiency in operations, maintenance and security, earning an almost legendary reputation in the aviation industry.

The time was also ripe for an illustrated book on El Al. Coincident with the celebration of El Al's 40th anniversary in 1988-89, many of its employees developed a heightened awareness and interest in the airline's dramatic history. This book would not have been possible without the cooperation of these dedicated personnel of El Al. In addition, although many records and memorabilia of the early days unfortunately have not been preserved, I could still gather considerable materials and interview many of the original pilots and other employees.

Within El Al, I am particularly grateful to Nachman Klieman, Company Spokesman, for his constant support, enthusiasm and a stream of information. Nachman, together with the other devoted members of El Al's public relations department, including Baruch Tirosh, Aviva Lavi and Sheryl Stein, gave me the necessary access to El Al's photographic archives and memorabilia, as well as important introductions to other El Al personnel. I am also most appreciative for the help of Mike Acharkan, Director of Technical Operations for El Al until his recent retirement. Mike is El Al's "in-house" historian and, like Nachman, kindly reviewed and commented on my manuscript.

Many others in the El Al family generously helped through interviews, access to photographs and documents, and other contributions. Among current El Al personnel, may I especially thank President Rafi Harlev for his Foreword, Corporate Secretary Ruth Arbel, Deputy Director of Training Moshe Stern, E. Lanir of El Al Cargo, Capt. Amitai Levin, Yacov Margolin and Nilly Neuberger of the Marketing Division, M. Daaman, Dvora Laish, and senior steward and trainer Yigal Levy.

My thanks also to the many former El Al personnel who similarly assisted, including Capt. Oded Abarbanel, Joyce Perlman Baron, past President Mordechai Ben-Ari, Herb Bornstein, Livia Eisen Chertoff, Capt. Sam Feldman, Capt. Yitzhak Hennenson, Joram Kagan, Capt. Bill Katz, Capt. Gad Katz, Yehuda Koppel, Capt. Maurice and Lynn Kouffman, Herbert and Greta Kweller, Ze'ev "Bubo" Landa, Capt. Sam Lewis, Capt. Norman Moonitz, Dunio and Francie Oberlander, and Capt. Danny Rosin.

Capt. Hal Auerbach, Capt. Gordon Levett, Harold Livingston and Ben Sklar, foreign volunteers for Israel who flew aircraft in El Al markings before commercial service began, provided helpful information, and useful materials were furnished by Danny Reisinger, El Al's independent design artist, and Yaacov Katz, photographer to El Al. For assistance on Arkia Israel Airlines, my special appreciation to Arkia's Corporation Secretary, Dan Yaari.

Aviation enthusiasts play a major role in any book of this nature. Among those in Israel, may I especially thank Noam Hartoch and Yehuda Borovik. Noam, the leading authority on civil aviation history in Israel, contributed the Preface, reviewed my text and made outstanding contributions to the fleet lists. Yehuda is the publisher and editor of *BIAF—Israel Aviation & Space Magazine*, a superb publication in its field.

From the wonderful cadre of aviation enthusiasts in the United States, I am grateful for the helpful information and encouragement from R.E.G. Davies, Curator of Air Transport at the Smithsonian's National Air and Space Museum and the dean of airline historians, Capt. Stanley Baumwald, David Cohen, Harvey Cohen of the Israel Government Tourist Bureau, David Farer, Richard Laurence, Jon Proctor, and the person who first introduced me to the joys of airline history, Allan Van Winkler. From England, another heartland of aviation buffs, may I thank Graham Alliance, J.M.G. Gradidge, John Havers, Peter R. Keating and Peter Marson, and from France my appreciation to Jacques Guillem and Jean-M. Magendie for providing photographs.

My quest took me to many specialized archives, and I received welcome help from John Wheeler, Public Relations Manager of Boeing Commercial Airplane Company, British Aerospace Civil Aircraft Division Photographic Department, Lt. Col. Ze'ev Lachish of the Israel Air Force Historical Branch, Micha Kaufmann of the Israel Defense Forces Archive, Israel Palgi and Zvi Zeira of the Israel Civil Aviation Administration, David Brauner of the Jerusalem Post Archives, the Israel Government Press Office Photography Department, Reuven Koffler of the Central Zionist Archives in Jerusalem, and Esther Togman of the Zionist Archives and Library in New York.

I am also indebted to Jack and Helene DeLowe and Leon and Shira Marcus for their great help to me over the years in Israel, as well as to special photography consultant William Fink.

Finally, my deepest appreciation to my wife Marilynn, and to our children, Daniel, Sharon and Haviva, for their help, patience and encouragement.

A postscript: In a book of this type an enormous amount of information has to be sifted and selected. Often I encountered different versions of particular data and events. I have included what I believe is accurate, and there is a source that I considered reliable for everything in the book. However, while numerous persons kindly assisted me, the ultimate responsibility for the final text falls on myself. I would welcome receiving additional information from readers, and comments may be addressed to me in care of the publisher, World Transport Press, Inc., P.O. Box 521238, Miami, FL 33152.

Marvin G. Goldman
May 1990

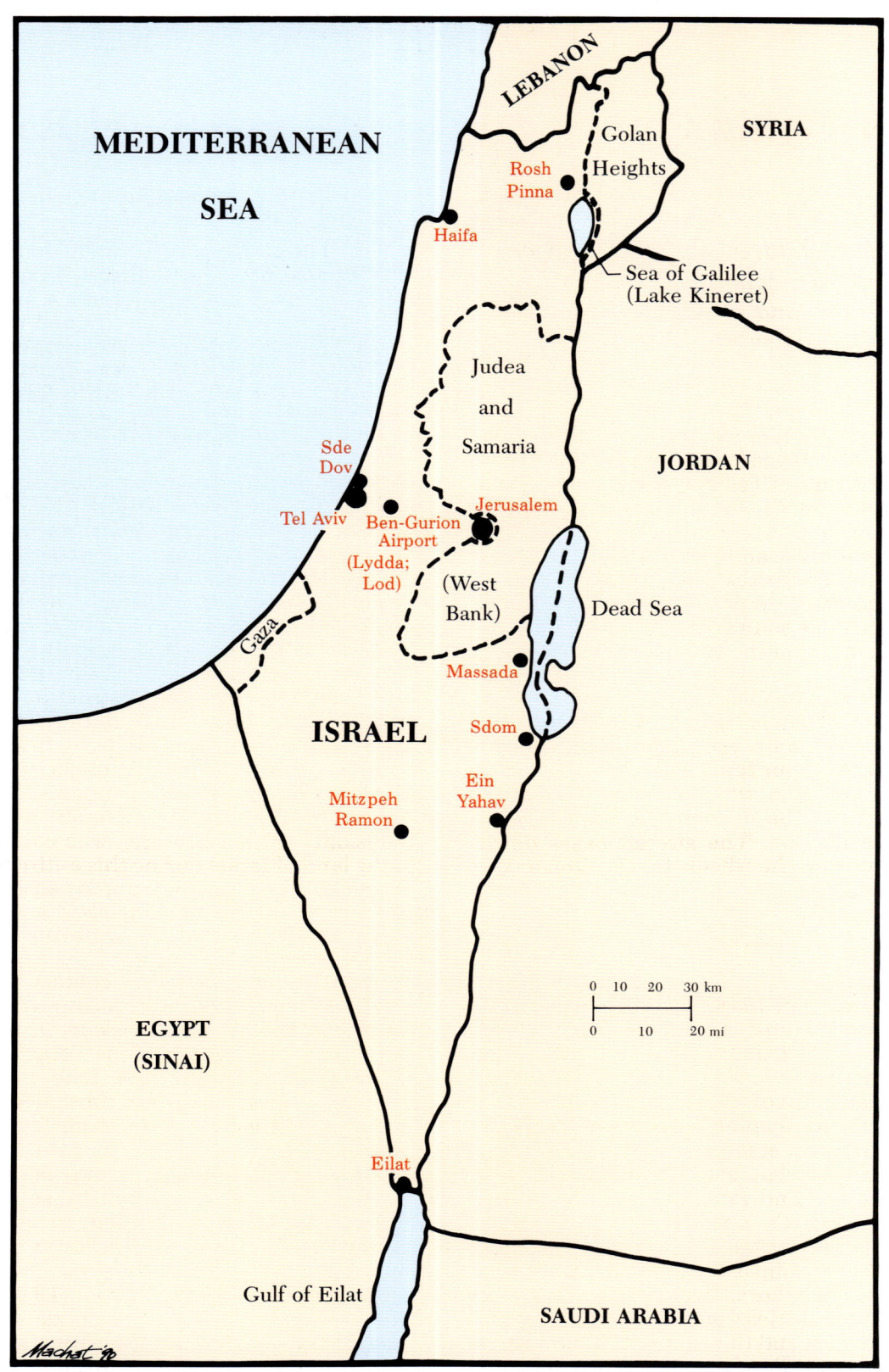

"Lydda Airport" was originally built by the British near the city of Tel Aviv and the town of Lydda, and opened for scheduled service in summer 1936. Following the establishment of the State of Israel on 14 May 1948, the Israelis renamed the town of Lydda, calling it by its biblical name of "Lod", and the airport became known as "Lod Airport". On 15 January 1974, a few weeks after the death of Israeli leader David Ben-Gurion, Israel renamed the airport "Ben-Gurion Airport". Accordingly, references to the airport at "Lydda", "Lod", "Ben-Gurion" and "Tel Aviv" are to one and the same place. In this book, "Lydda" will be used prior to 14 May 1948, "Lod" from that date through 14 January 1974, and "Ben-Gurion" thereafter.

There is a smaller airport in north Tel Aviv, but that is known as Sde Dov or Dov Field.

CHAPTER ONE

From Flying Camels to Flying Aces: Israel Reborn

"Your children shall come back to their own country ... and I will give you the land of Israel"
(Jeremiah 31:17; Yehezkiel 11:17)

"Ladies and gentlemen, we are approaching the coast of Israel now. If you look out the windows you will see the shoreline of Tel Aviv, and in another few minutes we will be landing at Ben-Gurion Airport". From your seat in El Al's jumbo 747, you see the glistening Mediterranean Sea slide by below, and Tel Aviv's hotel row on the coast appears in view, catching the golden glow of the late afternoon sun. You hear the rushing sound of the descending wing flaps and a thunk from the lowering of the landing gear as the plane crosses the shoreline and continues its smooth glide over Tel Aviv. The music of *Havenu shalom aleichem*, Israel's hopeful song of 'let there be peace unto you', fills the passenger cabin. Whether it's your first trip to Israel or one of many, your heart stirs with emotion. Now Ben-Gurion Airport and the surrounding fields and orchards fill the horizon. The aircraft eases down towards the runway, the wheels touch—you are in the Holy Land.

A mere vision in 1948, El Al today is one of the world's most advanced and efficient airlines and a true success story of international civil aviation.

The birth and rise of El Al are directly tied to the dramatic events shaping the State of Israel. El Al Israel Airlines emerged from the same desperate struggle that established Israel as a renewed homeland and sanctuary for the Jewish people. Upon Israel's declaration of independence on 14 May 1948, it was immediately attacked by the combined armed forces of its surrounding Arab neighbors. Israel's only outlet to distant friendly countries was to the West, over the Mediterranean Sea, and this route could be swiftly accessed only by air. Foreign air carriers could not be relied on to meet Israel's vital needs during hostilities. El Al was thus created as the "chosen instrument" of the State to be its civil aviation lifeline.

Miraculously, Israel's ground and air defense forces and the determination of its people repulsed the invading armies and preserved the new freedom of the fledgling State. The way was thus cleared for El Al to develop as Israel's principal airline. The path to development, however, started from almost nothing. The airline had virtually no money, no experienced executives, and little in the way of suitable aircraft or trained technical personnel. To fully appreciate the meager resources—and the imposing challenges—facing El Al at its creation, we must begin with a flashback to the struggle for the birth of the State of Israel and the crucial role of aviation.

Israel as a Jewish Homeland

The Jewish people have regarded the land of Israel as their legitimate homeland from time immemorial, promised to their Patriarchs and descendants in the Bible. For over 1,200 years until the year 70 (with only a brief interruption) a Jewish State existed in the Holy Land, with its spiritual seat at the Holy Temple in Jerusalem. That year witnessed the destruction of the Jewish State by the Romans, and thereafter the land suffered a wave of conquests by foreign interests over the centuries. The vast majority of Jews were scattered among the other nations. Yet they were joined in keeping the Jewish faith alive by thousands of their brethren who continued to live in the land of Israel during this entire period. Over these centuries the yearning for an ingathering of the Jewish people to Jerusalem and the land of Israel was repeated daily by devout Jews in their traditional prayers.

By the end of the 19th century, Palestine (as Israel was then called) was an impoverished backwater of the crumbling Turkish Ottoman empire and an insignificant part of the Turks' Arab lands in the Middle East. At this time many Eastern European Jews, faced with continued persecution in their countries, started to transform into reality their dreams and hopes of returning to their original Jewish homeland. From the 1880s through the start of World War I in 1914, several waves of Jewish immigrants returned to Palestine and settled into a harsh pioneering existence in the Holy Land.

At the end of World War I in 1918, the British and French had ousted the Turks from the Arab lands in the Middle East. Palestine, with its mixed population of Jews and Arabs, and amounting to only about 1% of the area of these Arab lands, was handed over to the victorious British under a League of Nations Mandate.

In carrying out the Mandate, the British tried to perform a balancing act between the Jewish and Arab population in Palestine. Already England's Balfour Declaration of November 1917 had acknowledged the right of the Jews to have a homeland of their own in the area of Palestine.

Jewish immigration resumed after World War I, and Jewish interests purchased and developed increasing areas of land. The Arabs, however, pressed the British in the opposite direction and also applied physical pressure on Jewish settlements in the Holy Land, culminating in a series of riots against the Jews during the 1920s and 1930s. For political reasons the British tended to side with Arab demands. Immigration of Jews to Palestine became subject to strict limits, and by the start of World War II in 1939 the British banned such Jewish immigration completely. Against this dual background in Palestine between the two world wars—that is, the politics of the British Mandate government and the rise of civil strife between the Jewish and Arab populations, civil aviation was born in the Holy Land.

Civil Aviation Under the British Mandate

Coinciding with the end of World War I in 1918, when the British took over control of Palestine, surplus military aircraft became readily available and converted to civilian use. This led to the formation by the early 1920s of the world's first significant civil airlines.

The first airfields in Palestine had been built by the Turks (with German assistance) in 1917 for military use. There were about a dozen, mostly primitive landing strips, with the more important ones located at Tzemach in the north near Tiberias (at the south shore of the Sea of Galilee), Ramle in the center (southeast of Tel Aviv), and Gaza at the southwest coast.

The first airline to operate in the Holy Land was Britain's Imperial Airways. The British governed Palestine from 1920 to May 1948 under a League of Nations Mandate. Handley Page H.P. 42 Hannibal, a giant aircraft in its day, is shown at a primitive landing strip in Gaza, Palestine, in the 1930s with the Mediterranean Sea in the background. The "G" on the aircraft signifies British registration. (Central Zionist Archives, Jerusalem)

Imperial Airways

Quite naturally, the British, as the governing authority in Palestine at the time, initiated the first civil airline service in Palestine. In 1924 the British Government consolidated a number of small British airlines into Imperial Airways, whose purpose was to connect London with the Empire. The first route to Palestine was established in January 1927 when Imperial Airways' D.H. 66 Hercules landplanes flying from Cairo to Baghdad and Basra stopped enroute at Gaza. A second Imperial Airways route to the Holy Land was started in October 1931 and continued through October 1936, using Short S.8 Calcutta and S.17 Kent flying-boats. These operated between Castelrosso (Cyprus) and Haifa Bay, and included a mail route between Cyprus, Haifa, and Alexandria (Egypt).

A third route was launched by Imperial Airways when it made Palestine a stopover on through air service between London's Croydon Airport and India. In the early morning hours of 21 October 1931 the first aircraft on this route, a Short Kent flying-boat named *Scipio*, landed on the Sea of Galilee near Tiberias. Passengers were then taken from Tiberias to Tzemach airfield on the southern lakeshore, where they continued their flight by landplane to Baghdad and Karachi. In October 1937 Imperial introduced the larger new Short S.23 C Class flying-boats, with the landings in Palestine being made either on the Sea of Galilee or the Dead Sea or Haifa Bay.

An Imperial Airways Short S.17 Kent flying-boat of the Scipio *class on the Sea of Galilee (Lake Kineret) in the early 1930s. This was a transit point linking Imperial Airways' service between Europe and the East. Passengers would continue by landplane, from Tzemach Airport at the southern shore of the lake, to Baghdad and onwards to India. Only three* Scipio *class flying-boats were built and they were in service from 1931-37. (Central Zionist Archives, Jerusalem)*

Benjamin Kahane (pointing) of the Jewish-run Flying Camel gliding club, later a hero aviator in Israel's 1956 Sinai Campaign, and Yitzhak Hennenson (seated), later a career pilot captain with El Al, with a Schneider Grunau Baby glider prior to takeoff on the beach at Bat Yam, Palestine, in June 1939. On the nose of the glider appears the name Sion *(meaning highest point or record) in Hebrew. Due in part to British limitations on the use of motorized aircraft by residents under the Mandate, early Jewish aeronautical activity had to resort initially to gliders.* (Israel Government Press Office)

The Birth of Jewish Civil Aviation

Gliders and Flying Camels

Aviation by Jewish residents in the Holy Land remained only a dream in the 1920s. The two earliest visionaries were Yisrael Shochet and Tzvi Nadav. Both foresaw the importance of aviation, not only as a commercial venture but also as a means to link and protect the Jewish settlements in Palestine. Shochet tried in the 1920s to form an aviation school and light-plane airline in Palestine. However, the British refused permission for such a venture, and in any event he lacked sufficient financial and other resources. Nadav, on the other hand, recognized that the Jews could probably get started in aviation by learning to fly gliders, in that the British would view gliding as a sporting activity and not object. In 1927 Nadav traveled to Paris to study aeronautics and gliding, with a view to starting Jewish aviation activity in Palestine upon his return.

In the early 1930s, with the increasing flow of Jewish immigrants from Europe to Palestine, a number of settlers arrived who had been active in aviation in Germany and Poland for some time. Their experience included powered aircraft as well as gliders and aircraft engineering. However, outlets for their aviation activity in Palestine were still almost nonexistent, and they had no access whatsoever to motorized aircraft. In March 1933 these early Jewish aviation enthusiasts, led by Shochet and Nadav, established the first aviation club in Palestine, called the "Flying Camel Club". The club promoted aeronautical studies, aircraft modeling and the flying of gliders. It especially attempted to interest Jewish youth, and it hoped that its activity would later expand to motorized aircraft. The official name of the club soon changed to the "Israel Aero Club", although the original "Flying Camel" name lived on in popular usage throughout the 1930s and, as we shall see, was reborn as the crew emblem for Israel's first international airline flight after independence in 1948.

Members of the Flying Camel gliding club in towing vehicle, signalling to the pilot of a Grunau Baby glider before takeoff on the beach near Bat Yam, Palestine, June 1939. (Israel Government Press Office)

Members of the Flying Camel gliding club with two of their gliders (a Wrona on the left and a Grunau Baby on the right) and a towing vehicle, setting out for training on a hill near Bat Yam, Palestine, June 1939. (Israel Government Press Office)

The Israel Aero Club remains active today and has introduced thousands of Israeli youngsters to the joys of aviation.

In April 1935 the Second Maccabiah (Jewish Olympic Games) was held in Tel Aviv. By a stroke of good fortune, it included flying competitions, and a group of Jewish glider fliers arrived from Germany with two German-built Schneider Grunau Baby gliders. One of the participants, Ernst Rappaport, was a judge by profession, a fine track and field athlete and, most importantly for Israeli civil aviation, one of the best glider pilots in Germany. After the Maccabiah Games, the participants from Germany left their gliders in Palestine, and Rappaport and others decided to settle there. He became the main glider instructor of the Jewish aviation enthusiasts. One of his initial pupils was Yitzhak Hennenson, who later rose to become a captain with El Al. Another early glider enthusiast, Uri Breier, became, in August 1952, the first native Israeli to captain an El Al aircraft on international flights.

Training courses in gliding started in 1935 at Mount Carmel in Haifa, and activity soon spread to other locations. Two additional gliders were purchased, each Polish, a Chaika and a Wrona. During 1937-39 the principal courses were held at Givat Hamoreh, near Kfar Yeladim in the Jezreel Valley. Dozens of enthusiasts thus received their introduction to aeronautics on gliders.

"Our Own Very First Airplane"

Simultaneous with the formation of the Flying Camel Club, another Jewish settler in Palestine, Yitzhak Chizik, set out to transform the dream of motorized aircraft into reality. He traveled to England to study aviation and returned to Palestine in 1934 holding a commercial pilot's license. He then met with two key figures, David Ben-Gurion and Dov Hoz, urging the purchase of an aircraft and the establishment of a school of Jewish aviation. Ben-Gurion was a political leader who later became Israel's first Prime Minister, and Israel's main international airport is now named after him. Dov Hoz was another advocate of Jewish aviation, and the north Tel Aviv airport in Israel is now named Sde Dov or Dov Field in his memory. Chizik received expressions of support from both of them and managed to scrape up enough money from national Jewish institutions in Palestine to purchase the first airplane for Jewish aviation in the Holy Land. It was a new single-engine de Havilland D.H.82A Tiger-Moth (British registry G-ACYN) acquired by Chizik and Dov Hoz in England in September 1934. That fall, David Ben-Gurion whispered to a gathering in Warsaw of Jewish leaders supporting increased immigration to Palestine, "we even have our own very first airplane".

Above: *A rare photograph of the first motorized aircraft of the Jewish settlement in Israel, a British-registered de Havilland D.H.82A Tiger Moth acquired through Israeli aviation pioneers Yitzhak Chizik and Dov Hoz in September 1934, taken at Lydda Airport, about 1938. In the background are two KLM (Royal Dutch Airlines) DC-3s being refueled enroute from Holland to the Far East. (Capt. Yitzhak Hennenson collection)*

Above, left: *Instructor Uri Breier, later one of El Al's first native Israeli pilots, with one of the members of the Flying Camel gliding club, during training on a Polish Wrona glider near Bat Yam, June 1939. (Israel Government Press Office)*

Left: *Ernst Rappaport, the first leading Jewish instructor on gliders in the Holy Land (on left), seen with future El Al pilot Yitzhak Hennenson, at a meteorological station at Lydda Airport, about 1938. (Capt. Yitzhak Hennenson collection)*

Aviators of the Aviron flying school, secretly run by the Jewish Haganah defense forces, near Kibbutz Afiqim, Jordan Valley, on 10 June 1938, with an RWD 8 Polish-built training aircraft (VQ-PAK). Sitting (left to right) are Israeli aviation pioneers Yitzhak Ben Yaacov (head of Aviron), Immanuel Zur (chief instructor of Aviron, and head of Lod Airport in December 1948), Emil Pohorilla (head engineer and maintenance manager) and Dov Hoz (a leader of Aviron, in charge of operations to help Jewish security). Yitzhak Ben Yaacov and Dov Hoz were tragically killed in an auto accident in 1940. Today the airport at Rosh Pinna, Israel, is named after Ben Yaacov, and the airport at north Tel Aviv, Dov Field, is named after Dov Hoz. (Israel Government Press Office)

Aviron

On 21 July 1936, the first Jewish civil aviation company was formed in Palestine, called Aviron—The Palestine Aviation Company Ltd. Aviron, which in Hebrew means "airplane", was established by various Jewish national institutions in Palestine, including the *Histadrut* Federation of Labor and the Jewish Agency. Behind the scenes it was also supported by the *Haganah*, the Jewish group dedicated to the defense of Jewish settlements and the precursor of the present-day Israel Defense Forces. Aviron's stated goals were to conduct a flying school for Jewish aviators and to develop internal commercial flights between Tel Aviv and Haifa and the Jordan Valley. It also had a third goal—to serve the *Haganah* in reconnaissance and defense missions—but this had to be carried out secretly because such activities were discouraged by the British authorities who viewed them as a threat to the balance of forces between the Arab and Jewish communities.

Aviron's flying school started in Afiqim near the Sea of Galilee in March 1938 with the sole Tiger Moth, a two-seat Polish RWD 8, and a high-wing, three-seat Polish RWD 13. By early 1940 Aviron owned nine aircraft, all single-engine: two RWD 8s, two RWD 13s, a five-seat RWD 15, three American-built Taylorcrafts, and one British Miles M.3A Falcon Major. These aircraft were mainly used as civil trainers, but they also served Jewish national interests by acting as spotter planes to protect groups of workers engaged in road and building construction in remote locations and by dropping essential supplies of food and ammunition to settlers in new outposts, especially during

the harsh winter periods. Other Aviron activities included the purchase and sale of small civilian aircraft and the operation of an aircraft repair and mechanical workshop.

Many Israelis received their first training on motorized aircraft through Aviron, including two of El Al's original Israeli pilots, Uri Breier and Yitzhak Hennenson. Aviron also flew some charter flights within Palestine and eventually flew regular service to Tiberias on the Sea of Galilee in the north, until World War II curtailed all activity in 1942.

Israeli Postal Service first day cover issued in 1985 showing the D.H.82A Tiger Moth pictured opposite. (Marvin Goldman collection)

Palestine Flying Service

Another Jewish flying school, called the Palestine Flying Service, started in January 1939 at Lydda Airport itself, with the open approval of the British Mandate authorities. The school was the brainchild of an American Jew, Moshe Chaim Katz, who teamed up with Edwin (Leibowitz) Lyons, an American who arrived in Palestine in a Taylorcraft, fleeing from Spain where he had participated in air operations for the Spanish Republicans, and Avraham Schechterman, a leader of the then-illegal Jewish underground movement called *Etzel*. Training was given on three Taylorcrafts and other small single-engine aircraft, and instruction covered aeronautics and aircraft repair. The first class graduated on 21 April 1939 in an impressive gathering at Lydda

Airport, presided by British High Commissioner Harold McMichael.

The graduates were the first Jews to receive pilot licenses in the Holy Land. Like Aviron, this school also had a secret mission—to train Jewish settlers in aviation skills for defense purposes. However, whereas Aviron conducted its training in the relatively remote Jezreel Valley, remarkably the Palestine Flying Service did it under the very nose of the British Mandate authorities at Lydda. Nevertheless, the advent of World War II brought the courses of the Palestine Flying Service to a close.

Flying cadets and instructors in front of U.S. Taylorcraft training aircraft at the Palestine Flying Service school, Lydda Airport in April 1939. The school was founded in March 1937 by Moshe Chaim Katz, assisted by head instructor Ed Lyons (Leibowitz), both originally from the U.S. Unknown to the British, the school served to train members of the Jewish underground Etzel *organization. (Israel Government Press Office)*

Pilot training at the Palestine Flying Service at Lydda Airport, April 1939. (Israel Government Press Office)

The graduation of the first class of the Palestine Flying Service, Lydda Airport, April 1939. Aircraft include VQ-PAH, a Taylorcraft used as a trainer by the school; SU-ABQ, a de Havilland Dragon Rapide of Misrair, an Egyptian airline serving Palestine; G-ABTJ Artemis, an Imperial Airways Armstrong Whitworth Atalanta, serving the Middle East, Africa and the Far East; G-AAUE Hadrian of Imperial Airways, a Handley Page 42 of the Hannibal class, flown on routes as far as India; and VQ-PAF, a three-engine Fokker XVIII of Hevra Avirit Miskharit, a company that transported fish from Aqaba, Transjordan, to Lydda. The two aircraft in front of VQ-PAH are Taylorcrafts VQ-PAI and PAJ and have graduating pilots standing by them. In the foreground are members of several Jewish organizations. (Israel Government Press Office)

Airport Development Under the British

Meanwhile, the British started developing additional airfields in Palestine. A small airfield was opened in 1934 at Haifa, originally to serve the Anglo-Iraqi petroleum company, and another was paved in 1938 in north Tel Aviv, the present Sde Dov or Dov Field.

The main development by far, however, was the British decision in the early 1930s to construct a major international airport at Lydda (renamed "Lod" by the Israelis, and today Israel's main airport, "Ben-Gurion"). Politics motivated the British decision, as they envisioned Lydda Airport as an alternative international center for their Middle East operations and routes to the East if for any reason they were forced out of neighboring Egypt.

Work started on Lydda Airport in 1934, and two years later it was ready for scheduled passenger services. In summer 1936 the Egyptian airline Misrair started regular service to Lydda, using de Havilland D.H.89A Dragon Rapide aircraft, on its routes linking Cairo, Nicosia, Beirut and Baghdad.

By April 1937 Lydda boasted four fully operational concrete runways of about 800 meters (2,600ft) each, two of which were soon extended to 1,200 meters (3,900ft). Together with a remarkably modern passenger terminal building of three stories, topped by a glass-enclosed control tower, Lydda Airport provided the finest facility of its day in the Middle East. This proved to be an open invitation to international air carriers, and from July 1937 through 1938 many airlines introduced regular scheduled service to and through Lydda. Holland's KLM started utilizing Lydda to refuel its Fokker aircraft enroute from Amsterdam to Batavia in the Dutch East Indies (now Indonesia). LOT Polish Airlines started weekly service from Warsaw, via Sofia and Athens, using Douglas DC-2 and Lockheed 14 aircraft. CSA, the Czechoslovakian carrier, started service from Prague, via Rome, using Douglas DC-3s.

Britain's Imperial Airways also started flying into Lydda to refuel its giant aircraft of that era, the four-engine Handley Page 42 Hannibal Class and Armstrong Whitworth XV Atalanta Class, on the London–Bombay route. Each H.P. 42 aircraft had a wingspan of 40 meters (130ft), and to service them Imperial built a huge hangar at Lydda in 1937. This hangar is still in use today by El Al for some of its Boeing jets. Meanwhile, Imperial Airways (which became BOAC in April 1940) continued its regular flying-boat passenger service to the Sea of Galilee until 1942 when, following the crash of a flying-boat there due to stormy weather, it shifted its water operations to the Dead Sea and to Haifa Bay.

In 1938 Air France, SABENA and Swissair, all using DC-3s, joined the international airlines serving Lydda, with routes from Paris, Brussels and Zürich respectively. Also, starting in April 1937, Italy's Ala Littoria provided service from Brindisi to Haifa Bay with its unusual three-engine twin-hulled Savoia Marchetti S.66 flying-boats.

Palestine Airways Limited

The British, Jewish and international aviation activity in Palestine was joined by yet another entrant. In December 1934, the first purely commercial airline based in Palestine was established by Pinchas Ruttenberg, the Jewish head of the electric company in Palestine, with funds from Jewish and British sources. Ruttenberg's approach differed from that of Chizik, Ben-Gurion and other Jewish pioneers. By emphasizing the commercial aspect, including an affiliation with Imperial Airways for crew and technical assistance, and by deferring the goal of Jewish aviator training and aviation defense as pursued by Aviron, Ruttenberg obtained British permission to form Palestine Airways Limited (in Hebrew, Land of Israel Airways Limited).

British-built Short S.16 Scion of Palestine Airways Limited, the first airline based in the Holy Land. Scheduled service started in August 1937 between Lydda Airport and Haifa, Israel, and was extended to Beirut, Lebanon, in June 1938. For aircraft registration purposes, the letters "VQ" were assigned to British Mandate Palestine. Shown is VQ-PAA, the first aircraft registered in Palestine, at Beirut Airport, about 1938. (Noam Hartoch collection)

Palestine Airways started by acquiring two Short S.16 Scion high-winged fabric-covered aircraft, with twin Pobjoy engines and seating six passengers. These were the first two aircraft registered in the Holy Land, obtaining registrations VQ-PAA and -PAB, "VQ" being one of the prefixes allocated to British colonies and protectorates. The Scions could fly at a top speed of 206kph (128mph) and had a maximum range of 630km (390mi). In 1939 the airline also acquired a fabric-covered twin-engine de Havilland D.H.89A Dragon Rapide biplane (VQ-PAC) and a Short S.22 Scion Senior (VQ-PAD).

In August 1937, with its Short S.16 Scion aircraft and Imperial Airways crew, Palestine Airways commenced thrice-weekly service between Lydda and Haifa. In June 1938 it extended its route to Beirut, inaugurating the first international service by a local airline. Soon thereafter Palestine Airways moved its operations to the newly-constructed Dov Field north of Tel Aviv, boosting its Haifa service to daily frequency. At the end of 1939 the airline added regular service to Larnaca, Cyprus, and charter flights to Egypt.

A rare photograph of the only four-engine aircraft with British Mandate Palestine civil registration, Palestine Airways' Short S.22 Scion Senior (VQ-PAD), in service only for a few months during 1939-40 prior to impressment into the Royal Air Force. The name on the aircraft in Hebrew reads "Land of Israel Airways Limited". (Noam Hartoch collection)

Weighing in for a Palestine Airways flight, February 1939. Imperial Airways crew piloted and serviced the aircraft and handled passenger check-in. Note the posters of Imperial Airways and Palestine Airways on the wall and the KLM poster on the table. (Israel Government Press Office)

The Impact of World War II

The outbreak of World War II shattered the rising international position of Lydda Airport. By June 1940 all foreign carriers except Britain's Imperial Airways and Egypt's Misrair halted service to Palestine. The aircraft of Palestine Airways were impressed in August 1940 by Britain's Royal Air Force for use as transport and communication aircraft in the war effort, and it was never revived as an airline. The Palestine Flying Service school closed, and its light aircraft were acquired by Aviron. While Aviron continued in existence, its activities were sharply reduced, and its scheduled flights were suspended by 1942. Lydda Airport was converted mainly to military use. In fact, as part of the Allied war effort, during 1943-44 it came under the control of the United States Air Force. During 1943 its four runways were all extended to lengths ranging from approximately 1,100-2,000 meters (3,600-6,560ft). In 1944, as the German threat in the Middle East subsided, Aviron initiated service four times a week between Lydda and Haifa. The following year, at the end of World War II, Aviron looked forward to route expansion. However, all attempts at regular international passenger service were stifled by the negative attitude of the British Mandate Government. Aviron therefore was limited to operating some charter flights with small aircraft. Its "fleet" included a de Havilland Dragon Rapide, two Polish RWD 13s, an RWD 15, and a handful of assorted even smaller aircraft. Most charters were within Palestine, but a few using the Dragon Rapide ventured to Nicosia, Cyprus, and even to some European capitals including London.

Aviron's post-war civil aviation activity, however, was short-lived as it was soon engulfed by the impending battle over the future of the Holy Land.

Inside the Short S.16 Scion aircraft of Palestine Airways, February 1939. The fabric-covered metal frame aircraft seated six passengers. One passenger is reading the Hebrew newspaper Ha'aretz, *still published today in Israel.* (Israel Government Press Office)

Israeli Postal Service first day cover issued in 1985 as part of a four-stamp set commemorating the beginning of aviation in the Holy Land, showing Short S.16 Scion VQ-PAA, the first aircraft of Palestine Airways. (Marvin Goldman collection)

Palestine Airways Short S.16 Scion at newly paved Dov Field ("Sde Dov"), named after Dov Hoz, in north Tel Aviv, 1938. Note the words Tel Aviv in the circle in Hebrew and English. The airport today serves as the base of Arkia Israeli Airlines and several smaller Israeli domestic carriers. (Israel Government Press Office)

End of the British Mandate

With World War II over, the British announced their intent to end the Mandate and pull out of Palestine as soon as practicable. The Jewish population, witnessing a continuing rise of Arab violence, desperately sought the means to defend themselves. Secretly they tried against seemingly impossible odds to circumvent the British prohibitions against Jews immigrating to Palestine or holding arms. On 29 November 1947 the United Nations General Assembly voted to partition Palestine into two separate countries. One would be a new Arab state. The other, only one-eighth the size of the homeland originally envisioned in Britain's Balfour Declaration and Mandate, would be the first Jewish state to exist in 2,000 years. The British then announced the date of their anticipated withdrawal from Palestine as 14 May 1948. The official Jewish institutions in Palestine reluctantly accepted the United Nations decision, but the Arab leaders immediately denounced it. Soon the Arabs, determined to wipe out the Jewish state before it was born, streamed infiltrators across the borders and began attacking Jewish settlements. The British did little to prevent these attacks, jeopardizing the Jews' already precarious position.

From the aviation standpoint, the Jews had only a rag-tag collection of antiquated civil aircraft. Moreover, the use of these few aircraft for defense or military purposes was prohibited by the British. Nevertheless, an illegal, secret Jewish air force called *Sherut Ha'avir* ("Air Service") was formed in November 1947 to airlift supplies to the beleaguered Jewish settlements until the British withdrawal and to help defend the new State of Israel immediately thereafter. Aviron, the only civil air service in Palestine, collaborated with the Sherut Avir, providing several of its few aircraft for specific missions against Arab infiltrators and even procuring additional small civil aircraft that could later be used if necessary for military purposes.

Although the Arabs living alongside the Jews in Palestine had no air force capability of their own, the surrounding Arab states—Egypt, Transjordan and Syria—as well as nearby hostile Iraq, amassed numerous fighter and bomber aircraft and threatened to attack the Jewish settlement immediately upon withdrawal of the British.

The Aviron airline ground transportation fleet at Lydda Airport, 25 October 1947. Note the Aviron logo plaque on the wood door of the car in the foreground. The stylized bird with wings outstretched over Israel became the first symbol of Arkia Israeli Airlines upon its formation with 50% El Al ownership in late 1949. (Israel Government Press Office)

Inspecting passenger documents on 25 October 1947 for an Aviron flight at Lydda Airport in front of Dragon Rapide VQ-PAR. In the background at left is the tail of a British Royal Air Force C-47 Dakota. The female passenger is Rachel Cohen, then with the Va'ad Le'Ummi (the governing council of the Jewish settlement in Palestine) and later a member of the first elected Knesset, the legislative body of the State of Israel. (Israel Government Press Office)

De Havilland D.H.89A Dragon Rapide, VQ-PAR, at Lydda Airport, 25 October 1947. It was the main aircraft of Aviron (Palestine Aviation Co. Ltd.), the first passenger airline owned by Jewish interests in the Holy Land, with secret ties to the Haganah Jewish defense forces. To the left of the cockpit, mounted on the wing, is a wind generator which powers the aircraft's instruments. Behind the cockpit, on the top of the fuselage, is a radio direction finder. (Israel Government Press Office).

The Mahal

By late 1947 the *Haganah* Jewish defense force possessed fairly capable military ground personnel, but a trained Israeli air force was virtually nonexistent. Faced with a woeful and dangerous mismatch in the air war defense effort against its neighboring hostile Arab countries, the Jewish population in Palestine turned to foreign volunteers—for trained pilots, supplies and aircraft. These volunteers, from the United States, Canada, England, South Africa, Holland and other countries, became known as *Mahal*, the Hebrew acronym for *Mitnaddevei Hutz la-Aretz* (Foreign Volunteers).

From the United States, one of the principal volunteers for the Jewish cause of independence was Al Schwimmer. In 1947, with the backing of the *Haganah*, Schwimmer formed an aviation company, Schwimmer Aviation in Burbank, California, to purchase and recondition war-surplus transport aircraft for the eventual purpose of assisting Israel in its struggle for independence. The acquisitions, in late 1947, included three Lockheed C-69s (the military version of the Model 49 Constellation) and ten Curtiss C-46 Commandos. Eventually, the C-69s became El Al's first three Constellations, and many of the C-46s also formed part of El Al's early fleet. However, there was no El Al in anyone's mind in 1947. The goal at that time was to somehow fly these aircraft to Israel to help during the anticipated war of independence.

Schwimmer's group also recruited experienced air crews and conducted pilot retraining. He was assisted by two other Americans from Boyle Heights in East Los Angeles who served with Schwimmer in the U.S. Air Force during World War II, Sam Lewis and Leo Gardner, both of whom were to later become captains for El Al.

A tremendous obstacle, however, soon confronted Schwimmer. The United States and

Al Schwimmer, who acquired the World War II-surplus Curtiss C-46s and Lockheed Constellation that were spirited out of the U.S. via Panama to Israel for use as arms transports from Czechoslovakia to Israel in the Israeli War of Independence in 1948. Several of the C-46s and the Constellation became early El Al aircraft. Schwimmer himself later settled in Israel and founded Israel Aircraft Industries. (Israel Aircraft Industries collection, via BIAF—Israel Aviation & Space Magazine)

virtually all other nations imposed an embargo against shipments of arms (including large transport aircraft) to Palestine—even though this action assisted the Arabs because they already had substantial supplies. To circumvent the embargo, Jewish interests formulated a clandestine scheme worthy of a spy thriller. Among the participants were Schwimmer, Teddy Kollek (later to become Mayor of Jerusalem) and Yehuda Arazi of the *Haganah*, one of the master spies of all time. The secret connection became Panama! Tocumen Airport in Panama City had just been built and was sadly under-utilized, a veritable white elephant. The Panamanian Government, eager to develop Tocumen, accepted warmly a proposal by these

Jewish interests to set up a new private commercial airline in Panama, to be known as Lineas Aéreas de Panama, S.A. ("LAPSA"). The war-surplus aircraft purchased by Schwimmer would be registered to LAPSA and flown to Panama, ostensibly for commercial service based at Tocumen. In reality, however, LAPSA would serve as a cover to spirit the aircraft out of the U.S. and eventually fly them to Israel if and when war with the Arabs appeared inevitable.

In preparation for the risky flights to Panama and Israel, Schwimmer Aviation started overhaul work on the aircraft at its Burbank base during winter 1947-48. On 13 March 1948, the first of the C-69 Constellations, in LAPSA colors and with a Panamanian registration (RX-121), was flown by Capt. Sam Lewis to Tocumen Airport from an interim base in Millville, New Jersey, via Kingston, Jamaica. The C-46 Commandos followed a few weeks thereafter, although one was lost in a tragic crash on takeoff from Mexico City. Each had been severely overloaded with electronic equipment urgently needed for the anticipated war. Meanwhile, the United States Federal Bureau of Investigation, having received information that the aircraft were ultimately destined for Israel, set off in hot pursuit of the two remaining Constellations and, at the last minute, seized them before they could leave the U.S.

In Palestine itself, civil strife between Jews and Arabs escalated sharply in January 1948, and the violence intensified with each succeeding month. The only country willing to sell arms to the Jews was, astonishingly, Czechoslovakia. Ironically, the Soviet Union, motivated by anti-British policy, supported the birth of the State of Israel. While the Soviets would not sell arms to Jewish interests directly, it allowed its satellite Czechoslovakia to do so.

The Jewish interests in Palestine, however, lacked any means of transporting the Czech arms in quantity. Moreover, by April 1948 Arab belligerency forced them to evacuate Lydda Airport and, when the British withdrew two days later, the Arabs were left in sole possession of the airport. External air communications by Jewish interests were then shifted north to Haifa and Ein Shamer. At the same time, the international air carriers abandoned Lydda and re-routed their services via Cairo. Thus, the Jewish community in Palestine was isolated from international air service.

Meanwhile, as the fateful day of British withdrawal from Palestine approached, the Jewish volunteer pilots and technicians at Tocumen, Panama, hastened to prepare their aircraft for the trans-Atlantic flight to Africa and then to the anticipated new State of Israel, but time was running out. On 8 May 1948, with aircraft preparation and crew training only partially complete, the first five C-46s took off for Israel via Paramaribo, Dutch Guiana (now Surinam); Natal, Brazil; Dakar, French West Africa (now Senegal); Casablanca, Morocco; and Catania, Sicily.

As planned, on 14 May 1948, the British withdrew their remaining troops from Palestine and the Mandate ended. Immediately, David Ben-Gurion and other Jewish leaders proclaimed the independence of the State of Israel. The very next day the newborn State was attacked. Without warning, but not unexpectedly, Egyptian Douglas C-47s bombed Tel Aviv and their Spitfires attacked airfields, unopposed. With Israel blockaded on all sides, its very existence depended on sea and air communications with a few friendly, but distant countries. Soon, however, the "LAPSA" aircraft flown out of the U.S. through Panama started to arrive. Two of the C-46s (registered RX-135 and -138) landed in Israel at Ekron Air Base south of Rehovot on the night of 18 May. After disgorging their loads of precious equipment, they lifted off the next morning for Zatec, Czechoslovakia to help in the arms airlift. The other C-46s proceeded directly to Czechoslovakia to pick up arms.

Meanwhile, the lone C-69 Constellation (RX-121) slipped away from Tocumen on 19 May, under the command of Sam Lewis and with Maurice Kouffman as co-pilot, destined for Zatec, Czechoslovakia via Paramaribo, Dakar and Casablanca. The new Israeli government then forged the Constellation and the C-46s into a somewhat autonomous group called the "Air Transport Command" (in Hebrew, *Lahak Tovala Avirit* or "LATA") under the direction of Munya Mardor, a Haganah arms-acquisition specialist who had been based in Europe. Sam Lewis was appointed the chief pilot in charge of operations at Zatec.

The C-46s and sole Constellation proved invaluable to the arms airlift from Czechoslovakia. The arms included disassembled and crated Czech-built Avia C.210 (Messerschmitt Bf 109G) fighters, which on arrival in Israel were hurriedly assembled for immediate action. By 29 May the first four Messerschmitts were launched over Israeli skies, ending the dominance of the Egyptian Air Force during the first two weeks of the War of Independence. The Israeli fighter pilots managed

---

Panamanian-registered Curtiss C-46 RX-138 later became El Al aircraft 4X-ACG. (via Noam Hartoch)

21

The Lockheed C-69 Constellation flown from the U.S. to Israel for use as an arms transport during Israel's War of Independence in 1948. To circumvent the then-existing U.S. arms and aircraft embargo on the Middle East, it was registered in Panama under the guise of a fictitious Panamanian airline, Lineas Aéreas de Panama, S.A. ("LAPSA"). The Panamanian registration RX-121 together with the flag of Panama is painted on the tail of the Constellation. The photo is actually taken from a postcard produced in Panama to advertise the airline LAPSA and to promote the illusion that it was a real operating airline! The Constellation RX-121 later became El Al's 4X-AKC. (BIAF—Israel Aviation & Space Magazine)

to shoot down some Egyptian bomber and fighter aircraft, and the Arabs unexpectedly abandoned their air offensive shortly thereafter. The Czech airlift continued until shut down by the Czechs in August 1948. Ninety-five precious trips were flown, carrying to Israel 25 Avia/Messerschmitt fighters, spare parts, flying personnel, and 350 tons of munitions.

Early in July 1948 the Israel Defense Forces managed to recapture Lydda Airport (now renamed Lod by the Israelis). However, the airport had been extensively damaged by the Arabs and required much reconstruction. Not until 24 November 1948 was Israel able to announce that Lod Airport was ready for regular civilian air traffic.

Meanwhile, two war-surplus Douglas C-54s (the military designation for the DC-4) were acquired in May 1948 in Europe and used as arms transports, as bombers, and as the lead aircraft for flights of Spitfires (also acquired in Europe) from Czechoslovakia to Israel. Also that month four Douglas C-47 Dakotas (a military version of the DC-3) were acquired in South Africa and flown to Israel where they were used for local transport and bombing. Another transport was acquired when an Air France DC-3 at Dov Field was damaged by an Egyptian strafing attack on 15 May. France abandoned the DC-3, but the Israeli Air Force retrieved the plane and restored it to flying condition.

On 22 August 1948 Israel launched the appropriately-named *Operation Dust* to save Jewish settlements in the south (the Negev) cut off

from the main part of Israel by Egyptian troops and only accessible by air. A 1,230-meter (4,030ft) dirt runway was built near the desert settlement of Ruhama in the Negev, about 40 kilometers (25 miles) south of Ekron Air Base. Due to the danger of Egyptian attack, flights to the Ruhama airstrip had to be at night, and there were no radio beacons or other navigational aids. As each plane approached in the dark, it would flash signals, kerosene-filled smudge pots lining the runway would be lit, and the plane would land in a cloud of dust. This operation lasted two months and totaled 417 flights, mainly between Ekron and Ruhama, moving 2,200 tons of supplies and 1,900 men into the Negev, and returning many wounded and exhausted men to central Israel. Six C-46 Commandos, five C-47 Dakotas, one C-54 Skymaster, and six single-engine Noorduyn Norsemen were involved in *Operation Dust* which helped saved the Negev during the War of Independence.

The heavy transports were piloted almost exclusively by *Mahal* volunteers as almost no Israelis had the necessary experience. The few who might have been qualified were assigned mainly to other tasks such as procurement, recruiting and administration.

By late summer 1948 the Israelis had at last secured the upper hand in the conflict. Although the signing of an armistice was still months away, the nation could at least see the way clear to the start of normalcy, including the resumption of civil aviation. The stage was set for the founding of El Al, Israel's national airline.

CHAPTER TWO
El Al to the Skies: The DC-4 Era

"Ve-el al yik-ra-u-hu"—*"And they (the Prophets) shall call them to the above"*

(Hosea 11:7)

On 18 August 1948, just three months after Israel's declaration of independence, the Israeli Provisional Government formally decided to establish a civil airline for the State. The official document, issued by the Ministry of Transport headed by David Remez, called for the State to create and invest in one airline as a "chosen instrument" for international civil aviation.

The blockade against Israel during and immediately before the War of Independence sharply emphasized the need for a strong civil airline. Israel was bordered on three sides by hostile Arab States—Syria, Jordan (formerly Transjordan) and Egypt (plus nonsupportive Lebanon). Only the Mediterranean Sea, forming the western boundary, offered some kind of security. Foreign airlines had cut their service to Israel during the war, and the new State obviously could not rely on them to meet its basic needs. From the beginning, therefore, Israel required its own airline to serve as a "lifeline" with the outside world. Moreover, its new air force would require a nonmilitary aviation entity to provide parallel technical capabilities and a reservoir of aviation skills. These are some of the special circumstances that led to the creation of El Al, and they have decisively influenced its role ever since.

The problems of founding a new airline were overwhelming. The State remained locked in a bloody war, struggling for its very survival. Its economy was in shambles, its Government financially insolvent. Meanwhile, the remnants of European Jewry from the Nazi Holocaust languished in displaced person camps in Germany, Cyprus and elsewhere in Europe. Upon arrival in Israel these refugees had to be housed, fed, re-educated and re-established. At the same time, Jews in other Middle East countries, threatened and often attacked in their native Arab lands, urgently needed evacuation to safety and a new life in Israel.

Yet where would the experienced airline pilots and crew be found? The British, during their Palestine Mandate, had sharply curtailed the ability of local Jewish interests to engage in flying, so very few native Israelis managed to acquire any aviation training. Also, the scarce transport aircraft possessed by the State were already over-extended for the war effort.

The Israeli military Air Transport Command, where the *Mahal* foreign volunteers were especially active, contained the sum total of air transport experience at the time. David Remez therefore turned to the Air Transport Command's Director, Munya Mardor, for assistance in starting the newly authorized airline. However, even before Remez and Mardor could begin, the State was suddenly thrust into creating a so-called "national airline" when none really existed. This was the setting for the first flight—the one that brought Israel's first President, Chaim Weizmann, home.

The First Flight of the National "Airline"

In late September 1948 the newly designated first President of Israel, Chaim Weizmann, was on a temporary stay in Geneva, Switzerland. The Israeli Government, eager to show the world that Israel was now a truly independent State, wanted to bring him home in an Israeli aircraft. However, all of the Israeli aircraft capable of making the trip were in service with the military Air Transport Command. Israeli military aircraft were not permitted to land in the United States or in Europe, due to the existing arms embargo policy of the nations concerned, so it became necessary to make the flight in an aircraft with civilian markings and registry. Yet Israel had no airline! The pre-war Aviron had been disbanded and melded into the Israeli Air Force, and the new civil airline proposed by the Ministry of Transport in August 1948 had not yet been formed.

Improvising, it was decided to commandeer one of the two four-engine C-54 transports of the Israeli Air Transport Command and to quickly convert it into an airliner. The selected C-54 was acquired in May 1948 through clandestine intermediaries of the *Haganah* defense arm from United States Overseas Airlines. It bore Israeli Air Force serial number 1701 and had been used to airlift arms and materiel from the sole country willing to supply Israel—Czechoslovakia.

The new "airline" needed a name. David Remez, Minister of Transport, adopted the suggestion of an Israeli aviation lawyer, J. Sczupak, and named the airline "El Al", inspired by the biblical phrase "el al" from the book of the Hebrew prophet Hosea, meaning "to the above" or more poetically "to the skies".

The C-54 received a hurriedly-applied civilian paint scheme featuring "El Al Ltd." and "Israel National Aviation Company" titles in English and Hebrew, and an Israeli flag on the tail. A sofa and other fine furnishings were installed for the comfort of the honored guest and his companions. Extra fuel tanks were fitted since there was no country that would permit a landing between Israel

The first aircraft to bear the name "El Al", 4X-ACA, at Ekron Air Base in the Negev, southern Israel, shortly before the historic flight to Geneva, Switzerland, on 29 September 1948 to bring Chaim Weizmann home to become Israel's first President. El Al had not yet been incorporated, but with the sudden need to launch a regular "civil airline" flight to Geneva rather than a military one, a C-54 (military version of the DC-4) was commandeered from the Israeli Air Transport Command and quickly painted with a new "airline" name and livery. (State of Israel Ministry of Defence, Military (I.D.F.) & Defence Establishment Archives)

and Geneva. The aircraft received the first entry in the new registration book of civil aircraft of the State, with the registered owner shown as "El Al". This first entry, dated 27 September 1948, assigned the registration letters 4X-ACA; "4X" was the new international code designating "Israel" for civil aircraft registration purposes.

The crew for this first civilian flight of the new State was all-Jewish and mainly recruited out of the *Mahal* foreign volunteers in the Israeli Air Force. Hal Auerbach and Arnold Ilowite, Americans with *Mahal*, together with Yitzhak Hennenson, one of the few native Israeli-trained aviators, were the three pilots for the Weizmann flight; Munya Mardor coordinated the operation.

Founders of Israeli aviation transport on the steps leading to 4X-ACA prior to the Weizmann flight at Ekron Air Base, Israel, about 26 September 1948. Left to right: Munya Mardor, head of the Israel Air Transport Command; Uri Michaeli, head of the Jewish airline Aviron in the 1940s and the first head of civil aviation with the Transport Ministry after Israel became a state; Bar Kochba Meerovitch, Deputy Minister for sea and air transport within the Transport Ministry; Aharon Remez, early Commander of the Israeli Air Force; and (front right) David Remez, Minister of Transport, who selected the biblical words "El Al" as the name of the airline. (Capt. Yitzhak Hennenson collection)

Some of the crew members of the Weizmann flight on steps leading to 4X-ACA at Ekron Air Base, Israel, about 26 September 1948. Left side, top to bottom: Yehuda Shimoni (navigator); Leah Melamed (assistant to Aharon Remez of the Israeli Air Force); Milt Shatan (flight engineer); Arnold Ilowite (co-captain). Right side, top to bottom: Yitzhak Hennenson (co-captain); Herb Bornstein (flight engineer); Leah (flight attendant); Coby (Israel Defense Forces representative); Norbert Solomon (steward); Joe Segal (radio operator). The blue uniforms with gold trim were custom made for the flight by a Tel Aviv tailor. The hat insignia is a "Flying Camel", reminiscent of the Jewish settlement's Flying Camel glider club of the 1930s and of a flying camel statue at an exposition hall in Tel Aviv. (State of Israel Ministry of Defence, Military (I.D.F.) & Defence Establishment Archives)

Blue uniforms, including cuffs and caps adorned with gold braid, were tailor-made in Tel Aviv for the crew. A flying camel was chosen for the hat insignia, reminiscent of the Jewish settlement's Flying Camel glider club of the 1930s and of a flying camel statue at an exposition hall in Tel Aviv. New airline registration records, logbooks, airworthiness certificates and Israeli passports were specially prepared to give the semblance of a civilian flight with an all-Israeli crew. Upon arrival in Geneva on 29 September 1948, the hastily contrived documentation was fortunately accepted by the Swiss authorities. Chaim Weizmann and his wife boarded the plane which immediately took off for the ten-hour nonstop return flight to Israel's Ekron Air Base in the Negev. Approaching the Israeli coast before dawn the next day, several Spitfire fighter planes of the Israeli Air Force escorted the C-54 to Ekron. Just moments before arrival, an Israeli military Norseman aircraft crash-landed on the main Ekron runway, but the pilot escaped unscathed and the wreckage was hurriedly moved off to the side. The "El Al" aircraft landed smoothly, and Weizmann's arrival was greeted with impressive formalities, including a welcome by Finance Minister Eliezer Kaplan and other Government officials, a military band playing *Hatikva*, Israel's national anthem, and, in the words of Munya Mardor, "an armed guard that would have been creditable at the gates of Buckingham Palace".

The flight completed, the "El Al" C-54 was stripped of its fine furnishings and returned immediately to more mundane duty with the Air Transport Command.

Flight report prepared by Capt. Hal Auerbach (Hillel Bahir) over Cannes, France, on 29 September 1948, while on the return portion of El Al's first flight, bringing Chaim Weizmann to Israel from Geneva. On the report, Chaim Weizmann wrote in the upper right hand corner, in Hebrew, "It is a great privilege to travel for the first time in an Israeli aircraft so beautifully appointed and with such an amiable crew". In the lower right-hand corner M. Simon wrote "'To the Bird' was the first song of Chaim Nachman Bialik (the early well-known poet of Israel). This 'bird' that we are flying in now is the fulfillment of our dreams." (El Al Israel Airlines collection)

Meteorological briefing at Ekron Air Base, 28 September 1948, prior to takeoff on the first "El Al" flight, to pick up Chaim Weizmann in Geneva. Left to right: Yitzhak Hennenson (co-captain); Joe Segal (radio operator); ground staff member; Sy Cohen (navigator); Hal Auerbach (co-captain); Arnold Ilowite (co-captain); Abie Nathan (second officer) (in center pointing with pen); tower operator; crew member; ground staff member; meteorologist; military representative. (State of Israel Ministry of Defence, Military (I.D.F.) & Defence Establishment Archives)

Initial Meetings to Establish the Airline

In early October 1948, following the impromptu Weizmann flight, Transport Minister David Remez turned his focus towards implementing the August 1948 proclamation which called for the establishment of a true national civil airline. Remez selected Dr. Avraham Rywkind to help organize El Al from an administrative and commercial standpoint. For the technical, operational and piloting aspects of the proposed airline, Remez consulted with Munya Mardor, the Director of Israel's Air Transport Command, and Mardor selected Maurice Kouffman, one of the *Mahal* pilots. Kouffman had served as a pilot in the U.S. Air Transport Command during 1942-45 and then flew for Trans-Caribbean Airways prior to volunteering for service in Israel.

Present at the initial organizational meetings were David Remez, Bar-kochba Meerovitch (Deputy Minister for sea and air transport within the Transport Ministry), Aryeh (Louis) Pincus (then legal adviser to the Transport Ministry), Avraham Rywkind and Maurice Kouffman. In Kouffman's words, "We met several nights to see the practicality of how it could be brought about, and we were very limited, not only in resources but in people. We decided it could be done, so we did it . . . and this was the start of El Al". The participants decided to launch El Al with four-engine Douglas DC-4s, to seek foreign landing rights as soon as possible and to formally incorporate the airline.

First Landing Rights

That same month (October), Meerovitch and Kouffman flew to Paris and met with the director of French civil aviation and the managing director of Air France, seeking landing rights for El Al in Paris. The meetings, lasting several days, convinced the French that Israel was capable of maintaining a regular airline. As a result, France authorized Israel to land civil aircraft in Paris, thereby becoming the first foreign country to grant airline landing rights to Israel and El Al.

Having secured the authority, "El Al" (still not yet incorporated) initiated a special flight to Paris. The same military C-54 of Weizmann fame (4X-ACA) was utilized for this flight from Tel Aviv, under the command of Capt. Norman Moonitz and Capt. Gordon Levett, both of *Mahal*, with several high-ranking Israeli Government officials were on board. On the return flight, in mid-month, the aircraft carried former U.S. Secretary of the Treasury Henry Morgenthau to Israel on a fact-finding trip in his capacity as general chairman of the United Jewish Appeal.

Incorporation of El Al

On 15 November 1948 the new Israeli national airline was incorporated, under the official name El Al Israel Airlines Ltd., with a share capital of two million Israeli pounds. The Israeli Government held 80% of the capital stock, the remainder divided among various Israeli organizations, including the Zim steamship line. The original board of directors consisted of E. Bavli, Z. Isersohn, H. Issachar, Munya Mardor, Bar-kochba Meerovitch, and Avraham Ruttenberg.

El Al's principal objective was defined by the Government of Israel as being to "secure and maintain a regular civil air link between Israel and the outside world in time of peace and war, within the framework of the maximum possible profitability". The Government also wisely accepted the basic premise urged by El Al's original directors and head officers, namely, that El Al should be an independently run commercial entity, with its own management, based on competitive airline standards, and with policy-making decisions reserved for the board of directors representing the Government. This is probably the single most important reason for El Al's success.

Avraham Rywkind became El Al's first employee. An immigrant from Poland, he managed El Al while it was only a "paper" airline, working as a one-man show out of an office of the Keren Hayesod organization which was engaged in obtaining funding for immigrant absorption. In effect this was El Al's first office. Rywkind became a pacesetter for future El Al executives—an idealist caught up in a tide of commerce and economic development, convinced that by working for the Israeli national carrier, he was fulfilling his highest duty to his country.

On 1 January 1949 Hadassah Perlberg became El Al's second commercial staff employee, assisting Rywkind. Shortly thereafter El Al obtained the first office of its own—a single room on the second floor of a building at 31 Rothschild Blvd. in Tel Aviv. Hadassah later married Rywkind and worked her entire career with El Al.

Aryeh Pincus, then in his mid-thirties and originally a lawyer from South Africa, was selected from the Transport Ministry in 1949 to become the the first Managing Director (later called President) of El Al, with Rywkind serving as commercial director. Considered brilliant, Pincus, like Rywkind, had no prior airline background, but embraced his task at El Al with messianic devotion.

In the initial months of El Al's formal existence, from November 1948 through February 1949, El Al did not have any aircraft of its own. In fact, El Al was really a matter of paint. When the need for a special flight occurred, military planes were quickly redecorated with civilian registrations and El Al titles. Air force personnel were handed newly-printed passports and served as El Al crews. For example, on 31 January 1949 a Curtiss C-46 Commando (4X-ACG) was "borrowed" by El Al from the Israeli Air Force, which in turn had acquired it from the Panamanian "airline" LAPSA. On this special flight, Eliezer Kaplan, Finance Minister of the State of Israel, was flown to Europe. Commanded by Capt. Sam Lewis, the flight traveled from Lydda to Rome, Corsica and Athens, returning on 17 February to Israel.

Operation Magic Carpet

Upon the establishment of the State of Israel in 1948 and the War of Independence, many Jewish communities in other countries of the Middle East found themselves oppressed and fearing for their safety at the hands of the governing Arabs. One of these precarious communities was a centuries-old group of Yemenite Jews living in the remote southwestern tip of the Arabian Peninsula. A simple yet tough and resilient people, they had somehow clung to their Jewish religious tradition although cut off for over 2,000 years from the main body of Jewry. They also believed, from the biblical prophecy in the book of Exodus, that some day they would be delivered from exile to the Holy Land "on eagles wings".

With El Al's help, the State of Israel and the Jewish Joint Distribution Committee mobilized to save the Yemenite Jews from destruction. Formidable obstacles were faced. The Arabs would not permit Jews to travel through the Red Sea and the Gulf of Eilat. As a result, other then an arduous ship voyage around Africa, the only way to bring the Yemenites to Israel was by air. Aircraft fuel was so scarce in Israel that all was needed for the war effort, and none could be spared for the airlift. Moreover, the British who controlled Aden, the only place where the Yemenites could be assembled for transport to Israel, would not make fuel available. To make matters worse, planes with Israeli markings, such as those of El Al, were not permitted to overfly Arab airspace en route to and from Aden.

A Douglas DC-4 of Near East Air Transport, the early affiliate of El Al used in immigrant airlifts, picking up Yemenite Jews in November 1949 in Aden (then a British Protectorate), at the southern tip of the Arabian Peninsula, to bring them to safety and a new home in Israel. Although in Near East markings, this aircraft is painted in an Alaska Airlines color scheme. Alaska Airlines, through its adventurous President James Wooten, was the original supplier of aircraft for the Yemenite airlift. (Central Zionist Archives, Jerusalem)

To overcome these problems, El Al, in a program organized by Yoel Palgi, cooperated with a charter operation established by the Joint Distribution Committee and by the adventurer James Wooten of Alaska Airlines. In January 1949, planes with the markings of Alaska Airlines, and later Near East Air Transport (formed especially to carry immigrants) and a "paper" Cuban airline, began flying to Aden to airlift Yemenite Jews in *Operation Magic Carpet*.

Fuel supplies were finally located, but only in remote Asmara, Ethiopia, so the flights had to ply a

Yemenite Jews taking shelter in the shade at the wheel of an Avro Tudor 1 aircraft at the hot, dusty airfield in Aden, November 1949. The Yemenites had never seen an airplane before, and they sat in awe and nervous anticipation, awaiting the fulfillment of the biblical prophecy that they would be returned to the land of their forefathers "on the wings of eagles". (Central Zionist Archives, Jerusalem)

triangular route: from Lod Airport, Israel, southwest to Asmara, Ethiopia, for fuel; then east to Aden to pick up the Yemenites; and then back to Lod Airport.

The airlift relied on Curtiss C-46s and Douglas DC-4s, many of which came from Israeli sources including El Al. When used for the airlift, the El Al aircraft were repainted with the markings of the charter airlines. El Al also loaned pilots and cabin crew for the operation.

A DC-4 normally seated about 50 passengers. However, the Yemenites were thin, and five people usually could fit into seats designed for four. So the usual seats were removed, and wooden benches installed with seat belts across them, to hold more passengers. As Capt. Sam Lewis relates, "When a plane was loaded, a crew member would stand at the top of the stairway sizing up the passengers and, when necessary to crowd more on a bench, would yell 'give me a thin one'". This unusual arrangement was euphemistically called "special immigrant high-density seating". Thus, each plane took off with about 120 people packed inside.

At the peak of *Operation Magic Carpet*, planes flew round-the-clock schedules to Israel, seven to eight flights a day, on routes of 2,600km (1,600mi) that took about nine hours. They had to fly a narrow corridor up the middle of the Red Sea and Gulf of Eilat skirting the Arab countries, with instruments of dubious accuracy and deprived of radio guidance. Engines suffered because of desert sand and dust—a forced landing anywhere would have meant disaster—but, remarkably, no mishaps occurred.

The Yemenites had never seen a plane before, so one can imagine their numb astonishment at seeing this great bird and wondering how it flew. Once inside the aircraft they usually sat stoically and in awe. But the flights had their unusual moments. Once a pilot passed back to the cabin a request for some water. Soon a Yemenite youngster brought to the cockpit a cup of hot freshly boiled tea. The crew did a double-take

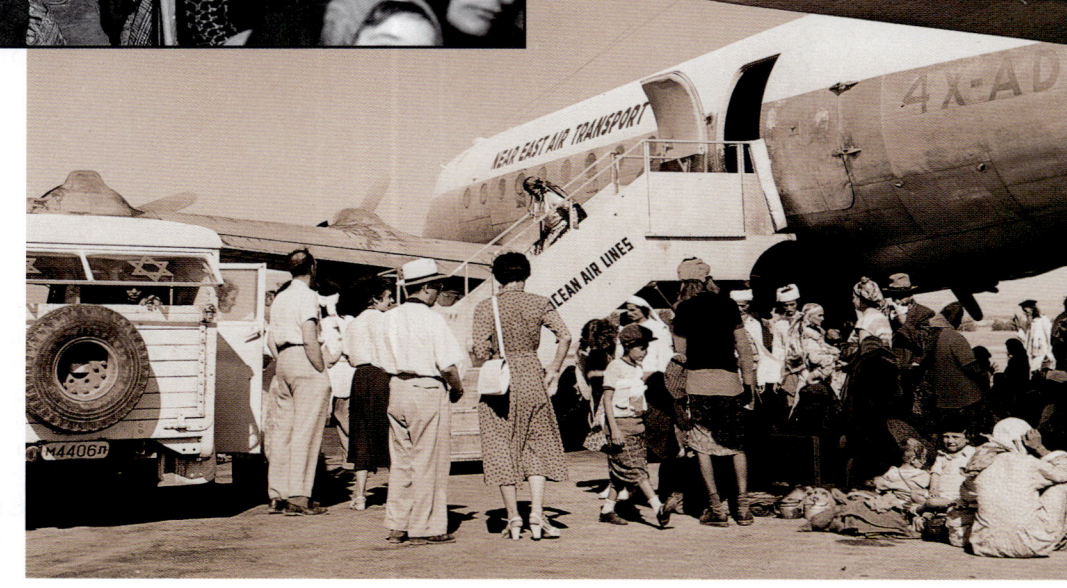

Above: *Yemenite airlift flight in a DC-4 operated by an El Al crew. Forty thousand Jews from Yemen were rescued in 1949 by* Operation Magic Carpet *through flights from Aden to Lod Airport, Tel Aviv. Note the crude wooden bench seating arrangements.* (Israel Government Press Office)

Below: *Habbanim Jews from the South Arabian Peninsula, airlifted from Aden, arrive at Lod Airport aboard El Al's DC-4 4X-ADN on 26 August 1950. As El Al could not fly planes in its own colors to many Middle Eastern points, liveries of associated charter airlines such as Near East Air Transport were usually used. Near East was funded in part by Israeli Jewish interests and commonly used El Al crews. Note also the stairs marked Transocean Air Lines, a pioneering post-World War II U.S. charter airline.* (Israel Government Press Office)

because they knew there were no facilities for boiling water on the plane. Hastening back to the passenger cabin, they were astonished to see the Yemenites operating a makeshift stove on the floor heating a kettle of water for tea!

Upon arrival in Israel, the Yemenites felt their prayers had been answered. Many kneeled and kissed the tarmac upon arrival. Truly they had realized their dream—being carried to the Promised Land "on eagles' wings". By the time the airlift ended in September 1950, 47,000 persons, almost all of Yemen's Jewish population, had been carried to Israel, together with some 3,000 Habbanim Jews who had resided in another remote area of the South Arabian peninsula.

Operation Ali Baba

The flights from Yemen were followed by an even more massive airlift of Jews from Iraq, called *Operation Ali Baba*. In March 1950, following Iraqi

persecution of the local Jewish communities, the Iraqi government allowed Jewish emigration, on condition that Jewish property be abandoned in favor of the government. Moreover, the airlift was allowed only with the reservation that there be no direct flights between Israel and Iraq. All flights had to land first in neutral Cyprus. On that basis, *Operation Ali Baba* started in May 1950. By its end in December 1951, 113,000 Iraqi Jews had been flown to Israel, with El Al playing a major role in the rescue.

Meanwhile, El Al also started special immigrant flights from Europe and many other areas, including India. These immigrant flights as well as the airlifts were often charged with emotion. In the words of early El Al stewardess Livia Eisen Chertoff, "many passengers would kiss the uniforms of the crew members upon seeing the Jewish Star of David insignia". El Al became the first visible symbol of a new life in a reborn land.

In 1950-51, El Al airlifted 113,000 Jews from Iraq to Israel in Operation Ali Baba. As Israeli-marked aircraft were not permitted to land in Iraq, foreign-registered planes of other airlines were utilized, although with El Al crew. Shown are Iraqi Jews disembarking from a DC-4 of Near East Air Transport bearing Cuban registration CU-T-465 in May 1951. This aircraft later became 4X-ADC of El Al's fleet. (Israel Government Press Office)

El Al's First Aircraft Purchases

At the beginning of 1949 El Al's plans to start its own fleet of aircraft with DC-4s finally became a reality. With funding from the Government of Israel, the Jewish Agency, and other Jewish organizations such as the Hebrew Immigrant Aid Society (HIAS), El Al purchased the first aircraft of its own—two used DC-4s that had earlier been converted from military C-54s. The DC-4s were acquired from American Airlines in February and March 1949 and registered in Israel as 4X-ACC and -ACD.

The DC-4 was a reliable four-engine transport built by Douglas Aircraft. It was normally configured for about 50 passengers and a crew of five, could cruise at 450km/h (280mph) at up to 4,300 meters (14,000ft), and had a range of 4,000km (2,500mi). However, it was not pressurized. This prevented it from flying at higher altitudes to avoid rough air and bad weather. By 1949 most of the major airlines were already flying pressurized aircraft, such as the Douglas DC-6, Boeing Stratocruiser and Lockheed Constellation. Given Israel's austerity economy at the time, however, the best El Al could do was to acquire secondhand DC-4s. Nevertheless, the DC-4s were tried and true aircraft, and their range was ideal for El Al's projected flights to Europe.

Capt. Maurice Kouffman personally took delivery of 4X-ACD from American Airlines at Tulsa, Oklahoma, on 26 February 1949 and flew it to Idlewild Airport, New York (now JFK Airport), for overhaul by the Willis-Rose aircraft company. Two weeks later, he accepted delivery of 4X-ACC, again from American, and also flew it to Idlewild to join its sister aircraft at Willis-Rose.

Meanwhile, the United States arms embargo on the Middle East was still in force. No aircraft could be exported from the U. S. without an export license from the Department of Commerce. However, following negotiations between the Israeli and U.S. Governments, on 1 March 1949 the State Department announced that export licenses would be granted for the DC-4s.

On 29 March 1949, export license in hand, El Al unveiled 4X-ACC at Idlewild Airport, painted in the first official livery of El Al. The name "El Al Israel Aviation Company" glistened in the sun above the window line in English and Hebrew. The name *Rechovoth* appeared smartly near the cockpit, in honor of the town of Chaim Weizmann's residence in Israel. A flying Star of David or *magen*

One of the first two aircraft purchased by El Al, 4X-ACC Rechovoth, acquired from American Airlines in March 1949. The DC-4 (converted from the C-54 military version) is shown at Idlewild Airport (now John F. Kennedy Airport), New York, 29 March 1949, prior to takeoff for Tel Aviv on El Al's first survey flight across the Atlantic. An SAS DC-4 is in the background. Note the Magen David (six-pointed Star of David symbol), with flying wings as part of the paint scheme to the right of the cockpit of the El Al plane. This became El Al's main symbol on its aircraft and advertising material until the introduction of an El Al block logo in 1962. (Worldwide Photo)

Capt. Maurice Kouffman, El Al's first pilot, next to DC-4 4X-ACC, with his wife Marilyn in the background. The cap and coat insignia worn by Capt. Kouffman are the first utilized by El Al in regular commercial service. They are made of metal and show the flying Star of David (Magen David) introduced in March 1949. (Capt. Maurice Kouffman collection)

david graced the window line behind the cockpit, and this became the first official El Al symbol. That afternoon, 4X-ACC took off from Idlewild on El Al's first trans-Atlantic flight, a survey trip to Tel Aviv via Gander, Shannon and Paris. Capt. Kouffman was in charge of the flight, and its seven man crew also included Capt. Martin A. Ribakoff (formerly with *Mahal*), Capt. John Greenacre of Pan American, other Pan Am crew members, and Kouffman's wife, Marilyn, as stewardess. On 3 April 1949, to the joy of the handful of El Al staff in Israel, 4X-ACC landed at Lod Airport—the first aircraft owned by El Al to touch down in Israel.

After six days at Lod Airport, 4X-ACC was flown back to the U.S. by Kouffman, this time with Aryeh Pincus on board, for the purpose of obtaining from the U.S. Government landing rights for El Al. Following two weeks of negotiations with aviation officials in Washington, D.C., El Al received the coveted authorization to land passenger aircraft in the U.S.

During 29-31 May 1949, Kouffman flew -ACD on a public relations tour, from Idlewild to Indianapolis, Oklahoma City and back to Idlewild. Thereafter, -ACD was flown to Israel where El Al personnel prepared to use it for the start-up of regular passenger service.

First Scheduled Passenger Service

With two DC-4s secured and one of them at Lod Airport in preparation for passenger service, on 15 July 1949 the State of Israel issued to El Al a formal Certificate to Commence Business as a regular scheduled airline.

On 31 July 1949, El Al initiated scheduled flights on a Tel Aviv to Paris route (via Rome for refueling), with DC-4 4X-ACD. This first scheduled flight began at the office of Bernard Wajnberg, Director of Globe Travel Service on Har Sinai Street in Tel Aviv. Wajnberg was considered Israel's most knowledgeable travel agent of his day, having started in the business in his native Poland in the early 1930s. From El Al's infancy he placed his professional advice and skill at the disposal of the new airline. For this first scheduled flight he booked 24 passengers who assembled at his Tel Aviv office for baggage weigh-in and for the bus that would take them to Lod Airport. Following a welcome at the airport by El Al's first Station Manager, Francie Oberlander, and greeted on board by a hastily trained but eager-to-please cabin crew, the passengers enjoyed a smooth ride on El Al's historic first flight. El Al was a true international scheduled airline at last! No matter that it was with one aircraft and one flight a week.

El Al's Capt. Maurice Kouffman being interviewed by well-known news personality Clete Roberts in front of DC-4 4X-ACC, while at the Douglas Aircraft plant in Santa Monica, California, early August 1949. (Capt. Maurice Kouffman collection)

The second of El Al's first two purchased aircraft, the DC-4 (converted C-54) 4X-ACD Herzl, shown at Orly Airport, Paris, following the arrival of El Al's first scheduled passenger flight, 31 July—1 August 1949. The stewardess is Miriam Gold and to her right in the photograph is Dr. Joseph Massis, head of El Al's Paris Office. On the far right are steward Herbert Kweller and navigator Kovacs. (El Al Israel Airlines collection)

Service Expands With Second DC-4

While 4X-ACD had the honor of inaugurating scheduled service, El Al's other DC-4, 4X-ACC, was still in the U.S. In early August 1949 it was checked out at the Douglas Aircraft plant in Santa Monica, California, to confirm its airworthiness for regular passenger service, and later that month it was flown back to Israel to join -ACD as part of the El Al "fleet". With two DC-4s in Israel, El Al expanded to two flights a week.

On 16-17 August 1949 El Al undertook one of its most emotional flights. Theodor Herzl, the founder of political Zionism, had been buried in Vienna, and the Israelis wanted to bring him home to Israel, the land of his dreams, for reburial. Using DC-4 4X-ACD, officially named *Herzl* for the occasion, El Al flew to Vienna and carried Herzl's remains to Israel, where he is now buried on Mt. Herzl in Jerusalem.

The honor guard is tense as the door of El Al's DC-4 4X-ACD Herzl swings open to lower the draped coffin of Theodor Herzl, founder of Zionism, flown from Vienna for reburial in Jerusalem, Israel, 16 August 1949. (Israel Government Press Office)

Home at last, as the draped coffin of Herzl reaches the soil of Israel, at Lod Airport, 16 August 1949. To the right of the saluting officer is David Remez, Minister of Transport, and to his right Yitzhak Gruenbaum, representative of the Jewish Agency. The carrier equipment bears the word "Aviron" in Hebrew and the flying bird symbol of Aviron, the Jewish airline later replaced by Arkia. (Israel Government Press Office)

Flight crew for the Herzl flight, 16 August 1949. Left to right: Bob Morse (captain); Herb Bornstein (flight engineer); Carmella Moyal (stewardess); Herbert Kweller (steward); Kovacs (navigator); Leo St. Denis (radio operator); Norman Moonitz (first officer). By this time El Al had introduced uniform insignia made of cloth (rather than metal), embroidered with gold thread. (Israel Government Press Office)

By October 1949 heavy bookings on El Al's flights to Paris, as well as special flights to Rome, caused El Al to charter Douglas DC-3s from Universal Airways, a small airline run by Jewish interests in South Africa and which primarily operated a Johannesburg–Tel Aviv route.

On 18 December 1949 El Al initiated scheduled service to its second and third destinations, Rome and Zürich, with 4X-ACD; and on 22 December 4X-ACC flew El Al's first scheduled service to London, with a stop in Rome. The total number of all El Al flights per week from Tel Aviv increased to three—one to Rome and Paris, a second to Rome and Zürich, and the third to Paris and London. The monthly passenger count rose from 400 to 750. Across the Atlantic, Maurice Kouffman opened El Al's first offices in New York, one at 250 West 57th Street in Manhattan and the other at Idlewild Airport. Israelis Yehuda Koppel and Dror Galezer soon arrived to run the city

office, and were joined by locally hired assistant Joyce Perlman Baron, who had previous experience with Trans-Caribbean Airways. Meanwhile, at Idlewild, Kouffman hired several of El Al's first pilots and maintenance technicians.

Arkia Is Born

Israel's first domestic airline, named Arkia, was founded in late 1949 with 50% ownership by El Al and the balance by the Israeli *Histadrut* Labor Organization. Arkia's affiliation with El Al continued until 1980 when Arkia was sold to private interests and its own employees. The first official Arkia flight was made on 28 February 1950 to Eilat, then a development town on the Gulf of Eilat at Israel's southern tip, in an Arkia-registered Curtiss C-46 Commando, with El Al crew. A more comprehensive history of Arkia is contained in Appendix I.

Lod Airport in the early years of El Al's operations, December 1950. The airport (called Lydda prior to the founding of the State of Israel in May 1948) as well as the terminal building shown, were built by the British during 1934-36. When it opened, it was one of the finest and most modern airports anywhere, and it soon became a prime Middle East stop for many European airlines, including Imperial Airways, Air France, CSA, KLM, LOT, SABENA, and Swissair. (Israel Government Press Office)

Above right: *El Al's first passenger check-in counter at Lod Airport in March 1951. Note the hand weigh-in of baggage at the left and the early El Al baggage label. Shown writing at the counter is Zvi Blumenfeld, traffic agent and assistant to El Al station manager Francie Oberlander. In the right background are, left to right, KLM station manager Baker and El Al's David Alsay and Zvi Yehudai.* (Israel Government Press Office)

Above: *Early El Al passenger terminal facilities at Lod Airport, 1951-52.* (El Al Israel Airlines collection)

Right: *One of El Al's first buses, manufactured by Chausson of France, in front of the Lod Airport terminal in January 1951, transporting passengers between the El Al office in Tel Aviv and Lod Airport.* (Israel Government Press Office)

El Al's First Cargo Operations

On 24 January 1950 El Al acquired two Curtiss C-46s (4X-ACE and -ACF) from the Israeli Air Force. The Air Force had employed them as transports in the 1948 War of Independence following their arrival from the U.S. and Panama via Al Schwimmer's Panamanian "airline", LAPSA.

The C-46 was a twin-engine medium-range transport developed at the start of World War II, earning fame as the prime mover of supplies over the Himalayan Mountain "Hump" run between India and China during the conflict. After the war many found their way to airlines around the world for use as cargo carriers, and others were converted to passenger use. The C-46 could cruise at 280km/h (175mph) at 3,000 meters (10,000ft), and had a range of 5,000km (3,100mi) with a usual crew of four. Compared to the legendary Douglas C-47 (DC-3), the C-46 had a more rotund fuselage accommodating up to 6,750kg (15,000lb) of cargo.

El Al used its initial two C-46s to launch a freight operation on 26 January 1950 between Israel and several European cities. With foresight it recognized the potential growth and value of air cargo revenue as well as the importance of air transport to the future increase of Israeli exports of flowers, fresh produce and other goods. In April 1951 El Al established one of the few regular cargo runs to London. Intermediate stops were made in various European cities as required. By 1955 the usual route to London was via Athens, Rome, Düsseldorf and Amsterdam, with the return to Tel Aviv via Brussels, Rome and Athens. Another freight service was established to Paris via Athens and Rome, returning via Düsseldorf, Zürich, Rome and Athens. Schedules were arranged to permit other ports of call as required.

Between 1950 and 1955 El Al operated a total of seven ex-Israeli Air Force C-46s, but not all at the same time. Besides carrying freight, some of El Al's C-46s were employed in passenger service, usually with 38 seats, and they supplemented the DC-4s (and later the Constellations) as needed for shorter or less traveled routes.

An El Al C-46 in freight operations at Lod Airport. El Al recognized early the future potential of air cargo and started all-freight service with two of the capacious C-46s on 26 January 1950. (El Al Israel Airlines collection)

First Casualty

By the start of February 1950 El Al's scheduled flights to Europe were running smoothly with its two DC-4s. This promising state of affairs, however, was soon shattered. On the night of 5-6 February, in a rare freezing winter storm, it started snowing in Tel Aviv and at Lod Airport. The DC-4 *Herzl* (4X-ACD) was on the tarmac that night, boarding passengers and baggage. Ice formed on the wings, and maintenance personnel removed it as it accumulated. A number of notables were on the aircraft, including Aryeh Pincus, El Al's President, and Bar-kochba Meerovitch of the Transport Ministry. Abba Eban, Israel's representative to the United Nations at the time, was scheduled to be on the flight, but the weather turned him back enroute to the airport. At about one in the morning, the aircraft's captain, Kenneth Fuller, made the decision to take off. Gaining speed on the runway, the DC-4 lifted off slightly, but immediately an engine failed and the aircraft plunged back to earth, careening off the side of the runway. All aboard somehow managed to escape and scramble to safety. However, flames soon engulfed the aircraft and reduced it to a total loss. The only surviving property was a consignment of diamonds, but only a few were recovered after a spirited search which did not lack for volunteers! With one-half of El Al's passenger fleet in smoldering ruins, a board of inquiry was assigned to investigate the crash, but the definitive cause was never established.

In May 1950 El Al purchased two DC-4s from United Air Lines (registered in Israel as 4X-ADB and -ADC) and conveniently adopted the United paint scheme, a blue window line rising in steps towards the front, as shown in this photograph. In the original photo the word "Mainliner" used by United appears faintly to the lower left of the door. (El Al Israel Airlines)

El Al's DC-4 4X-ACC in the hangar at Lod Airport after receiving a new color scheme in April 1951. Note that the round DC-4 windows are outlined by painted white rectangles, making the aircraft appear more like the newer and pressurized DC-6 which had square windows. The photograph is taken from underneath one of El Al's newly-arrived Constellations. Barely visible in the hangar at right is a camouflaged Curtiss C-46 undergoing an engine change. The hangar was originally built by the British in 1937 to house its giant Handley Page H.P.42 Hannibal class aircraft. (Israel Government Press Office)

El Al maintenance shops at Lod Airport, April 1951. The staff are working on Pratt & Whitney R-2000 engines which powered the Douglas DC-4. (Israel Government Press Office)

More Acquisitions and Routes

El Al moved quickly to close the gap caused by the loss of the DC-4 and also to implement earlier plans for an expansion of service in summer 1950. At first, a replacement DC-4 was leased briefly from the affiliated immigrant airlift charter operation of Near East Air Transport. Then three additional used DC-4s were purchased— 4X-ADB and -ADC, formerly with United Air Lines, and 4X-ADN from Trans-Caribbean Airways. Apparently El Al liked United's striking color scheme of dark blue and silver, because El Al retained the livery on the former United DC-4s and then repainted its other DC-4s to match.

With the increase of its DC-4 fleet to four aircraft, and the availability of its two C-46s when needed for passenger service, El Al was able to substantially expand its routes and frequency of service.

To the United States

El Al's main expansion objective was to launch service to the U.S. On 18 June 1950, just five days after Israel signed a bilateral air agreement with the U.S., El Al inaugurated trans-Atlantic service with a charter group organized by the Israeli youth organization, *Habonim*. The route was from Tel Aviv to New York, via Rome, Paris, Shannon, and Gander (Newfoundland), and employed a combination of El Al's newly-acquired DC-4s, 4X-ADB and -ADC, one for the Israel—Europe segments and the other for the trans-Atlantic portion. The return flight was made with a group charter organized by Pioneer Women, arriving at Tel Aviv on 25 June.

The crew of El Al's first flight to Johannesburg, South Africa, in November 1950. Left to right: Back row: Lou Mazerow (second officer); Pete Rivas (flight engineer); Livia Eisen Chertoff (stewardess); Chaya Tarnar (stewardess); Herbert Kweller (first El Al steward); Dell Webb (radio operator). Front row: Gaffe; Bob Moorehead (captain); Aryeh (Louis) Pincus (first President of El Al); Herbert Cranko (Director of Administration and Finance, and former managing director of Universal Airways of South Africa, acquired by El Al in 1950); Morty Leveseur; and Jay Webman (maintenance). (Livia Eisen Chertoff collection)

The same day, El Al operated its first "official" round-trip passenger flight between Israel and the U.S. With a charter group of passengers and the same combination of DC-4s, the flight stopped at Rome, Shannon and Gander enroute, arriving at Idlewild Airport, New York, on 27 June 1950. This marked the start of weekly DC-4 charter service by El Al between Israel and New York.

To Additional European Cities and Johannesburg

El Al started service to Istanbul in March 1950 with twice-weekly charter flights, followed by a start-up of regularly scheduled passenger service

One of El Al's first two offices in Europe, on Avenue de l'Opéra in Paris (the other was in Rome). The Paris office was shared with Israel's shipping line, Zim. The first scheduled passenger flight by El Al was made from Tel Aviv to Rome and Paris on 31 July 1949. (El Al Israel Airlines collection)

on 1 March a year later. Scheduled weekly service to Vienna started on 5 July 1950 with DC-4s. Flights to Athens and to Nicosia, Cyprus, started in late 1950 on a sporadic basis, with regularly scheduled flights being inaugurated early the following year.

In fall 1950 El Al acquired Universal Airways, a South African company. Universal had been flying to Lod Airport as part of a Johannesburg to London long-haul route, incongruously using short-haul DC-3s. Established by Herbert Cranko, a South African Jew, and by other South African Zionists, Universal contributed to the War of Independence by flying in needed supplies and equipment and providing another link to the outside world. Upon the 1950 takeover, Cranko

left his post as managing director of Universal to become El Al's Director of Administration and Finance. El Al immediately placed DC-4s on the route to replace Universal's DC-3s, commencing service to Johannesburg (Palmietfontein Airport), via Khartoum, Sudan, Nairobi, Kenya, and Livingstone, Northern Rhodesia (now Zambia), on 29 October 1950.

The pride of being El Al/Arkia's first stewardess to Eilat, upon arrival in Eilat on 28 February 1950 with the Curtiss C-46 in the background. El Al crew served the Arkia flight, the stewardess being Tova Mizrachi. Note the original El Al metal uniform insignia, the flying Star of David. The C-46 was originally one of the Panamanian-registered LAPSA aircraft ferried out of the U.S. via Panama to Israel, as can be seen by the obliterated Panamanian flag on the tail under the Israeli 4X-ACT registration. (Israel Government Press Office)

Below: Aboard El Al/Arkia's first official flight to Eilat, Israel, 28 February 1950, in Curtiss C-46 4X-ACT. Note the bare furnishings and absence of wall soundproofing. Left to right (first four persons): Yaacov Hozman (first President of Arkia); Aryeh Pincus (first President of El Al); Avraham Ryvkind (first head of commercial operations of El Al); Danny Rosin (in back) (El Al pilot). (Israel Government Press Office)

Following this flurry of route expansion, El Al maintained its network without any new additions for another five years.

The first anniversary of El Al's initial scheduled flight was celebrated on 31 July 1950. During this first year El Al had flown 172 round-trips covering 1,180,000km (732,000mi) with 10,405 passengers and 66,225kg (146,000lb) of freight. The number of El Al employees stood at 350, some 75 of whom, including 45 flight crew, were non-Israeli. This ratio would inevitably change in the years ahead, however, as native Israelis acquired the necessary skills to take over as pilots and technicians.

El Al's Sole "DC-3"

In early 1951 the receipt of Turkish Government approval for regularly scheduled service to Istanbul had an interesting sidelight. Upon receiving the approval, El Al wanted to initiate service as soon as possible, but found itself short of aircraft. It turned to the Israeli Air Force for assistance, and obtained one of the Air Force's C-47 Dakotas (a military version of the DC-3). The "DC-3" was painted with the El Al name, given a civil registration (4X-ATA), and placed in service for the first scheduled flight to Istanbul on 1 March 1951. The flight went round-trip on that day with stops in each direction in Nicosia, Cyprus. The aircraft was used for only a few more flights before being returned to the Air Force. Interestingly, when El Al acquired its first Boeing 707 jet in 1961, the 4X-ATA registration was revived and assigned to it.

The DC-4's Swan Song

The end of 1950 represented the height of DC-4 activity in El Al. In addition to the new Johannesburg service, there were eight weekly flights to Europe: three to Rome; two to Paris; two to London; and one to Istanbul, Vienna and Zürich. At this peak of DC-4 activity, however, El Al knew that the days of its "Fours" were numbered. All its competitors were already operating pressurized and larger aircraft. El Al could not exist forever on immigrant airlifts and loyal Zionistically-motivated air travelers. Already three used Constellations had been purchased by El Al and, following overhaul by Al Schwimmer's group in Burbank, California, the first arrived in Israel on 22 December 1950.

As the Constellations entered service in 1951, El Al started selling its DC-4s. However, one aircraft was lost on 24 November 1951 in another accident. On a freight run from Tel Aviv to Amsterdam via Rome and Zürich, a route ordinarily plied by a Curtiss C-46, El Al substituted a DC-4 (4X-ADB) with its seats removed. On approach to Zürich's Kloten Airport, the aircraft clipped some trees on a wooded hillside and crashed, killing six of the crew of seven, including Capt. Theodor ("Ted") Gibson of Miami, one of the first foreign volunteers for the Israeli Air Force. Ted Gibson was a former U.S. Navy dive bomber pilot and at the time was the chief instructor of the advanced flying school in Israel. El Al's commercial director, Avraham Rywkind, had been on the ill-fated flight, but suffering from exhaustion—caused by overwork—he got off at Rome for a rest and was spared.

By the end of 1951 only two DC-4s (4X-ACC and -ADC) remained in El Al's fleet. They were sold in January and April 1952 respectively, thus ending El Al's pioneering and emotional DC-4 era with the classic Douglas airliner.

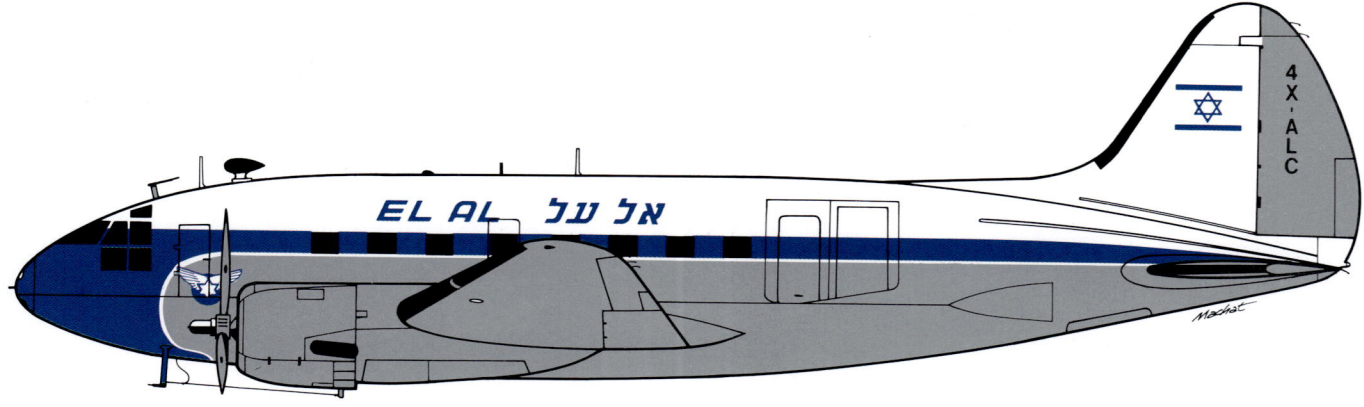

The barreness of Eilat may be seen in this October 1955 photograph with a parked El Al C-46 (4X-ALC). The flights were operated by El Al's subsidiary, Arkia, and the Arkia symbol appears just to the right of the blue nose of the aircraft. (Israel Government Press Office)

Constructing the first terminal at Eilat, 28 February 1950. Eilat, now a thriving tourist sun resort at the Red Sea, was barren land at the time. In the background are (left) an El Al C-46 (4X-ACT) and a DC-3 named **Galilee** of South Africa's Universal Airways, operated to Eilat by an El Al crew. El Al acquired Universal Airways later the same year. (Israel Government Press Office)

An ambulance flight between Eilat and Tel Aviv in April 1951. The aircraft is a Curtiss C-46, either 4X-ALC (formerly -ACT) or 4X-ALB (formerly -ACF), in a simple color scheme due to the common repainting of aircraft into non-Israeli liveries to allow refugee flights to land in other countries. The stairs say "Arkia" in Hebrew; the ambulance still says "Palestine", a leftover from the pre-Israel days preceding May 1948. (Israel Government Press Office)

Above and right: *Earliest El Al ticket jacket and baggage tag, 1949-50. (El Al Israel Airlines collection)* **Below:** *Flight cover flown on El Al's first official passenger charter flight to the United States. The DC-4 flight left Tel Aviv on 25 June 1950, arriving at Idlewild Airport, New York, the next day following stops in Rome, Italy; Shannon, Ireland; and Gander, Newfoundland. (Marvin Goldman collection via Stanley Baumwald)*

CHAPTER THREE

The Lean Years: Vintage Constellations

"Bring back my sons from afar and my daughters from the ends of the earth"

(Isaiah 43:6)

T he years 1951-1957 are known as the "lean years" in El Al's history. The drama, euphoria and harried improvisation of the first twenty-four months of operation had subsided. Now the airline was settling into trying to run a regular commercial operation—and times were hard on Israel and on El Al.

The young country faced the huge task of providing food, lodging, work, education and medical care for hundreds of thousands of penniless new immigrants from all parts of the world.

The economy was in shambles, and travel and trade in Israel confronted austerity and severe limitations. Serious doubts persisted as to whether a small country like Israel could maintain an airline that could successfully compete in the international air market and still not drain the weakened economy.

Meanwhile, El Al was still struggling with its small fleet of unpressurized Douglas DC-4 and Curtiss C-46 aircraft. Its direct competitors from Europe and the United States were already using larger and pressurized aircraft, such as Lockheed Constellations and Douglas DC-6s.

Given the constraints on equipment and finance, the entire El Al organization struggled to survive. Every facet needed improvement, from company organization and management policies to technical, operational and customer service standards. Added to this was the desire to integrate Israeli personnel, particularly into the higher ranks of captains.

This page and opposite; *Constellation-era (1951-57) El Al baggage labels, each featuring the flying Star of David.* (Marvin Goldman collection)

Schwimmer's Constellations

As for aircraft, El Al turned to Al Schwimmer for assistance. Schwimmer had been instrumental in acquiring the Curtiss C-46s spirited out of the U.S. to Israel via Panama for use in the War of Independence, several of which eventually joined El Al's early fleet. Schwimmer had also purchased five World War II-surplus Lockheed C-69 Constellations from obsolete U.S. Air Force supply stocks at Wright Field in Dayton, Ohio, three of which received some basic rehabilitation by his company with a view towards service as transports in Israel's War of Independence. Only one eventually found its way to Israel, via Panama. The other two were impounded by the FBI (see Chapter 1). With Israel's War of Independence over, Schwimmer regained ownership of all three aircraft, and through his company, Intercontinental Airways, started to completely refurbish them for airline use at Burbank, California.

Schwimmer's three Constellations were all of the earliest type, but they were just what El Al needed. Now for the first time El Al would have pressurized aircraft, capable of flying higher than the DC-4s and C-46s and avoiding bad weather more frequently. The Model 49 Constellation (as the civil equivalent of the C-69 was designated) had a service ceiling of 7,710 meters (25,000ft), with a typical cruising speed of 440km/h (275mph) and an average range of 3,900km (2,400mi).

In October 1950 El Al purchased the first two of these "Connies"—as the type was affectionately called, and had them registered as 4X-AKA and -AKB. The third Connie was purchased in April 1951. This aircraft (4X-AKC) was the same one that had served in the Czech arms airlift of the Israeli War of Independence, while under Panamanian registration.

To refurbish the Constellations, Schwimmer had to re-design the interiors from their bare military layout. Improvements were made in the cabin heating, ventilation and insulation. Extra cabin

One of El Al's first Lockheed 49 Constellations being refurbished for passenger service by Schwimmer Aviation at Burbank, California, 1950. (BIAF—Israel Aviation & Space Magazine)

windows were cut, and the top cockpit windows removed. The engines were also improved, allowing increases in maximum gross and landing weight. The Connies were then painted in El Al's new royal blue and silver colors and tested by Lockheed.

The first Constellation ready for delivery proved to be 4X-AKB and, following a flight from New York to Israel under the command of Capt. Sam Lewis and First Officer Leo Gardner, it arrived at Lod Airport on 22 December 1950. The dignitaries aboard the plane included Al Schwimmer himself; Yehuda Arazi, the Israeli undercover agent who helped mastermind the acquisition of arms for the War of Independence; and Levi Eshkol, Treasurer of the Jewish Agency and later Prime Minister of Israel. It was a momentous occasion to have those who contributed so much to the birth of the State of Israel now participate in a major step forward in the development of El Al.

The new Constellation received the name *Mazal Tov* (Good Luck), and it was placed into immediate service with a charter flight from Tel Aviv to New York on 28-29 December 1950 carrying members of the Israel Philharmonic Orchestra. At the end of January 1951, 4X-AKB launched the first regular El Al Constellation service to Paris and London.

El Al's first Constellation (4X-AKA) on a test flight over Southern California in late 1950 while still under U.S. registration (N90827, visible under the left wing) prior to delivery to El Al. (El Al Israel Airlines collection)

On 25 March 1951 the second El Al Connie (4X-AKA), arrived in Israel. It was fitted with larger fuel tanks than AKB, allowing it to fly for two hours longer. El Al's Connies generally flew in an all-tourist configuration of about 63 seats. This was unusual at the time, since all other scheduled airlines ordinarily flew with an all first class seating configuration until economy class was introduced in 1952.

Inauguration of Regularly Scheduled Service to New York

Although El Al had been flying to the United States since June 1950, all of these early flights had been charters. Now, with the arrival of El Al's second Constellation, El Al decided to inaugurate regular scheduled service between Tel Aviv and New York. On 29 April 1951 an El Al Constellation lifted off the runway from Lod Airport on the inaugural scheduled flight to New York, via Athens, London and Shannon. With this flight El Al became the eleventh airline at the time to have regularly scheduled service on the North Atlantic route—and the first such airline to be based outside North America and Europe.

Connie Routes

The Constellations plied the same routes that had been pioneered for El Al by its DC-4s. With the route expansion of late 1950 and early 1951, the cities served by El Al numbered twelve: the home base at Tel Aviv; London, Paris, Zürich, Rome, Athens, Vienna, Nicosia and Istanbul in Europe; Nairobi and Johannesburg in Africa; and New York. Gander, Newfoundland, and Shannon, Ireland, were common refueling stops on the trans-Atlantic route. The first known comprehensive published schedule of El Al is dated 29 April 1951, the same day as the inaugural scheduled flight to New York. The schedule included two Constellation round-trips a week between Tel Aviv and New York, with three to five stops, depending on the flight and direction, selected from Athens, Rome, Paris, London, Shannon and Gander; one Constellation round-trip to Paris, with stops each way in Zürich; one Constellation round-trip to Johannesburg, with stops each way in Nairobi; one DC-4 round-trip to Vienna, with stops in Rome; and one DC-4 round-trip to Istanbul, with stops in Nicosia.

On 8 August 1951 the third of the three Constellations purchased by El Al from Schwimmer's company (4X-AKC), arrived at Lod Airport, allowing the phase-out of the DC-4s by April 1952. El Al then substituted some C-46s, acquired from the Israeli Air Force, for two of its shorter routes—a weekly round-trip to Vienna (with stops in Rome and Athens) and a weekly round-trip to Istanbul (with a stop in Nicosia).

During 1952-54, while the details of El Al's passenger schedules changed from time to time, the basic structure remained the same, with flights between Tel Aviv and New York via stops at various European capitals; Tel Aviv and Vienna (via Rome and Athens); Tel Aviv and Istanbul (via Nicosia); and Tel Aviv and Johannesburg. In 1954 El Al acquired a fourth Constellation (4X-AKD) from California Hawaiian Airlines. This allowed El Al, by July of that year, to increase its trans-Atlantic service to thrice weekly.

Route expansion occurred in March 1956, as El Al added its first new scheduled destinations in five years—Brussels and Amsterdam.

By summer 1957 El Al was operating an all-Constellation passenger service. Each week there were three round-trips to New York (via Athens or Rome, Brussels or Paris, and London); one to Paris (via Zürich); one to London (via Vienna and Amsterdam); and another to Istanbul. In addition, leased Douglas DC-6Bs (and later DC-7Cs) were utilized on a weekly round-trip to Johannesburg.

First arrival of an El Al Lockheed 49 Constellation (4X-AKB) at Lod Airport, on 22 December 1950, commanded by Capt. Sam Lewis with Leo Gardner as first officer. Hillel Simon, operations officer at Lod Airport at the time, is directing the aircraft in with upraised flags. (Israeli Government Press Office)

ISRAEL AIRLINES

EL AL
ISRAEL AIRLINES

אל על
נתיבי אויר לישראל

TIME TABLE

EFFECTIVE APRIL 29 1951

Earliest El Al published timetable known to the author, dated 29 April 1951. Issued in connection with the inauguration of El Al scheduled flights to the United States, the schedule called for two round-trips weekly between Tel Aviv and New York, with two or three European stops each way selected among Athens, Rome, Paris and London, and refueling stops in Gander, Newfoundland, each way and also at Shannon, Ireland, westbound. Four other weekly flights went from Tel Aviv to Rome/Vienna, Zürich/Paris, Nicosia/Istanbul, and Nairobi/Johannesburg. In just 2½ years after its founding, El Al was serving 12 countries in four continents. Constellations were now used on all flights except for DC-4s on the routes to Vienna and Istanbul, and Curtiss C-46s were used as freighters. Note the use of "EA", the original two-letter airline code for El Al. Eastern Airlines was already using "EA" and it objected, thus by 1952 El Al adopted "LY" instead, drawn from LYdda Airport. The middle digit of each flight number was originally keyed to the ultimate destination from Tel Aviv, the "0" meaning Johannesburg, "1" New York, "2" Europe, and "3" Istanbul. As flights became more complex and computerization was introduced, this system had to be dropped. Note also the absence of service during the Jewish Sabbath, Friday eve to Saturday eve, a hallmark of El Al during most of its existence as well as today. (Marvin Goldman collection)

U.S.A., NEWFOUNDLAND, IRELAND, ENGLAND, FRANCE, SWITZERLAND, AUSTRIA, ITALY, GREECE, TURKEY, CYPRUS, SOUTHAFRICA, KENYA, ISRAEL

EASTBOUND		EA 112 Constellation	EA 102 Constellation	EA 122 DC4	EA 114 Constellation	EA 124 Constellation	EA 132 DC4
		Saturday	Sunday	Monday	Wednesd.	Wednesd.	Wednesd.
NEW YORK	Dp.	23.59			10.30		
GANDER	Ar.	Sunday 06.00			16.30		
	Dp.	07.00			17.30		
SHANNON							
LONDON	Ar.	19.30			Thursday 06.00		
	Dp.	20.30			07.00		
PARIS	Ar.	22.00					
	Dp.	23.00				10.15	
ZURICH	Ar.					12.00	
	Dp.					13.00	
VIENNA	Dp.			18.00			
ROME	Ar.			20.45	11.45		
	Dp.			21.45	12.45		
ATHENS	Ar.	Monday 06.15					
	Dp.	07.15					
ISTANBUL	Dp.						15.00
NICOSIA	Ar.						18.00
	Dp.						19.00
JOHANNESBURG	Dp.		00.30				
NAIROBI	Ar.		08.30				
	Dp.		09.30				
TEL AVIV	Ar.	11.30	18.30	Tuesday 06.45	20.15	23.00	21.15

ISRAEL, KENYA, SOUTHAFRICA, CYPRUS, TURKEY, GREECE, ITALY, AUSTRIA, SWITZERLAND, FRANCE, ENGLAND, IRELAND, NEWFOUNDLAND, U. S. A.

WESTBOUND		EA 111 Constellation	EA 121 DC4	EA 123 Constellation	EA 131 DC4	EA 113 Constellation	EA 101 Constellation
		Sunday	Sunday	Tuesday	Wednesd.	Thursday	Thursday
TEL AVIV	Dp.	22.00	23.00	09.00	09.00	09.00	23.30
NAIROBI	Ar.						Friday 08.30
	Dp.						09.30
JOHANNESBURG	Ar.						15.30
NICOSIA	Ar.				09.15		
	Dp.				10.15		
ISTANBUL	Ar.				13.15		
ATHENS	Ar.	Monday 00.30					
	Dp.	01.30					
ROME	Ar.		Monday 05.00			13.30	
	Dp.		06.00			14.30	
VIENNA	Ar.		08.45				
ZURICH	Ar.			16.00			
	Dp.			17.00			
PARIS	Ar.			18.45		18.00	
	Dp.					19.00	
LONDON	Ar.	09.00				20.30	
	Dp.	10.00				21.30	
SHANNON	Ar.	12.05				23.35	
	Dp.	13.05				Friday 00.35	
GANDER	Ar.	19.35				07.05	
	Dp.	20.35				08.05	
NEW YORK	Ar.	Tuesday 00.25				11.55	

Passengers originating their passage in ROME, PARIS, ZURICH and NICOSIA are accepted only to ISRAEL and onward connecting points.

Ar. = Arrival
Dp. = Departure

משען אויר מתקבל לכל חלקי העולם

Air Freight accepted to all parts of the World

All times are local summer times.
All fares are in accordance with IATA tariffs.
Meals and refreshments served (KOSHER כשר)

Welcoming festivities at Lod Airport for El Al's first Constellation (4X-AKB) to arrive in Israel, on 22 December 1950. The Constellation was El Al's first "modern" pressurized aircraft, enabling it to open regular scheduled passenger service across the Atlantic to the United States (as opposed to the earlier sporadic charter flights with DC-4s). (Israeli Government Press Office)

Problems, Problems

The Connies were temperamental planes. Mechanical problems were frequent and a general shortage of spare parts plagued the industry, causing frequent delays and schedule disruptions. Often an aircraft would be grounded, perhaps in Iceland or Khartoum, waiting for a scarce replacement engine or spare parts to be flown in. One of the Connies was dubbed "The Turkish Bath" as its air conditioning was "temporarily" out of order most of its life with El Al. The Connies also were not that well insulated, and the high interior noise level from the engines and propellers made the long flights seem even lengthier.

The published schedules only compounded the problem. They were usually issued late, with numerous errors, and schedule changes were frequent. More importantly, they called for El Al's Connies to be flown between two and four hours per day more than the average utilization of similar aircraft by other airlines. This over-ambitious plan just couldn't be carried out in practice.

Public relations had a hard time. One of the carrier's biggest jobs was to convince the public that it was a real commercial airline and not just an immigrant carrier. (Most of the airline's early income came from carrying immigrants to Israel.) Yet the frequent delays meant that El Al still appealed mainly to air travelers sentimental about its ties to Israel. With good nature, they joked that El Al really was an acronym for "Every Landing Always Late", and the Constellations were called the "El Al Cancellations". Nevertheless, during this period El Al maintained a flawless safety record, and its load factor remained one of the highest of all trans-Atlantic airlines.

Another problem confronting El Al was that most of the crew members were still non-Israelis, which rankled the Israeli public. Pilots in the early years of El Al could be divided into three distinct groups—*foreigners* (airmen recruited from *Mahal* and foreign air carriers, predominantly Anglo-Saxon in language and culture); *semi-foreigners*, former U.S. Air Force and Royal Air Force fliers, mostly Jewish, suspended between two worlds, Zion and the rest of the universe—from New York, Los Angeles and London—captivated by the new State yet uncommitted in terms of their future, and who because of language, interest and salaries tended to gravitate toward the foreign element; and *Israeli citizens*, such as Oded Abarbanel, Yitzhak Hennenson, Zvi Tohar and Shmuel Wedeles.

By 1954, however, the slow but steady shift to an Israeli crew emphasis had become decidedly noticeable. There were many Israeli radio operators, some co-pilots and assistant flight engineers. Zvi Tohar became the first Israeli to be licensed to captain Constellations, in 1953. Only 50 foreign air crew remained by 1954, and some of the foreign pilots, such as Bill Katz from Florida, George (Gad) Katz from Rhodesia, and Danny Rosin from South Africa, became residents.

Above: *Capt. Sam Lewis in the cockpit of an El Al Constellation, 1952. At his right is Uri Cohen, flight engineer, and later a captain with El Al.* (Capt. Sam Lewis collection)

Right: *El Al in-flight meal service aboard a Constellation in March 1951, served by Herb Kweller, El Al's first steward on scheduled passenger flights.* (Israeli Government Press Office)

Below: *An El Al Constellation (4X-AKA) at Paris (Orly Airport), about 1952, attended by an El Al Citroën vehicle.* (El Al Israel Airlines collection)

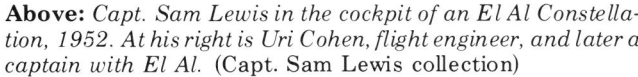

El Al Constellation (4X-AKB) with the Lod Airport terminal building in the background, 22 December 1950. (Israeli Government Press)

Maintenance

El Al's early maintenance was mainly contracted out. For example, maintenance on its Constellations was initially performed by aircraft service companies operating out of Idlewild Airport, New York. From the beginning, El Al established a goal of developing its own complete maintenance facilities and technicians at Lod Airport. It was slow going, but by dint of hard work, local capabilities developed. Early Israeli technicians of El Al, such as Dov Rafaelovitch and David Yaacov, furnished the ambition and helped develop the skills that later transformed El Al maintenance into a premier operation admired by the industry. By 1954 70% of all maintenance work was handled at Lod, and only 60 of the imported technicians remained.

Meanwhile, Al Schwimmer was also hard at work to help make the State of Israel self-sufficient in aircraft maintenance and servicing. In October 1953, with input from his own maintenance company, Israel Aircraft Industries (IAI) was established at Lod Airport under the original name of Bedek—Government Aircraft Overhaul Depot (*Bedek* means "inspection and maintenance"). Its mission was to act as an overhaul and maintenance center primarily for the Israeli Air Force, with the servicing of commercial transports transiting Tel Aviv as a secondary function. Within three years

IAI completed an impressive new aircraft overhaul base at Lod, with the capability to do complete engine repairs and 1,000-hour checks. In March 1956 IAI's success led to a proposal to transfer El Al's line and engine maintenance work to IAI. This change was vigorously resisted by El Al's mechanics. A government investigating committee was convened and decided in favor of independent El Al maintenance, a policy that has continued with beneficial results to this day.

The Search for New Aircraft

By 1953 El Al realized that its early model Constellations were becoming obsolescent. As in the DC-4 era, its competitors on the trans-Atlantic run were already flying more advanced types, with greater comfort, range and reliability.

Yet El Al's financial resources were extremely limited. It simply couldn't afford to buy any better aircraft. At first, in July 1953, it considered a novel plan to upgrade its piston-engine C-46 aircraft with a small turbojet engine, developed by aeronautical engineer Dr. Erich Schatzki. They were to be mounted in pairs, like jet pods, allowing the capacious aircraft to carry an additional 4,500kg (10,000lb) of payload. The engine would be manufactured by Société Turboméca of France. However, this plan was never implemented, as El Al decided instead to add a fourth Model 49 Constellation to its fleet.

Refueling a Constellation at Lod Airport, April 1951. Unlike underwing pressure hoses used today, refueling in the piston-engine era was by overwing gravity methods. (Israeli Government Press Office)

A year later El Al considered buying some Model 1049 Super Constellations to replace the 49s, but deferred a decision. Plans were also formulated for the possible sale of $1-3 million of stock to the public; again, this did not go through.

El Al's competitive disadvantage in aircraft had become even more acute by 1955. Other alternatives were advanced. Bob Prescott, head of The Flying Tiger Line, a well-known U.S. charter and cargo airline, proposed to supply El Al with new Lockheed 1049G Super Constellations and Flying Tiger expertise in exchange for a 26% ownership interest in El Al. Prescott also said he would help phase-in jet aircraft when these were available for commercial use. It was an attractive offer, but the temper of the times in Israel was for El Al to become less dependent on foreign sources, so the Flying Tiger proposal was turned down.

Also considered, in October 1955, was the purchase of two later model Constellations from Compania Cubana de Aviacion. One was to have been placed in trans-Atlantic service in late 1955 and the other in January 1956, so as to allow El Al to increase its service to five trans-Atlantic flights a week during the 1956 season. This plan, too, was never consummated.

Meanwhile, El Al's President, Aryeh Pincus, preferred a bold leap forward. Britain's Bristol Aeroplane Company was designing a new type of aircraft—a four-engine turboprop with a passenger capacity nearly twice that of the Connie and a long-range capability and speed ideal for El Al's requirements. The aircraft, called the Britannia, was still in the design stage and would cost the then staggering sum of $4.5 million (four and a half times the cost of a used Connie)—but it represented a technological revolution! The turboprop engines would offer a new dimension in smooth and quiet flight, with greater economy and ample power to fly nonstop across the Atlantic even against the prevailing winds.

With a lot of hard work and sweat, Pincus convinced the Government to select the Britannia alternative, and a firm order for three Britannias, with an option for a fourth, was signed on 22 June 1955. El Al thereby became the first airline outside of Britain's State-owned British Overseas Airways Corporation (BOAC) to order this innovative "jet-prop" aircraft.

El Al Constellation flight crew with earliest uniforms during Constellation service, 1951. Left to right: Max Diamant (steward), another unidentified steward, Joe Debsky (steward), Kitty Lowenthal Tohar (stewardess), Bernie Hoffman (captain), Livia Eisen Chertoff (stewardess), Herb Bornstein (flight engineer), Dan Lichtenstein Alon (radio operator), and Sam Feidman (captain). (El Al Israel Airlines collection)

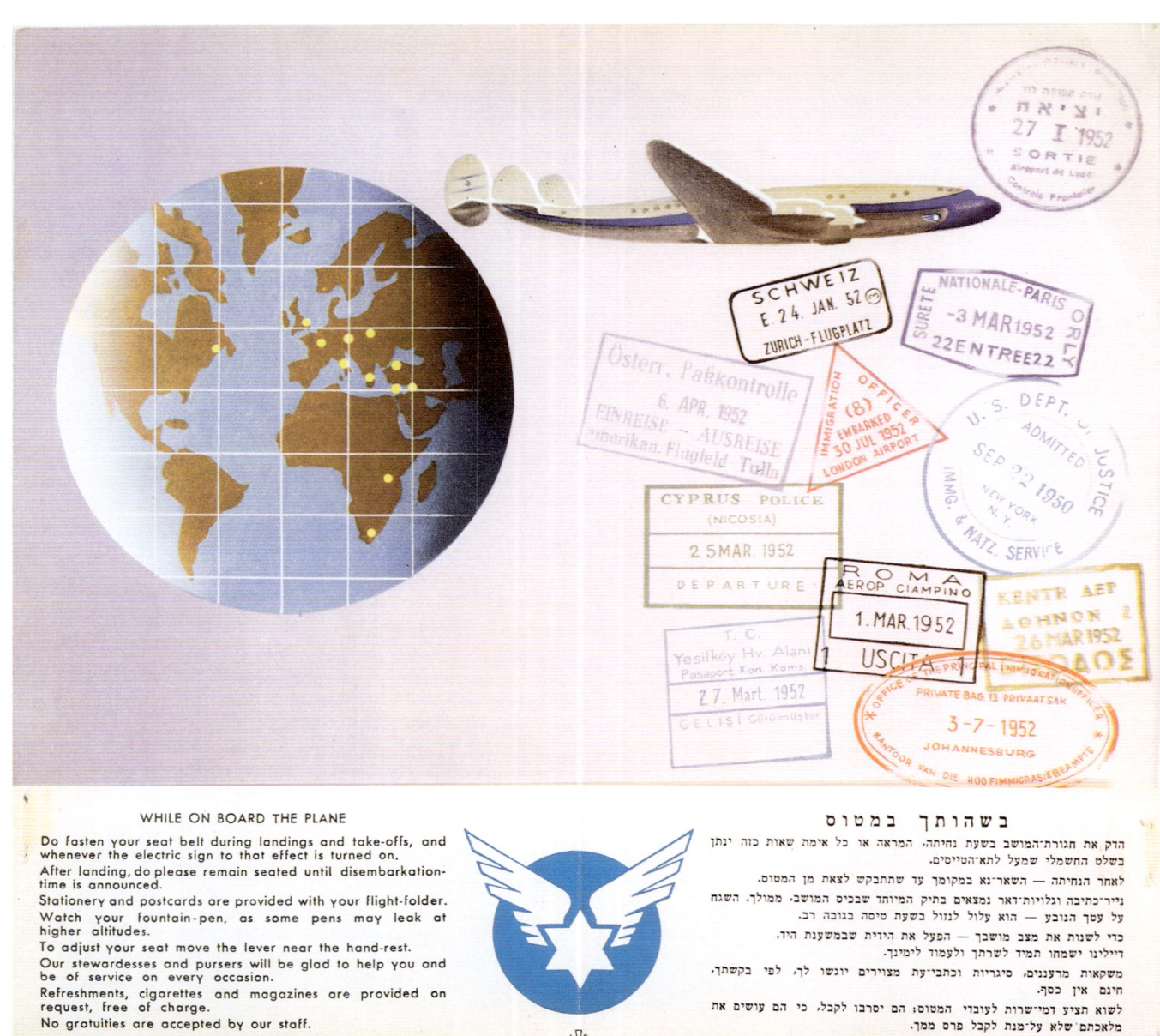

WHILE ON BOARD THE PLANE

Do fasten your seat belt during landings and take-offs, and whenever the electric sign to that effect is turned on.

After landing, do please remain seated until disembarkation-time is announced.

Stationery and postcards are provided with your flight-folder.

Watch your fountain-pen, as some pens may leak at higher altitudes.

To adjust your seat move the lever near the hand-rest.

Our stewardesses and pursers will be glad to help you and be of service on every occasion.

Refreshments, cigarettes and magazines are provided on request, free of charge.

No gratuities are accepted by our staff.

בשהותך במטוס

הדק את חגורת־המושב בשעת נחיתה. המראה או כל אימת שאות כזה ינתן בשלט החשמלי שמעל לתא־הטייסים.

לאחר הנחיתה — השאר־נא במקומך עד שתתבקש לצאת מן המטוס.

נייר־כתיבה וגלויות־דאר נמצאים בתיק המיוחד שבכיס המושב, ממולך. השגח על עטך הנובע — הוא עלול לנזול בשעת טיסה בגובה רב.

כדי לשנות את מצב מושבך — הפעל את הידית שבמשענת היד.

דיילינו ישמחו תמיד לשרתך ולעמוד לימינך.

משקאות מרעננים, סיגריות וכתבי־עת מצווירים יוגשו לך, לפי בקשתך, חינם אין כסף.

לשוא תציע דמי־שירות לעובדי המטוס: הם יסרבו לקבל. כי הם עושים את מלאכתם שלא על־מנת לקבל פרס ממך.

Inside of one of El Al's earliest ticket jackets, introduced in 1952. Replicas of Government passport stamps from each of El Al's eleven foreign destinations appear on the right. (Marvin Goldman collection)

Symbols of El Al's destinations and a hearty "Bon Voyage" appear on the outside of a 1952 Constellation-era ticket jacket. (Marvin Goldman collection)

Following page, top left: *An early El Al advertising poster from the Constellation era, probably post-November 1952. (El Al Israel Airlines collection)*

Following page, top right: *One of El Al's first advertising posters. The pointed "A" in El Al indicates the poster was in use prior to November 1952, as subsequent El Al liveries and advertising used a flat-topped "A". (El Al Israel Airlines collection)*

Following page, below: *El Al's network from April 1951 through February 1956. Within two years after inaugurating scheduled service, El Al linked 12 cities on routes covering 30,000km (19,000mi). The reference in the illustration to "15 countries" includes those utilized for refueling stops. (Marvin Goldman collection)*

Tragedy Strikes

Just as El Al was glowing over the signing of the Britannia order, it suffered a stunning loss. On 27 July 1955 Constellation 4X-AKC lifted off from Vienna bound for Tel Aviv with 51 passengers and a crew of seven. The flight, regularly scheduled LY402, had originated in London the day before and also stopped at Paris. Its route from Vienna channeled it down a narrow air corridor over Yugoslavia near the Bulgarian border. The crew was Stanley Hinks, Captain; Pinchas Ben-Porat, First Officer; Rafi Goldman, Radio Operator; Sydney Chalmers, Flight Engineer; Sara Acharkan, Stewardess; and Albert Alkhadaff and Leon Tiser, Stewards.

The Constellation was flying at a height of 5,400m (17,700ft) in the early morning twilight. Suddenly the plane was intercepted by a covey of Bulgarian MiG-15 jet fighters. They directed the aircraft to lower its landing gear and proceed to a military air base west of Sofia. The plane descended to an altitude of about 600m (2,000ft) as it prepared to touch down in Bulgaria. Suddenly, without warning, the MiGs opened fire with machine guns and 20-mm cannon and the aircraft crashed in flames near the Greek border. There were no survivors.

Overcoming obstacles imposed by Bulgarian officials, the bodies were eventually allowed to be returned to Israel, and those of the El Al crew are buried at a memorial site in Tel Aviv's Kiryat Shaul cemetery.

The shooting down of the Constellation plunged El Al into gloom. It canceled further flights pending a study of the tragedy and a reassessment of its future. Skeptics stepped up their criticism of the airline as an unnecessary luxury. The Britannia decision was still under fire. Strong vocal opposition existed to the losses accruing from the trans-Atlantic routes. To reach profitability, the load factor (i.e. the number of passenger seats occupied as a percentage of those available) would have had to rise to 102%! Suggestions arose that El Al confine itself to "essential" flights and regular scheduled service to Europe. It seemed that El Al had reached the nadir of its fortunes.

Management, however, was convinced that the only way out was development, not retrenchment. They believed that no country, and particularly not Israel, could afford the luxury of depending entirely on foreign carriers to keep the lines of exterior communication open. They also believed in the ultimate economic viability of Israeli commercial airline operations. Flights were resumed, and another used 049 Constellation (4X-AKE) was purchased in October 1955 as an interim measure to replace the destroyed aircraft.

Laying wreaths at the memorial burial site in Kiryat Shaul (Tel Aviv), Israel, of the crew of the El Al Constellation (4X-AKC) tragically shot down by Bulgarian MiG fighter aircraft near the Bulgarian-Greek border on 27 July 1955 with the loss of all 51 passengers and seven crew members aboard. This photograph was taken on one of the anniversaries of the event. Shlomo Lahat, President of El Al in 1966-67, is standing in front wearing dark glasses. (El Al Israel Airlines collection)

The Sinai War

The despair and doubts about El Al changed dramatically with the outbreak of the Sinai War on 29 October 1956. In the months preceding the war, Israel confronted fierce guerrilla warfare along its eastern border with Jordan, while the Gaza Strip at its southwest had been turned into an Egyptian-supported *fedayeen* guerrilla base. Meanwhile, directly south at Eilat, Israel's communications by sea were under attack. The Suez Canal had been illegally nationalized by Egypt's President Nasser, and Egypt proclaimed a blockade of Israeli shipping through the Red Sea by sealing off Eilat from Sharm-el-Sheikh. The guns of Ras Nasrani were pointed at the 72m (235ft)-wide lane that Israeli shipping would have to navigate to keep Eilat and the southern Negev alive.

In coordination with the British and French who were particularly concerned about protecting their own interests in the Suez Canal, Israel invaded the Sinai peninsula in an effort to keep its Red Sea shipping lanes open.

All foreign airlines immediately stopped flying to Israel; the country was surrounded by unfriendly States to the north, east and south. As in the War of Independence, Israel's only swift line of communication to its nearest friends and allies was over the Mediterranean Sea by air.

One of El Al's earliest airline-issued postcards, printed in Israel, 1951-52. (Marvin Goldman collection)

El Al was the only airline that flew passengers in and out of Israel during the 1956 War. It was difficult, as many of its pilots were called to active duty by the Air Force. Other pilots were requisitioned to fly El Al aircraft that transported ammunition and supplies from Paris to Israel.

The Sinai War ended public doubts about El Al and galvanized support. The Israeli Government understood anew that in times of war, when all foreign airlines suspend flights to Israel, only El Al can be counted on to continue scheduled service. Pride replaced criticism in the public's mind. There were no more calls to cut back El Al's routes. Now the Government of Israel committed itself to building El Al into a major international airline by firmly supporting the airline's decision to pursue the acquisition of the Bristol Britannia.

A New Era, and New Leadership

The Sinai Campaign also signaled the beginning of a new era. Sweeping managerial and organizational changes were about to transform El Al, as the debt-ridden airline moved swiftly from piston- to turbine-engine aircraft, from adolescence to maturity, from losses to profitability, and from an immigrant carrier to a significant international competitor.

Moshe Carmel, then El Al's chairman, decided that El Al needed a new leader who would reduce the losses and respond more quickly to technological innovation. He chose Efraim Ben-Arzi. Pincus left to become top man of the Jewish Agency.

Born in Poland, Ben-Arzi was an engineering graduate of Grenoble University and ended World War II with the highest rank obtained by a Palestinian Jew serving in the British Army—Lieutenant Colonel. Later he rose to the position of Major General in the Israeli Defense Forces and head of logistics and supply. A strong and controversial leader, he attracted both admirers and critics.

Ben-Arzi worked for a more efficient utilization of manpower and equipment and emphatically endorsed the decision to purchase the Britannia. His main policies and views are as strikingly modern today as they were then: that the small size of the host country does not limit the traffic potential of its national carrier; high equipment utilization is a must—it reduces unit costs; and the successful airline must emphasize manpower skills, the best exchange of information, and active participation in spare parts pools. Ben-Arzi also maintained that the usefulness of an airplane is not always related to age, as fashion and "having the latest" are important factors; and one can only compete through publicity and advertising—publicizing new equipment will draw the public away from the older airplanes.

With these policies in place, and the Britannia order firmly on the books, El Al was poised for one of its boldest steps forward.

The dramatic royal blue and silver paint scheme of one of El Al's first Constellations. Capt. Sam Lewis, a hero in air transport during Israel's War of Independence and later Chief Pilot of El Al for many years, is on the left, with Pete Rivas, flight engineer, on the right. Capt. Lewis was with El Al 22 years, logging 28,000 flying hours. Following mandatory retirement at age 60, he started yet another flying career, becoming the chief instructor of 707 crews for Ecuatoriana and later the personal pilot for a luxuriously fitted 707 owned by a wealthy Israeli industrialist. (Capt. Sam Lewis collection)

El Al's Constellation 4X-AKD in a rare color photograph taken at London-Heathrow. (Brian Stainer via Peter R. Keating)

Above: *Shimon Peres, then Director-General of Israel's Ministry of Defense and later Prime Minister of Israel, boarding an El Al Constellation at Lod Airport in the mid-1950s. El Al's Joe Klein is at the foot of the stairs.* (El Al Israel Airlines collection)

Below: *First flight cover carried on El Al's first official scheduled passenger flight from Tel Aviv to Amsterdam, 5 March 1956.*

CHAPTER FOUR

No Goose No Gander: The Record-Breaking Britannias

"I carried you on eagles wings"
(Exodus 19:4)

As 1955 dawned, El Al was still coping with a fleet of outdated, World War II-vintage Model 49 Constellations and C-46 Commando aircraft. It dreamed of the day when modern aircraft could be operated, enabling El Al to join the world's leading airlines. New aircraft, utilized efficiently, could also increase passenger traffic, restore profitability and earn badly needed foreign currency for the young State of Israel.

Many alternatives had been considered, including the acquisition of later model Constellations and improved engines for the Commandos. However, El Al's management had kept their eyes focused on a bold venture taking shape at the Bristol Aeroplane Company at Filton, England, and they were transfixed. A new engine was being developed—for a new airliner called the Britannia—that would substantially improve speed and operating economy.

Britannia production at the Bristol Aeroplane Company Ltd., Filton, Bristol, England, about 1956. (Bristol Aeroplane photo via El Al Israel Airlines collection)

The Britannia was powered by four Proteus turbopropeller engines in place of the traditional piston power. The projected Series 300 longer-bodied version, which particularly appealed to El Al, would accommodate some 100 passengers, nearly twice that of a Constellation, and a new dimension in quieter flight and comfort was promised due to the smoother operation of the turboprop engines. The Britannia's long-range capability of nearly 6,900km (4,300mi) with maximum payload, and its cruising speed of nearly 640km/h (400mph) at an altitude of 7,900m (26,000ft), were also significant improvements over the piston-engine Constellations. The Britannia's performance would allow regular nonstop

service in both directions across the Atlantic, ideal for El Al's requirements. Each Britannia would cost $4.5 million (nearly five times the cost of a used Connie), an enormous sum in its day for the young airline and State—but it represented a technological revolution!

After painstaking internal analysis and tough pleading and cajoling with its Government shareholder representatives, El Al announced on 17 March 1955 its bold decision to invest up to $18 million for four Britannias to replace its outmoded fleet, with the hope of operating them on its trans-Atlantic route by early 1957. On 22 June 1955, at a time when only British Overseas Airways Corporation (BOAC) had committed to purchase any Britannias, El Al signed an order with Bristol, covering three aircraft and an option for a fourth. El Al thereby became the first overseas airline to order the British-built Britannia.

Only one month later, in July 1955, one of El Al's Constellations was shot down by Bulgarian MiGs when it accidentally strayed into Bulgarian airspace. Strong demands in Israel were made on El Al to cancel the Britannia order and to cut back to "essential" routes only. Debates on these issues were even held in the Knesset, the Israeli legislature. El Al's management, however, staunchly supported the Britannia decision, and when Efraim Ben-Arzi was appointed President of El Al after the 1956 Sinai War, he also strongly backed the decision.

The Britannia became a matter of sink or swim for El Al because of the required heavy financial and technical commitment. Success would mean a technological leap into the heart of the international airline arena—the highly competitive North Atlantic run. Failure would leave El Al with its fleet

Viewing a prototype of the Bristol Proteus turboprop engine for El Al's Bristol Britannias, about 1956-57. Left to right: Moshe Carmel (El Al Chairman of the Board); Efraim Ben-Arzi (El Al President and a prime supporter of the decision to acquire the Britannias); Uri Michaeli (pioneer in early Israeli civil aviation, and head of Israel's Department of Civil Aviation).

of second-line uncompetitive aircraft and would fuel the arguments of the skeptics who preferred cutbacks in the airline's role.

El Al wisely made elaborate preparations to assure a smooth introduction of these innovative turbine-powered aircraft. By the delivery date of the first Britannia, over 450 El Al employees received specialized training for the aircraft at El Al's own training headquarters, and some 140 employees received training abroad.

order. El Al had entered a new era, one that would establish it for all time within the ranks of the world's leading international airlines.

With 4X-AGA now at Lod Airport, intense crew training started. Soon this expanded with the arrival in Tel Aviv of the second Britannia (-AGB) on 19 October and the third (-AGC) on 29 November.

El Al embarked on a series of carefully prepared Britannia proving flights, seeking to

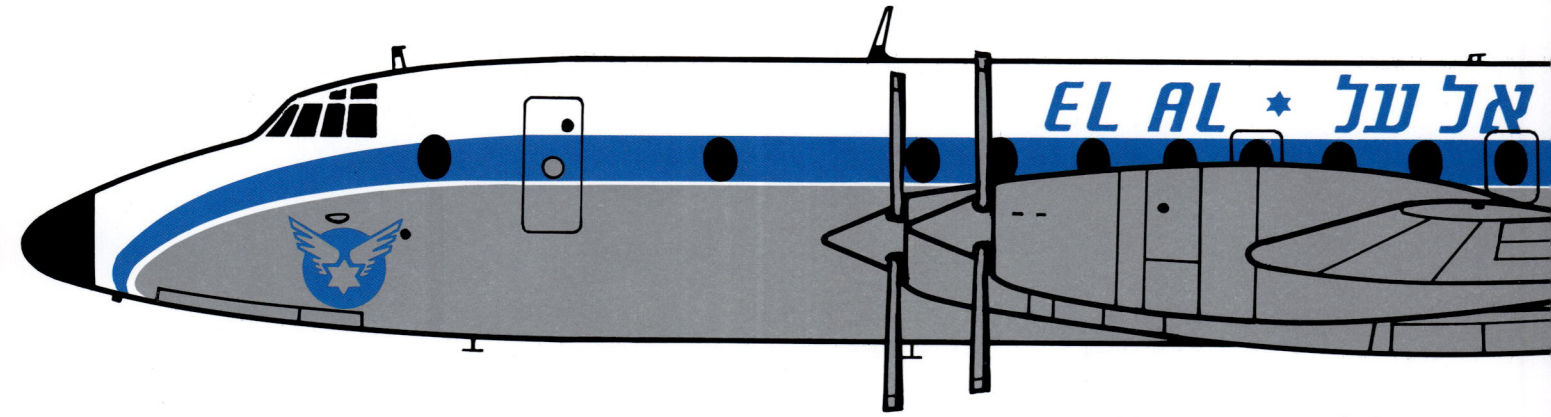

Unfortunately, the development of the Britannia during 1955-1957 was plagued with delays, mainly due to unforeseen problems with ice formation in the intakes of the Proteus engines. The planned delivery dates of early 1957 slipped away, frustrating expectations of securing a longer headstart against airlines which had not ordered long-range turboprops.

El Al's first Britannia, registered 4X-AGA, was finally delivered to the airline at Filton, England, on 5 September 1957. The nonstop delivery flight to Tel Aviv one week later was made in 5hr 59min at an average speed of 645km/h (401mph). The arrival occasioned a great celebration at El Al and coincided with its announcement of the conversion of the option on a fourth aircraft to a firm

H.R.H. the Duke of Edinburgh leaving El Al Britannia 4X-AGC after inspecting it during a visit to the Bristol Aeroplane Company, 1957. (Bristol Aeroplane photo via El Al Israel Airlines collection)

establish the best possible operating techniques for these revolutionary aircraft. The first round-trip proving flight was completed 30 October 1957, allowing El Al to check out the sophisticated flight deck equipment, all of which performed beautifully. Early in November 1957, the first of four trans-Atlantic proving flights was completed, with the New York to London sector of 5,665km (3,520mi) being flown in 9hr and the London to Tel Aviv segment in 6hr 50min. In contrast, typical flying time in an El Al Constellation had been 14hr from New York to London, plus the time for a refueling stop at Gander, Newfoundland. On 8 December 1957 another El Al Britannia covered the New York to London segment in only 8hr 3min. The setting of new speed records by El Al had begun.

The most significant accomplishment of all, however, occurred on 18/19 December 1957 when El Al, with Britannia 4X-AGC on a proving flight under the command of Capt. Zvi Tohar, covered the 9,270km (5,760mi) from New York to Tel Aviv in 14hr 46min at an average speed of 645km/h (401mph) thanks to a helpful tailwind. At the time this was the longest distance ever covered nonstop by a commercial airliner.

Turboprop Service

On Sunday, 22 December 1957, when all other intercontinental airlines except BOAC were still operating piston-engine aircraft, El Al launched its scheduled turbine-powered Britannia passenger service with 4X-AGB. This followed BOAC by just three days. The route was Tel Aviv to London (Heathrow) to New York (Idlewild, now Kennedy). In the words of *Jane's All the World's Aircraft*, "Showing an appreciation of the competitive potential of the aircraft which would have done credit to a company of greater size and much longer experience, El Al . . . put these new aircraft into Atlantic service".

On the New York to London return segment of its inaugural Britannia scheduled service, El Al set a speed record for the trans-Atlantic passenger service crossing between the two cities, known as the *Blue Riband* record, with a flying time of 8hr 3min. Although BOAC broke that record on 6 January 1958 with a time of 7hr 57min, El Al snatched it right back two days later, shaving

ISRAEL AIRLINES

נת"ב אויר לישראל

4X-AGA

Machat

13min off the flight time. Initially, service was flown once a week, departing Lod Airport each Sunday afternoon. Following a refueling stop and embarking additional passengers, the Britannia left London at 2340, arriving at Idlewild Airport at 0530 local time the following morning. The return started each Wednesday evening at 1900, stopped at London, and arrived in Tel Aviv late Thursday afternoon. By 16 January 1958 all three El Al Britannias were operating on the trans-Atlantic route via London.

El Al's Britannias featured a cockpit crew of four or five, with a typical passenger configuration of 18 first class seats, of which four were special "sleeperette" seats and another four were unusually luxurious curtained-off berths, and 72 tourist class seats. As in other propeller-driven aircraft of the day, the first class seats were in the rear of the cabin because it was the quietest part.

Eager to promote their new turboprop Britannia service, El Al launched one of the most famous airline advertising campaigns of all time. With eye-catching proclamations, "No Goose . . . No Gander", El Al pointed out that the Britannia eliminated the frequent need on westbound trans-Atlantic crossings (because of prevailing winds) for refueling stops at Goose Bay, Labrador, or Gander, Newfoundland. With another bold advertisement, "We Have Cut the Atlantic Ocean by 20%", El Al ignored the then-existing taboo of drawing attention to long-range over-water operations by successfully emphasizing the Britannia's dramatic improved speed over other aircraft in crossing the Atlantic. The quieter ride was publicized by dubbing the Britannia "The Whispering Giant". El Al established a substantial advertising budget, under its New York public relations head J. Peter Brunswick, a former Royal Air Force officer and journalist. Brunswick chose an advertising agency that was relatively new at the time, Doyle, Dane

and Bernbach, which produced some of the greatest airline advertisements ever.

The successful introduction of the Britannias was borne out by El Al's sharp rise in passenger numbers. In the first four months of turboprop operations, El Al achieved higher passenger load factors than any other trans-Atlantic carrier, reaching almost 70% by the end of April 1958, a remarkable accomplishment in those days. Ever since, El Al has retained one of the top positions of any carrier on the North Atlantic as measured by load factor.

Reception for the El Al Britannia 4X-AGB at the Farnborough Air Show, England, September 1957. The Britannia catapulted El Al into the forefront of trans-Atlantic travel, with a new standard of comfort and the setting of numerous speed records. (El Al Israel Airlines collection)

An El Al Britannia over the coast of Israel, April 1958.
(Israel Government Press Office)

Above: *An El Al Britannia (4X-AGC) at Lod Airport, around late 1957.* (British Aerospace collection)

Below: *Graduating class of new El Al flight attendants, sporting the new uniforms introduced by El Al upon starting Britannia service, in late 1957.* (El Al Israel Airlines collection)

African Service

Following the 1956 Sinai War, El Al was foreclosed by hostile Arab states from passing over their airspace, and thus the direct route to Johannesburg down the east coast of Africa, opened by El Al in 1950, was no longer possible. The only other route was through North Africa, but the countries concerned objected to El Al-marked aircraft landing in their territories.

El Al accordingly chartered aircraft from SABENA, the Belgian airline. Using Douglas DC-6B and later DC-7C aircraft, El Al flew from Tel Aviv to Benghazi or Tunis on the North African coast and then south via Kano, Nigeria, or Fort Lamy, Chad, and Leopoldville or Brazzaville, Congo, to Johannesburg. This system continued until 1962 when El Al introduced its own new Boeing 720B jets to Johannesburg on an even more circuitous route, via Teheran, Iran (see Chapter 5).

Via Britannia to the Top

El Al's utilization of the Britannia dramatically illustrated how a small airline, with top quality planning and training, could become a shining example of a first class operation.

Before scheduled service with the Britannia started across the North Atlantic, El Al set a primary goal of making almost all trans-Atlantic flights without any intermediate refueling stop at Gander, Goose Bay or elsewhere. J.E.D. Williams, El Al's Manager of Technical Planning and Development at the time, initiated an intensive study to see how the Britannia could be operated most efficiently so as to eliminate these stops. All known variables were studied, including prevailing winds, payload, and fuel burn. El Al also invested in some 365 hours of crew training and route proving.

El Al learned that if westbound flight time exceeded 12hr 20min, an intermediate refueling stop at Goose Bay, Gander or Boston would be required—a stop that El Al was determined to avoid. The airline also noted that, by departing from the Great Circle route (the shorter distance route) in search of better wind conditions, an average of 55 minutes could be saved. Also, as fuel was burnt and the aircraft became lighter during flight, optimum performance and fuel consumption could be achieved by allowing the aircraft to drift upwards about 245m (800ft) per hour, with the aircraft initially cruising at about 6,700m (22,000ft) and slowly rising to 9,150m (30,000ft). Procedures were also adopted to vary this general plan according to the winds experienced at these levels.

With these techniques El Al consistently outstripped BOAC (as well as everyone else) in nonstop performance across the Atlantic. In fact, during the first eleven months of its Britannia operations, El Al completed over 300 trans-Atlantic flights, and more than 90% were nonstop. Whenever a stop was made, it was due to unusual weather, traffic or load conditions.

Moreover, El Al consistently was faster across the Atlantic than BOAC, both in scheduled and in actual flying times. El Al scheduled 10hr 50min for the London to New York run, with the return at 8hr 30min—both less than BOAC's timetable. Yet El Al often beat its own schedule. For example, on 10-11 March 1958, a London-New York flight by 4X-AGA commanded by Capt. Sam Lewis made the crossing in 9hr 23min—a new westbound speed record and 87 minutes less than the

---

With the start of Britannia turboprop service, in late 1957 El Al launched an impressive advertising campaign, created by the Doyle Dane and Bernbach agency. The prize-winning advertisement "No Goose . . . No Gander" pointed out that with the Britannia, El Al could regularly fly across the Atlantic without stopping for refueling at Goose Bay, Labrador, or Gander, Newfoundland. (Marvin Goldman collection)

Another award-winning advertisement from late 1957, implying that El Al's jet-prop Britannia will fly across the Atlantic Ocean 20% faster than regular piston-powered aircraft. This was a risky pitch, because in those days oceans and mountains were considered dangerous for flying and taboo in advertisements. But the advertisement caught on and further contributed to the success of El Al's image. (Marvin Goldman)

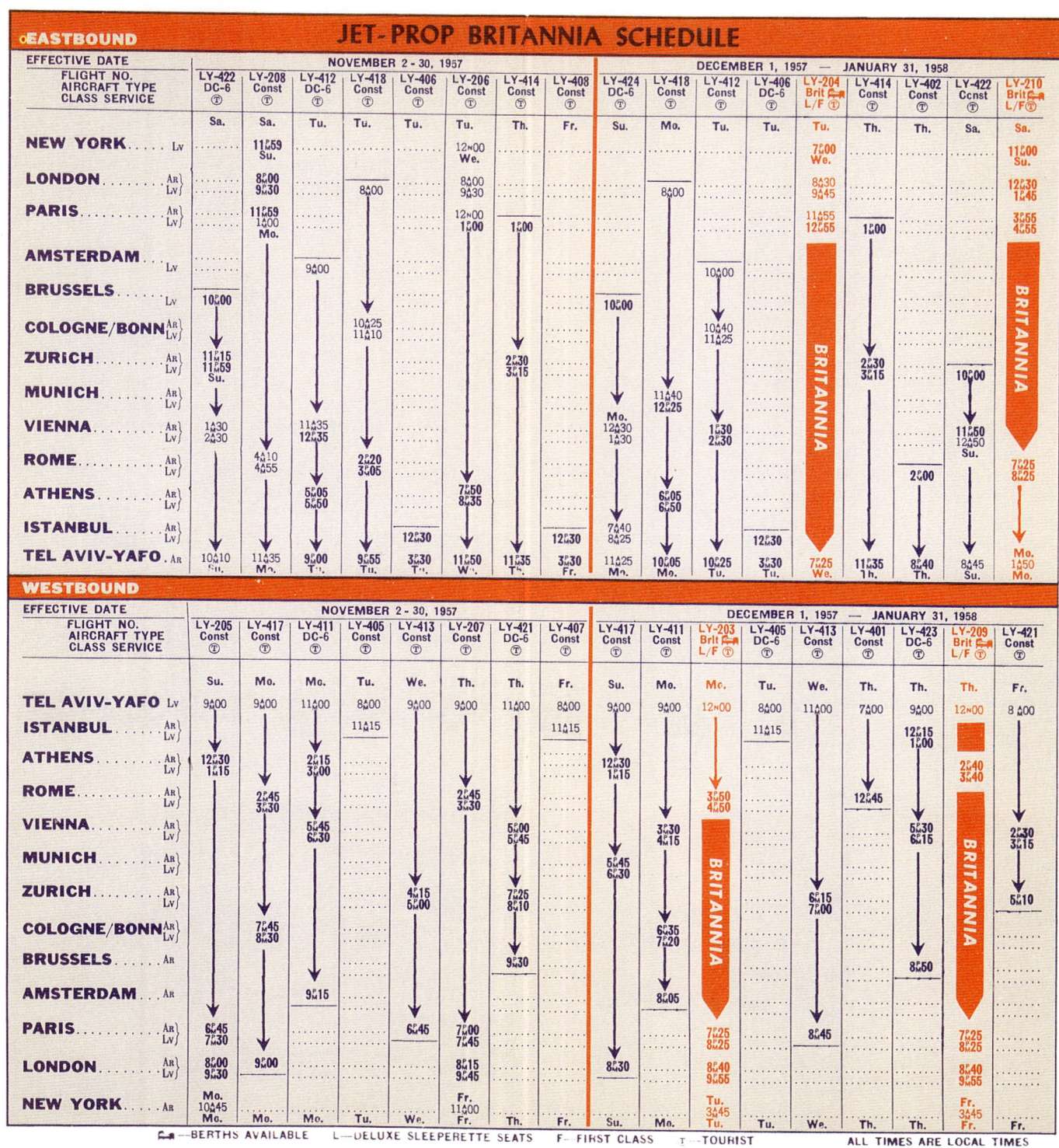

Winter 1957/58 schedule, the first showing El Al's new Britannia service. Service actually started 22 December 1957 with one flight per week, becoming twice a week in January 1958 and building up to five times weekly by summer 1958. (Marvin Goldman collection)

scheduled time. In another typical example, an El Al Britannia would leave New York for London eight minutes later than its BOAC counterpart, and be parked on the ramp at Heathrow by the time the BOAC aircraft landed!

This performance made El Al the envy of other trans-Atlantic carriers and allowed it to operate its Britannia fleet with maximum efficiency.

A Brief Reign

For summer 1958, El Al's first peak tourist season with Britannia aircraft, all three Britannias flew regularly between Tel Aviv and New York. At the height of the summer, there were five trans-Atlantic flights per week in each direction. Stops enroute were either in London or Paris or both. Passenger demand proved so great that an additional Britannia (4X-AGE) was leased from the manufacturer pending delivery of the fourth aircraft. Trans-Atlantic boardings more than

Capt. Tom Jones, a Welshman who became one of El Al's early captains and later Chief of Flight Operations, photographed about 1958. (El Al Israel Airlines collection)

Capt. Zvi Tohar, one of El Al's most beloved pilots, in the cockpit of a Bristol Britannia at Lod Airport, about 1958. He was one of the first native Israelis to become an El Al's captain and eventually rose to become Chief Pilot and later Chief of Flight Operations. (El Al Israel Airlines collection)

doubled, from 8,000 to 19,000 passengers, and El Al's percentage share of traffic on the route also doubled—within one year.

The Constellations were now completely displaced from the trans-Atlantic route, and remained in service on El Al's European schedules, flying regularly between Tel Aviv and Amsterdam, Athens, Brussels, Istanbul, Nicosia, Rome, Vienna and Zürich, as well as to two new destinations added in early 1958—Cologne and Munich, Germany.

On 7 March 1959 El Al took delivery of its fourth and final purchased Britannia (4X-AGD) and returned the leased aircraft. North Atlantic operations continued basically unchanged through 1959 and 1960, although trans-Atlantic passengers rose further to 25,000 in 1959 and 32,000 in 1960. Within the European network, the Britannias started to replace the Constellations, as these could not match the aircraft of most of El Al's competitors. In August 1959 the Britannia inaugurated scheduled service to Teheran, Iran.

By summer 1960 the Britannias were flying six times a week on the trans-Atlantic route. They also took over all the European network flights, except for the Istanbul and Nicosia services which were still plied by the aging Constellations. This period

Aboard a Britannia around 1958, giving out Chanukah dreidels (spinning tops) as gifts to young passengers. (El Al Israel Airlines collection)

David Ben-Gurion (towards the foot of the stairs), then Prime Minister of Israel, arrives at Lod Airport (later named Ben-Gurion Airport in his memory) about 1958 on an El Al Britannia. Moshe Dayan is in military uniform on the stairs.

EL AL אל על

נתיבי אויר לישראל
ISRAEL AIRLINES

Britannia 4X-AGA at Idlewild Airport (later JFK), New York, in the first color scheme. (Airliners America/ATP)

represented the peak of El Al's Britannia operations, as the rising star of pure jet travel now loomed on the horizon.

As fate would have it, the Britannia entered service a year later than planned. Meanwhile in the United States at the Boeing plant at Seattle, feverish activity to develop the pure-jet 707 resulted in the type entering service a year earlier than originally anticipated. The Boeing 707 started operation over the Atlantic with Pan American in October 1958 and, just three weeks earlier, BOAC had introduced the British-built de Havilland Comet 4 pure jet on the same route—all less than a year after El Al placed its first Britannia into service. The entry of the Douglas DC-8 jet in 1959 also fueled the fierce competition.

It was accepted, of course, that jet aircraft would eventually supersede turboprops for long-range routes. However, it was originally thought that the Britannia would have a minimum life as an aircraft of first rank for five years. The delay in delivery of the initial Britannias coupled with the quick entry of the pure-jets cut the Britannia's dominant position back to ten months.

Fortunately, El Al did not sit back and merely savor its success with the Britannia. President Ben-Arzi moved quickly to start negotiations with Boeing for the purchase of three 707-420 Intercontinental pure jet aircraft, and in January 1961 El Al started operating Boeing 707s (see Chapter 5). As a result, only three years after El Al's stunning introduction of its Britannias, the latter had to

Eleanor Roosevelt, one of the many well-known international visitors carried by El Al, is greeted by an El Al hostess upon arrival at Lod Airport, about 1958. (El Al Israel Airlines)

Britannia 4X-AGB at Orly Airport, Paris, August 1965, in El Al's updated color scheme. (Jean-M. Magendie)

relinquish their role as the flagships of the El Al fleet. As new 707s were delivered to El Al, they gradually replaced the Britannias on the trans-Atlantic run and the turboprops were increasingly confined to the European network, in turn replacing the remaining Constellations on the Istanbul and Nicosia routes.

By summer 1962 nine of the ten competing European and U.S. carriers serving Tel Aviv were already using pure-jet equipment. Only the tenth, KLM (Royal Dutch Airlines), was operating to Tel Aviv with Lockheed Electra turboprop aircraft. That year El Al completely removed its Britannias from the North Atlantic run, and it leased two of them via the manufacturer to British United Airways. The two remaining Britannias continued on the European network until sold to Globe-Air of Switzerland in 1964-65, and the two leased ones were returned to El Al until withdrawn and sold by the end of February 1967. Thus El Al's Britannia service ended less than a decade after its dramatic beginning.

Orthodox Jews dancing around their rebbe (distinguished rabbi) to greet him upon arrival at Lod Airport, about 1958, with a Britannia (4X-AGC) in the background. (El Al Israel Airlines collection)

An Arkia/Aliza Sud Aviation SE 3130 Alouette II jet-powered helicopter arrives at Lod Airport to connect with an El Al Britannia international flight in February 1960. This was the first commercial helicopter service in Israel and the Middle East. (Noam Hartoch)

El Al cover commemorating its first scheduled Britannia flight from Tel Aviv to New York on 22 December 1957. (Marvin Goldman)

CHAPTER FIVE

The Jet Era Arrives: Boeing 707s and 720s

"Behold, He who keeps Israel neither slumbers nor sleeps"

(Psalms, 121:4)

Even while the Britannias were achieving unparalleled success and the airline was still trying to swallow its then-enormous $18 million investment, El Al's management realized they could not sit back and relax. They had to prepare for the swiftly-approaching age of pure-jet aircraft. So only months after the first Britannia entered service, El Al opened negotiations for the purchase of new 707s, a type then being developed by Boeing in Seattle, Washington.

The 707 four-engine jet prototype (known as the 367-80) arose out a desire by Boeing in the early 1950s to further develop its four-piston-engine C-97 military transport/tanker aircraft. By significantly modifying the C-97 fuselage and combining it with wing technologies derived from Boeing's B-47 and B-52 jet bombers, Boeing hoped primarily to exploit the military market for the new aircraft, with the civilian market being a secondary, albeit still important, consideration. Meanwhile, the British de Havilland Comet jet airliner had entered service in 1952, only to suffer a sharp setback from two crashes caused by catastrophic metal fatigue. By 1955 de Havilland had started work on an improved model, designated Comet 4, and Douglas had decided to go ahead with a competitive design that became the DC-8. Not to be outdone, Boeing invested heavily in its 707 program and made faster progress than anticipated. By October 1958 Boeing 707s were in service with Pan American, earning the acclaim of airlines and passengers alike.

El Al decided to order three Boeing 707s of the improved Intercontinental Series 420 for use on its trans-Atlantic routes. The 420 designation meant that the aircraft was powered by four Rolls-Royce Conway "by-pass" engines (rather than the Pratt & Whitneys in use on the 320 Intercontinental series). The Boeing 707-420 featured a maximum cruising speed of 965km/h (600mph), nearly 50% faster than the Britannia, and a range of 7,830km (4,865mi) while carrying a maximum payload of 28,850kg (57,000lb). The order entailed a new level of expenditure for El Al, particularly coming so soon after the Britannia acquisitions. Fortunately, however, El Al had developed a good credit standing with Chase Manhattan Bank since the Constellation days, and it managed to negotiate a loan for 80% of the cost of the new 707s.

El Al's first pure jet, a Boeing 707-420 "Intercontinental", under construction at Boeing's Renton factory in Seattle, Washington, 1960. At right is Chaim Pearlman, El Al Resident Engineer, conferring with Boeing Foreman B. L. Taylor. (Boeing Airplane Company, via El Al)

The 707s required longer and stronger runways for takeoffs and landings than those commonly in existence at the world's civil airports. To accommodate them, the main runway at Lod Airport was extended in November 1960 to 2,658 meters (8,720ft).

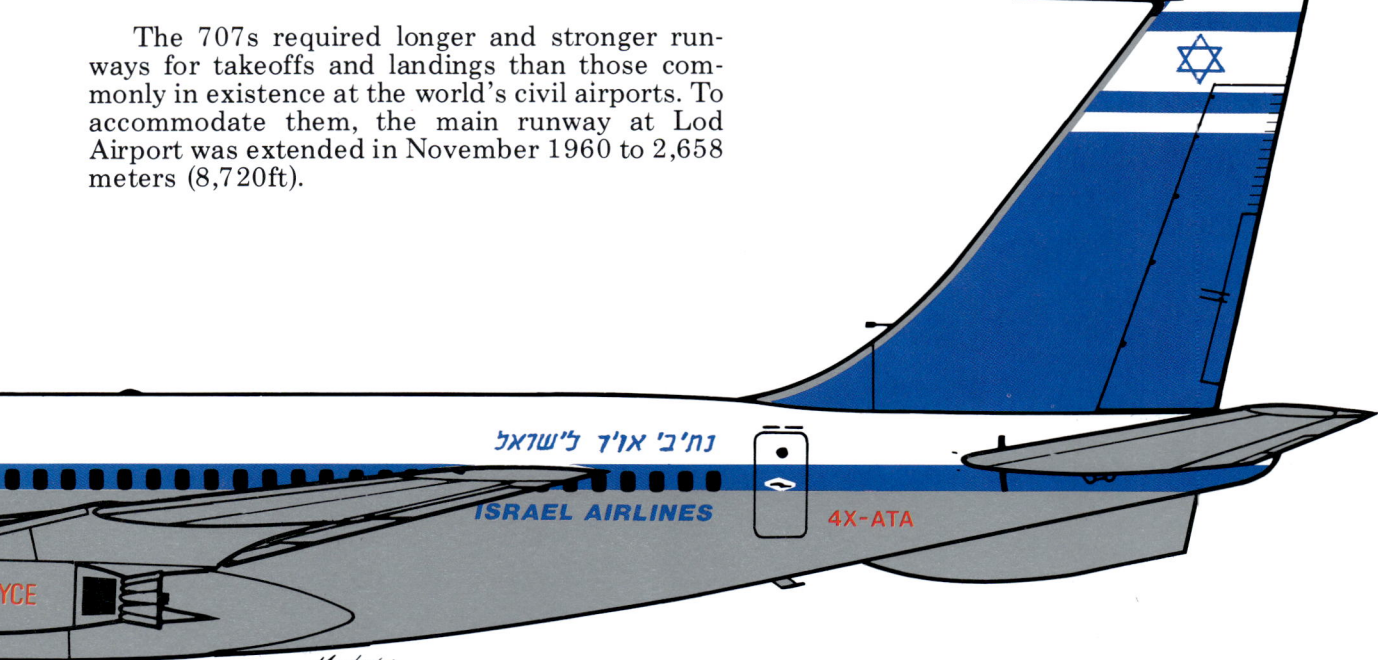

נת"בי אויר לישראל

ISRAEL AIRLINES 4X-ATA

The First 707s

El Al originally planned to introduce its first 707 in summer 1961. However, competition from other airlines did not allow El Al the luxury of waiting and, as other carriers were already flying jet aircraft, El Al was forced to advance its plans. It began weekly Tel Aviv—New York service on 8 January 1961 with a Boeing 707 leased from Brazil's VARIG. On 19 February 1961, this service was increased to twice weekly.

On 7 May 1961 El Al took delivery of 4X-ATA, the first of its initial group of three 707-420 jetliners. The ceremony was held at Boeing Field, Seattle, complete with blessing by Rabbis and 250 people in attendance. Captains Sam Feldman and Zvi Tohar were in command of the delivery flight to Israel.

The first aircraft had the honor of establishing two world records. On 15 June 1961, during the return portion of its maiden scheduled passenger flight from New York to Tel Aviv, 4X-ATA flew 9,270km (5,760mi) nonstop—a new distance record for a scheduled commercial flight. The aircraft was piloted by Captains Tom Jones and Danny Rosin and carried 97 passengers at a cruising altitude of 12,500 meters (41,000ft). Accomplished in 9hr 33min, this flight also set the speed record for a New York to Tel Aviv flight.

On 10 June 1961 El Al took delivery of its second Boeing 707-420 (4X-ATB). During the 1961 summer high-tourist season, with two 707s in its fleet, El Al started operating six round-trip New York flights per week with 707 aircraft, and two additional round-trips per week with Britannias. All flights called at either London or Paris, except that once a week El Al operated a 707 from New York to Tel Aviv nonstop.

The new nonstop 707 flight (LY 228) would leave New York at 2130 each Thursday evening and arrive in Tel Aviv on Friday afternoon, at 1425. With a seven-hour time difference, the scheduled flying time was 9hr 55min. Although this nonstop was discontinued during the winter schedule, it was a popular flight and was reinstated for summer 1962. A Tel Aviv—New York nonstop, which would have to confront unfavorable westerly winds, was also considered. However, it was rejected because even under optimum conditions only about 30-40 passengers could have been carried, a marginal operation from the the economic viewpoint at best.

Initially, El Al's 707s on the New York services carried only a limited payload—115 passengers and no freight. El Al soon found, however, that it could remove most of the restrictions. The passenger limit was raised to 156 (except for a maximum of 120 on the New York–Tel Aviv nonstop), although still without any cargo being carried.

El Al's pure-jet flights proved to be a great success. The increased frequency of service was complemented by trans-Atlantic load factors at or near the top figures among all airlines at the time, exceeding 60% on a year-round average. Israel was no longer so "far away" to passengers from the U.S. The 30-hour flights on vibrating and noisy Constellations were now but memories of the past. In 1961 El Al's share of total air passengers arriving in Israel rose to an estimated 55-60%. In all, El Al carried 171,068 passengers during its 1961/62 fiscal year (1 April 1961 —31 March 1962) compared to 116,502 the previous year and a mere 38,004 five years earlier.

On 15 October, following its 1961 peak-season summer schedule, the last two Constellations were retired from European schedules, marking the end of the piston-engine era for El Al.

El Al's "Bar Mitzvah" Year

On 15 February 1962, in ample time for the coming summer high season, the third and last of El Al's original order of three 707-420 jets (4X-ATC) was delivered.

For El Al's 1962 summer schedule, it operated three 707s and moved to a new high of nine round-trips per week to New York compared to seven the previous year. The weekly nonstop New York–Tel Aviv flight was resumed. Other flights were routed through European airports, including London, Paris, Amsterdam, Rome and Athens. On 11 June 1962 service was inaugurated to Frankfurt, Germany, with two round-trips per week from Tel Aviv.

The operation of all three El Al 707s provided a fitting background for 1962—celebrated as El Al's 13th or "bar-mitzvah" year. El Al carried its one-millionth passenger that year, and many special celebrations were held. The airline had come a long way since its first improvised flights on converted aircraft borrowed from the Israeli military air transport command.

El Al's Answer to Arab Boycott

In March-April 1962 El Al accepted delivery of two Boeing 720B medium-range jet aircraft, registered 4X-ABA and ABB. The acquisition of the 720Bs was directly related to the Arab boycott.

After the 1956 Sinai War, in order to reach Johannesburg, South Africa, without flying over or too close to Arab country airspace, El Al had to fly a circuitous route via North and Central Africa, using piston-engine aircraft leased from other airlines and without El Al insignia. The Boeing 720Bs had the necessary performance to allow El Al to resume flying to South Africa with its own aircraft—via an exaggerated route stopping at Teheran, Iran—and they were chosen for that reason.

The 720Bs, with their powerful Pratt & Whitney engines and improved wing over that of the 707, could takeoff from "hot and high" Teheran on long-distance flights. Accordingly, starting 14 June 1962, the 720Bs took over El Al's service from Tel Aviv east to Teheran. They were then flown from Teheran southwest across the Persian Gulf, to Central Africa, and then to Johannesburg. A direct route south via the narrow Gulf of Eilat, down through the Red Sea straits and then to Johannesburg was not feasible because of Egyptian hostility.

The service to Africa via Teheran established one of the world's most circuitous air routes—there were no fewer than 25 heading changes to prevent flights from straying over hostile areas. Radio aids were sparse. The Boeing 720B journey became a 16-hour endurance test and added 3,860km (2,400mi) to the trip. High elevation and temperatures, plus a heavy fuel uplift, limited air-

Roll-out of El Al's first 707 (4X-ATA) at the Boeing plant in Seattle, April 1961. (Boeing Airplane Company, via El Al)

To the skies over the State of Washington with El Al's first 707, which made its first flight on 14 April 1961. El Al selected Rolls-Royce engines for its first three 707s. This particular aircraft (4X-ATA) served for 23 years, carrying over two million passengers more than 58 million kilometers (36 million miles), equivalent to circling the world 1,450 times. (The Boeing Co. Archives No. K7710)

craft performance and thus the payload. Double crews had to staff the aircraft. To achieve the break-even point, the route had to show an 85% load factor.

The 720Bs also served to replace the Britannia on the Tel Aviv to Europe routes, starting with the 1962 summer schedule. Now with five new jets in its fleet, El Al was able to secure a large slice of the international travel market, and the ratio of non-Jewish passengers edged closer to 40%. El Al gained acceptance not just as an ethnic and immigrant carrier, but also as a successful and established international mover of passengers and cargo.

In 1965, to increase efficiency and performance of its 720Bs, El Al replaced their original JT3D-1 turbofan engines with more powerful JT3D-3Bs. This also enabled standardization with the Pratt & Whitney-powered 707-320B aircraft ordered for late 1965 delivery.

Demonstrating the 720B's versatility, in 1965 an El Al 720B became the first jetliner to land at Eilat's small airfield. Although a proving flight, it was a historic event as ten years would pass before the next landing of a jet airliner (a Sterling Airways Caravelle) at the Israeli resort town.

With a fleet of five new Boeing jet aircraft (three 707s and two 720Bs), and with a pair of supplementary Britannias, El Al settled in for expected steady growth during the mid- and late-1960s. Not all went as planned, however, and before the 'Sixties drew to a close, El Al had to survive many trials, including labor unrest, battles with charter flights, management changes, attempts at government political intrusion and—most serious of all—a war for the very survival of Israel.

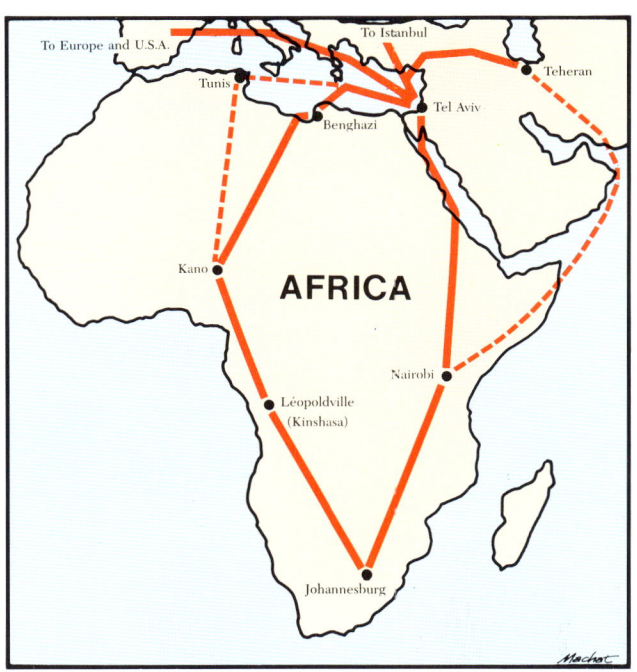

El Al's route to Johannesburg via Nairobi was one of its first, having started in November 1950. The route was severed following the 1956 Sinai War due to Arab hostility, and El Al had to fly via a North and West African route using leased aircraft of other airlines. With the purchase of Boeing 720Bs, El Al restored service with its own aircraft. However, hostile neighbors required El Al to fly an unusually circuitous route, via Teheran, Iran, and the Persian Gulf. (Mike Machat)

EL AL ISRAEL AIRLINES Announces

FIRST DIRECT BOEING 707 Jet Flights New York to Tel Aviv

EFFECTIVE JANUARY 5 THROUGH FEBRUARY 18, 1961

LY 206 L/F/Y B	LY 228 F/Y JET	LY 208 L/F/Y B	LY 210 L/F/Y B	FLIGHT NO. / CLASS SERVICE / AIRCRAFT TYPE	LY 221 F/Y JET	LY 205 L/F/Y B	LY 207 L/F/Y B	LY 209 L/F/Y B
Wed 19 00	Thu 20 30	Fri 19 00	Sat 22 00	Lv ... NEW YORK ... Ar	Sun 15 30	Wed 02 40	Fri 04 05	Sat 06 00
Thu 09 20 / 10 35	↓JET↓	Sat 09 20 / 10 35	Sun 12 20 / 13 35	Ar ... LONDON ... Lv	↑JET↑	Wed 20 35 / 19 20	Fri 22 00 / 20 45	Sat 23 55 / 22 40
↓	Fri 09 10 / 10 10	12 45 / 13 45	15 45 / 16 45	Ar PARIS Lv	13 35 / 12 35	↑	20 35 / 19 35	22 30 / 21 30
		15 55 / 16 35		Ar ROME Lv		17 10 / 16 30	17 10 / 16 30	
17 15 / 17 45	↓JET↓	↓	↓	Ar ATHENS Lv	↑JET↑	16 30	16 30	18 10 / 17 30
20 00 Thu	15 20 Fri	21 35 Sat	23 35 Sun	Ar ... TEL AVIV ... Lv	09 00 Sun	13 00 Tue	13 00 Thu	15 00 Fri

EFFECTIVE FEBRUARY 19 THROUGH MARCH 17, 1961

LY 224 F/Y JET	LY 206 L/F/Y B	LY 228 F/Y JET	LY 208 L/F/Y B	LY 210 L/F/Y B	FLIGHT NO. / CLASS SERVICE / AIRCRAFT TYPE	LY 221 F/Y JET	LY 205 L/F/Y B	LY 231 F/Y JET	LY 207 L/F/Y B	LY 209 L/F/Y B
Mon 20 30	Wed 19 00	Thu 20 30	Fri #19 00	Sat 22 00	Lv ... NEW YORK ... Ar	Sun 15 30	Wed 02 40	Wed 16 50	Fri #04 05	Sat 06 00
Tue 07 50 / 09 00	Thu 09 20 / 10 35	↓JET↓	Sat #09 20 / 10 35	Sun 12 20 / 13 35	Ar ... LONDON ... Lv	↑JET↑	Wed 20 35 / 19 20	Wed 14 20 / 13 20	Fri #22 00 / 20 45	Sat 23 55 / 22 40
↓JET↓	↓	Fri 09 10 / 10 10	12 45 / 13 45	15 45 / 16 45	Ar PARIS Lv	13 35 / 12 35	↑	↑JET↑	20 35 / 19 35	22 30 / 21 30
12 05 / 12 55			15 55 / 16 35		Ar ROME Lv		17 10 / 16 30	12 00 / 11 10	17 10 / 16 30	
↓JET↓	17 15 / 17 45	↓JET↓	↓	↓	Ar ATHENS Lv	↑JET↑		↑JET↑		18 10 / 17 30
16 45 Tue	20 00 Thu	15 20 Fri	21 35 Sat	23 35 Sun	Ar ... TEL AVIV ... Lv	09 00 Sun	13 00 Tue	09 00 Wed	13 00 Thu	15 00 Fri

#—No traffic rights LY 208/207 New York-London.

EFFECTIVE MARCH 18 THROUGH JUNE 10, 1961

LY 224 F/Y JET	LY 204 L/F/Y B	LY 206 L/F/Y B	LY 228 F/Y JET	LY 208 L/F/Y B	LY 210 L/F/Y B	FLIGHT NO. / CLASS SERVICE / AIRCRAFT TYPE	LY 221 F/Y JET	LY 203 L/F/Y B	LY 231 F/Y JET	LY 205 L/F/Y B	LY 207 L/F/Y B	LY 209 L/F/Y B
Mon 20 30*	Tue 17 00*	Wed 16 00*	Thu 20 30*	Fri 18 00*	Sat 22 00*	Lv ... NEW YORK ... Ar	Sun 15 30*	Tue 06 50*	Wed 16 50*	Wed 04 25*	Fri 04 25*	Sat 04 05*
Tue 08 50** / 10 00**	Wed 08 20** / 09 20**	↓	↓JET↓	Sat 09 20** / 10 20**	↓	Ar ... LONDON ... Lv	↑JET↑	01 25** / 00 25**	15 20** / 14 20**	Wed ↑	Fri ↑	Sat 23 50** / 22 50**
↓JET↓	↓	Thu 08 15 / 09 15	Fri 09 10 / 10 10	↓	Sun 14 15 / 15 15	Ar PARIS Lv	13 35 / 12 35	Tue ↑	↑JET↑	23 00 / 22 00	23 00 / 22 00	↑
	10 30 / 11 30					Ar AMSTERDAM Lv		23 15 / 22 30				
12 05 / 12 55		14 05 / 14 45	↓JET↓	13 00 / 13 45	20 05 / 20 45	Ar ROME Lv	↑JET↑	19 40 / 19 00	12 00 / 11 10	19 40 / 19 00	19 40 / 19 00	19 40 / 19 00
↓JET↓		↓		↓	↓	Ar ATHENS Lv		↑	↑JET↑	18 40 / 18 00	18 40 / 18 00	
16 45 Tue	19 00 Wed	17 00 Thu	15 20 Fri	18 45 Sat	23 00 Sun	Ar ... TEL AVIV ... Lv	09 00 Sun	15 30 Mon	09 00 Wed	15 30 Tue	15 30 Thu	15 30 Fri

*—EFFECTIVE APRIL 30, WHEN DAYLIGHT SAVING TIME BEGINS, NEW YORK DEPARTURES AND ARRIVALS WILL BE ONE HOUR LATER.
**—UNTIL MARCH 26, WHEN DAYLIGHT SAVING TIME BEGINS, LONDON DEPARTURES AND ARRIVALS ARE ONE HOUR EARLIER.

JET—BOEING 707.   B—BRITANNIA.   L—FIRST CLASS SLEEPERETTE.   F—FIRST STANDARD.   Y—ECONOMY.   ALL TIMES ARE LOCAL TIMES.

First El Al schedule showing Boeing 707 service, initiated with an aircraft leased from Brazil's VARIG, January 1961. (Marvin Goldman collection)

Basic Policies; El Al's Relationship to Israel

El Al's two main policies in the 1960s followed those established upon its founding. First, it should be operated as a profitable business, as independent as possible from State interference. As a result of this attitude, the expected financial strength would help El Al fulfill its second basic tenet, the standby one of serving as a lifeline to the world for the State of Israel in the event of war or other emergency.

On the other hand, with the maturing of El Al and the modernization of its fleet, other policies became prominent. Long-range planning objectives, more sophisticated budgets and financial safeguards, as well as uniform work procedures, were developed and constantly reviewed. El Al also had to deal with its new crucial role in Israel's economy. Its profits, as well as tourism to Israel promoted by El Al, represented valuable foreign exchange to the young State. With its world-wide network of offices and advertising activities, El Al became the leading promoter of tourism to Israel—to the point in the 1960s where it spent over twice the amount of the combined budgets of all the relevant tourist institutions in Israel to attract visitors.

With a policy of promoting Israel first, and itself second, El Al regularly brought travel and tourist writers, radio and TV personnel and sales agents on familiarization tours of Israel during the winter months, and the benefits in increased tourism were reaped throughout the year.

Labor Unrest

The year 1960 saw El Al turn its first annual profit following seven years of losses flying Constellations and making payments on the new Britannias. With the introduction of the more efficient pure-jets in 1961, El Al's profits started to soar, and for almost all the next 18 years (until 1978) El Al operated in the black.

Inevitably, with the onset of profits from 1960, labor started demanding more of a share for itself. Originally, an atmosphere of "one big family" prevailed at El Al, with a labor-management honeymoon. President Ben-Arzi, however, made it clear that he ran management and wanted no voice of labor in management matters. In 1960 the pilots started the first strike, seeking higher wages and professional recognition, rather than receiving inferior treatment compared to foreign airmen. The next year the mechanics went out on strike when 28 temporary employees were fired for creating labor problems. A bitter battle ensued, and El Al aircraft had to be dispatched for a time by hastily mobilized superintendents and foremen. In 1962 the pilots struck again, with many angry charges and countercharges. The following spring the first really disastrous labor walkout occurred when the airmen stopped flying during the peak Passover season.

EL AL knocks the props off

Starting January 5th, El Al goes from jet-prop to pure jet. We'll be flying the Boeing 707/420 Intercontinental Jet, latest and most powerful of the 707s, equipped with the superb Rolls Royce-Conway by-pass engines. We'll fly New York to Paris non-stop in 6 hours, 50 minutes, and one-stop to Tel Aviv in 11 hours, 50 minutes, without a change of planes. El Al jet flights to London begin in February, and Rome in March.
See your travel agent or El Al Israel Airlines, 610 Fifth Ave., New York 20, N.Y., PLaza 1-7500.

El Al postcard advertisement proclaiming the start of pure-jet service, replacing jet-prop (turbopropeller) aircraft, in January 1961. (Marvin Goldman collection)

Each time El Al was able to eventually settle the labor grievances. However, a pattern of labor disturbances emerged that continued to plague the airline for years to come and that adversely affected its competitive position.

Political Intrusion Fails

In 1962 the Israeli Government pressured El Al to open routes to West Africa. The Government had been working hard to develop close political and economic ties to West Africa's newly independent states, and it desired direct air routes to nurture this process. El Al knew, however, that these routes could not be operated profitably and that having a profitable operation was one of El Al's main policies and mandates. El Al fought this attempted intrusion into its business, and the Government backed down and agreed to allow El Al to continue to set route policy.

x

71

Similarly certain Government officials, trying to curry favor with Belgium, Holland and the Scandinavian countries, pressured El Al to allow those countries to obtain greater market shares for Israel-bound passengers. El Al complained that this would just reduce El Al's profits, and again the Government eventually conceded.

The principle of non-intervention by the Government in El Al's daily business operations, established since the first days of the airline, was thereby maintained and reaffirmed.

Battling the Charters

Until the 1970s, international air fares on scheduled airlines were rigidly controlled by widespread government regulations everywhere and by the international tariff system of the International Air Transport Association (IATA), of which El Al and almost all major carriers were members. This cartel arrangement encouraged high and rather inflexible fares.

On the other hand, many resourceful non-scheduled airlines had arisen, spawned by the surplus of obsolescent equipment and the growth of tourism immediately after World War II. These charter airlines started "affinity travel" featuring significantly reduced fares for groups of individuals ostensibly having a common relationship, and the impact of their activities started to be felt. Travel wholesalers began offering "inclusive tour" packages with attractive low tariffs geared to undercut scheduled operations and provide close

to a 100% load factor. In 1958 El Al discovered that 40% of all passengers entering Israel came via special charter flights. The effect on El Al can be appreciated even more when one realizes that at the time about 90% of El Al's traffic was tourist-stimulated and only 10% business-motivated.

Mordechai Ben-Ari, commercial manager of El Al, fought repeatedly at IATA meetings for a new, more flexible type of international tariff structure and for better ways to combat the rise of charter traffic. Within Israel Ben-Ari also made clear to the Government El Al's early and forthright stand against the uninhibited growth of charters to Israel, arguing that Israel needed a financially healthy national carrier. El Al could provide better, less expensive packages if the charter threat could be eliminated. Further, he argued, landing rights were a valuable commodity that should not be given away freely, and the charters would also undermine El Al's negotiating ability for wider and more flexible foreign landing rights.

In 1961 El Al negotiated a special resolution from IATA that allowed it, as a short-term approach, to utilize an affinity group fare system. These flights had some success in filling El Al seats. In 1962 Mordechai Ben-Ari pushed through IATA a new concept in airline tariffs—the non-affinity group fare on scheduled flights. He reasoned that the scheduled airlines needed a lower, more flexible fare to promote mass tourism and combat the nonscheduled operators. However, IATA demanded in return that all charter flights to Israel be banned.

Flight cover flown on El Al's first commercial Boeing 707 flight, from Tel Aviv to New York, 8 January 1961. (Marvin Goldman collection)

El Al's first 707, 4X-ATA, at the International Arrivals Building, Idlewild (JFK) Airport, New York, 1961. Behind the El Al aircraft are a Swissair DC-8 (HB-IDA), an Aerolineas Argentinas Comet 4, and the Pan Am terminal. (El Al Israel Airlines collection)

In December 1962 El Al succeeded in having the Israeli Transport Minister cancel all charters to and from Israel effective 1 April 1963, and El Al introduced the non-affinity group fare on scheduled flights. However, this proved to be only a temporary victory. The charter issue continued to resurface, and ultimately it contributed to a major management reshuffle at El Al in 1967.

Maximum Utilization

During the early and mid-1960s El Al carefully developed the practice of maximizing the utilization of each of its aircraft. In doing so, El Al had to contend with the fact that its fleet was very small (only seven aircraft), its routes were far-ranging (from New York in the west to Teheran in the east, and south to Johannesburg), and it had to limit (and eventually eliminate) operations on the Jewish Sabbath and on certain Jewish holidays.

These restrictions notwithstanding, El Al achieved one of the highest aircraft utilization rates in the industry. To illustrate, here is a typical Monday to Wednesday schedule for a single Boeing 720B during summer 1964: Monday 0700—leave Tel Aviv for Zürich, land at Tel Aviv 1530 on return flight from Zürich; Monday 1700—depart Tel Aviv for Rome, arrive back at Tel Aviv 2300; Monday midnight—leave Tel Aviv for Teheran and return to Tel Aviv by 0800 on

Crew of the nonstop New York—Tel Aviv return portion of the maiden scheduled passenger flight of El Al's 707 4X-ATA on 15 June 1961 which set a long-distance record for a commercial service. The co-captains were Tom Jones and Danny Rosin (fourth and third persons from the right, respectively). To their immediate left is Dov Arav, flight engineer, and to their right is Sam Boshes, first officer. (Capt. Danny Rosin collection)

El Al's first Boeing 720B (4X-ABA) being test flown over the State of Washington, March 1962. Five meters (15ft) shorter than the 707 Intercontinental, the 720 also featured aerodynamic refinements to the wing which improved takeoff performance and cruising speed. (The Boeing Co.)

Tuesday; Tuesday 1145—take-off from Tel Aviv for New York via one of the European gateways, land at Tel Aviv Wednesday 1630 after completion of return flight from New York and Europe.

During this 57½-hour period the aircraft will have accumulated about 40 hours flying time. It was then rolled into the hangar for an overnight maintenance check to be ready for an early flight the following morning.

Boeing 707s normally spent about 30 hours away from Tel Aviv on the New York run via Europe (except for the occasional nonstop flight). They typically would leave in the early morning from Tel Aviv and return the next day in the late afternoon for an overnight maintenance check before departing again on a similar schedule the following day.

El Al maintained such a heavy aircraft utilization rate that it had a reserve aircraft factor of almost zero or, as one employee put it, "one-half an airplane for three days a week, and none for the remaining four". During the Jewish Passover holiday in 1964, 707/720B utilization built up to an astonishing average of 15 hours per day. Nevertheless, El Al still managed to maintain an enviable on-time record and high safety standards.

Maintenance and Technical Efficiency

A prime reason for El Al's high aircraft utilization rate has been the fine maintenance facilities and procedures developed by the airline. Gradually building its own facilities and in-house capabilities, by 1964 El Al handled almost all of its own airframe-electronics maintenance and overhaul work—tasks previously farmed out to Israel Aircraft Industries across the field from El Al's headquarters. The drive for self-sufficiency in maintenance was also spurred by the political conviction that El Al always had to be ready to take care of itself, without the help of others, in the

State of Israel souvenir sheet featuring commemorative Israel postage stamp honoring El Al's thirteenth or "Bar Mitzvah" year. Note the introduction of the El Al block logo in the lower left-hand corner. On an El Al official first day cover dated 7 November 1962. (Marvin Goldman collection)

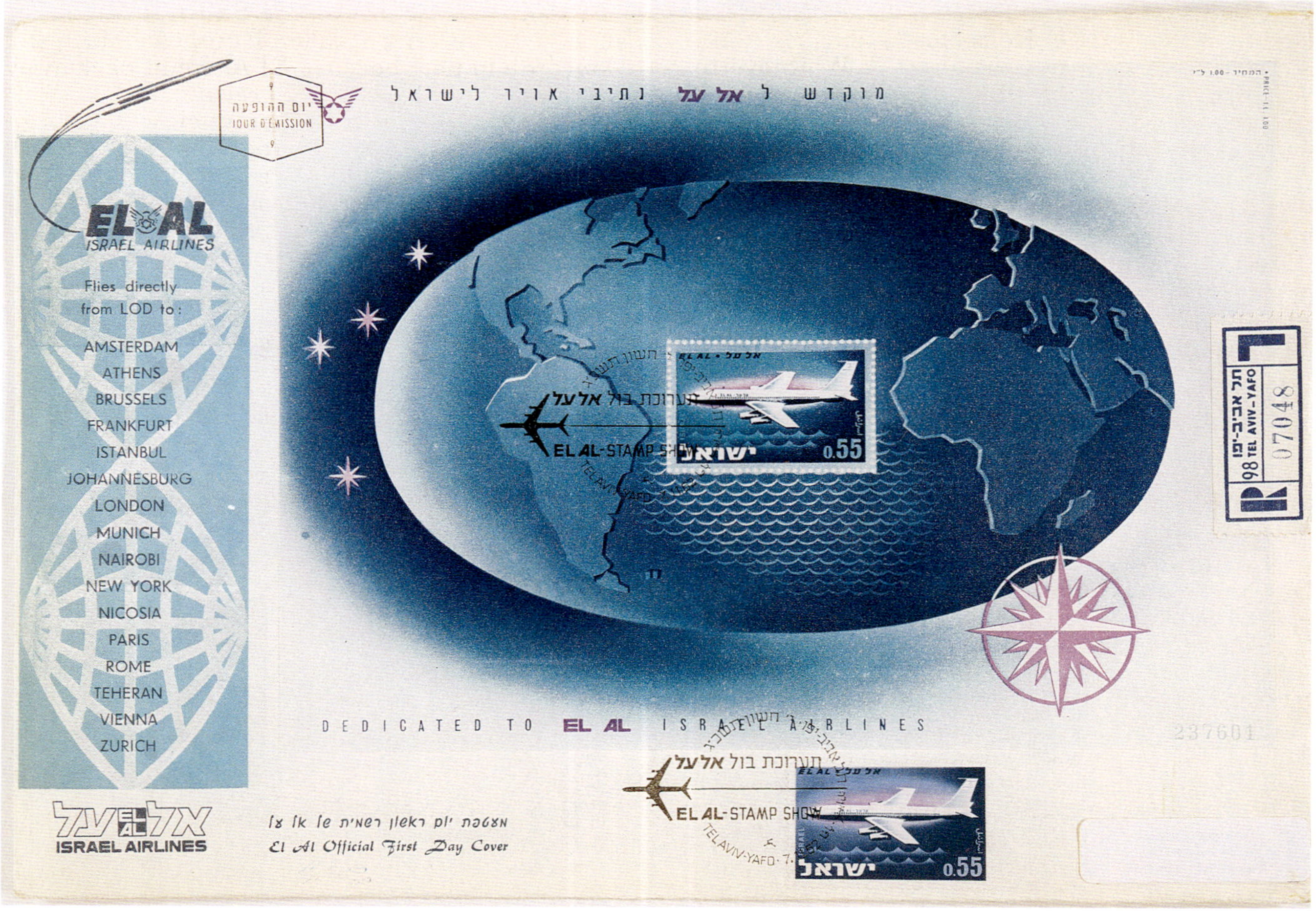

event of war or other emergency. In addition, striving for economy, El Al was then hand-building the majority of its test equipment in its electronics, radio and overhaul shops, at considerable savings over what would have been foreign purchases.

Maintenance checks came to be performed on an "equalized maintenance system", at intervals of 100 hours and requiring 10-12 hours to complete, fitted into overnight hours. Each check would include all items due every 100 hours, a quarter of all 400-hour items, 1/6 of the 600-hour items, etc. This system permitted the basic El Al operational pattern of scheduling the bulk of departures from Tel Aviv during the early morning so that the aircraft would return in the late evening, allowing the night-time period free for maintenance. In addition, an annual major overhaul, which would remove the aircraft from service for 12 days, was performed during the relatively slack four-month winter season.

The Fifth Pod

Engine overhauls in the early and mid-1960s, however, still had to be contracted out—to Rolls-Royce in England for the 707's four Conway bypass engines, and to SNECMA in France for the 720B's Pratt & Whitney JT3Ds. To accomplish this at minimum cost, El Al adopted the "fifth pod" procedure as a standard working tool. Designed by Boeing primarily as an emergency procedure for ferrying engines, the fifth pod was slung beneath the left wing of a 707, carrying a spare powerplant in a streamlined shape akin to the aircraft's regular engine nacelle. The Rolls-Royce engines were ferried to London and the Pratt & Whitneys to Paris on regularly-scheduled flights at almost no cost in payload or performance. El Al also modified the Boeing-designed kits for the two types of engines, cutting removal and installation time from the original three hours to an average of 35 minutes, the fastest of any airline. As a result, pod installation or removal caused no delay to the schedule.

Artist's conception of a Boeing 2707 supersonic transport (SST) in El Al livery (1964). El Al placed deposits on two SSTs, securing delivery positions 10 and 14. The SST, however, was never built by Boeing, and the range of the European-built Concorde was not suitable for El Al's main Tel Aviv—New York route. (El Al Israel Airlines collection)

SST Flirtation

In 1964 El Al placed deposits with Boeing for two Boeing 2707 supersonic transports (SSTs) designed to fly over Mach 2.5 or two and a half times the speed of sound. El Al obtained preferred slots for production numbers 10 and 14 and a hoped-for early slice of the American supersonic market. The SST would have cut the nonstop flying time over the New York—Tel Aviv route from 10hr 50min (for the 707) to a little over five hours. El Al opted for the U.S. SST rather than the slightly slower and smaller European Mach 2.2 Concorde in part because El Al could back away from its U.S. options and still recoup its down payments made to assure its production line positions. Such rebates would not have been allowed under the Concorde contract. Perhaps more importantly, it correctly anticipated that the Concorde as eventually built would not be able to fly the New York—Tel Aviv route nonstop with anything like a full load.

Six of El Al's fleet of 707s/720Bs, grounded during a strike in the late 1960s. The aircraft are in the second of three successive standard El Al 707/720B color schemes. The second livery is characterized by the "A" of "El Al" having a sloped left side and straight right side, and it was in use generally from 1964 through 1971. During that period the total number of aircraft in El Al's all-707/720B fleet ranged from five in 1964 to six in 1966 to ten in 1970-71. The longer 707s are distinguishable from the 720s in that they have two emergency exit doors over the wing instead of one. (El Al Israel Airlines collection)

As it turned out, the Boeing SST was never built, following concern in the U.S. over environmental noise and the basic commercial economics of the aircraft. This was actually a fortunate development for El Al (and other airlines) which already had a modern fleet and was still working hard to pay off the high financial costs of its Boeing 707 and 720B acquisitions.

On 7 January 1966 El Al acquired its first 707 of the -320B series (4X-ATR). However, due to a crew strike, El Al immediately leased the aircraft to The Flying Tiger Line as N317F and then leased it back with Flying Tiger pilots. On 3 October 1966 the aircraft was re-registered as 4X-ATR and acquired regular El Al colors. This photograph shows the aircraft during its brief El Al/Flying Tiger hybrid life in 1966. (John Wegg)

Minimum Equipment Acquisition

One of El Al's original premises, nurtured by Ben-Arzi in the 1960s, was that its aircraft purchases should be kept down to manageable numbers. El Al measured its needs by year-round requirements, not on peak seasonable demands which for El Al have traditionally been the Passover/Easter season and the summer months. During heavy traffic periods, therefore, El Al would lease or charter planes. While many airlines practice this rule today, El Al was one of the first to pursue it.

New Routes and Aircraft

Three new destinations for regular scheduled service were added in 1964—Copenhagen, Denmark; Sofia, Bulgaria; and the Greek island of Rhodes. This brought the total number of El Al destinations to 19. However, service to Sofia was discontinued after only a few months, and regular service to Rhodes ended in the late 1960s.

With the acquisition of two more Boeing 707s in 1965 and 1967, and the sale of the last surviving Britannias during the same period, El Al became the first all-pure-jet airline in the Middle East. Its entire fleet consisted of only seven aircraft, but it was a modern roster comprising five 707s (three Rolls-Royce-powered 420 series and two Pratt & Whitney-powered 320B series) and two 720Bs. The new 707-320Bs were not convertible to a cargo configuration; however, they were chosen because they had the long range that El Al needed on its routes. In making this choice El Al had to pass up, for the time being, other 707 cargo-capable aircraft.

The Six-Day War

By May 1967 war clouds were once again gathering over the Middle East. Egypt's President Nasser declared a blockade of Israel's Red Sea port of Eilat, announcing that the hour of confrontation had arrived. Egyptian guns at Sharm-el-Sheikh, a coastal fortress overlooking the Strait of Tiran, were trained on Israeli shipping navigating this link with the Gulf of Eilat. The Soviet-equipped forces of Egypt's army crossed the Suez Canal and began moving in the direction of Israel's Negev region. Egypt demanded that the United Nations forces in the Sinai evacuate their border positions, and the UN immediately sent their troops packing.

Most of the male employees of El Al under age 40, including more than half the aircrew, were mobilized. Despite being short of manpower El Al was again called upon to undertake a unique task—the evacuation of thousands of innocent tourists in Israel prior to the deterioration of the situation into actual warfare. From 14-24 May 1967, with only a minimum number of aircrews available, El Al transported 11,500 tourists from Israel. Remaining employees worked around the clock.

Meanwhile, Israelis overseas and foreign volunteers mobbed El Al offices desiring to return to Israel to help in the anticipated defense effort. In Holland, young people camped on the streets while waiting for accommodations on El Al flights. Later, there was a near riot in Amsterdam when someone spotted an El Al airliner at Schiphol Airport. The young volunteers demanded immediate accommodation and it took all the persuasion of El Al personnel to convince them that the plane was flying in an all-cargo configuration.

El Al also began to ferry military and other priority cargo to Israel. Its aircraft were reported at airfields not normally served by scheduled flights, including such odd spots as the airfields of Dassault and Sud Aviation in France. It picked up so-called "undisclosed freight", although the airline was quick to point out that nothing outside the terms of normal insurance coverage was carried.

El Al aircrew during the airlift were greeted cordially by air traffic controllers and ground personnel alike; some were applauded at the airport terminals, and controllers addressed crews with *shalom*—the traditional Hebrew greeting meaning "peace".

At the time, El Al had no pure cargo or convertible passenger-to-cargo aircraft among its fleet of seven Boeing jets. El Al was forced to make do by stripping the seats from aircraft outbound from Tel Aviv or, on some passenger flights, removing the seats at intermediate European points before picking up military and other cargoes.

Loading and unloading at Lod Airport were done by clerical and cabin staff and over-military age executives, pressed into service to replace the mobilized ground handlers. During evening hours they formed long lines and helped in unloading incoming aircraft. There was no change in the maintenance schedule. Maximum aircraft utilization was achieved with daily use reaching an astonishing 14 hours. The interiors of the planes became wrecks. Sharp-edged crates tore the linings out of cushions, upholstery was shredded by freight, decorative panels were mutilated, and carpeting ruined by accumulations of mud and grime.

El Al employees worked 12-hour shifts—and many contributed even longer hours to make up for the absence of their mobilized colleagues. Essential offices were kept open around the clock. Grounded stewardesses became drivers of minibuses, since the regular El Al airport buses had been commandeered for the defense effort. Aircrews would fly ten hours straight and then return to flight duty after six-hour intervals, except for the pilots who were not allowed to exceed the legal limits of 10 hours per day or 120 hours per month. Somehow the airline still managed to fly scheduled routes.

On 26 May 1967 the *New York Times* carried a two-page advertisement pointing to Israel's crisis and summing up El Al's confidence that "We'll be flying in 5728, 5729 [years on the Jewish calendar corresponding to 1968 and 1969]. In fact, we plan on flying there for a long, long time".

In the early morning of 5 June 1967 war erupted between Israel, on the one hand, and Egypt and Syria, later joined by Jordan, on the other. As in 1948 and 1956, all foreign airlines immediately stopped flying to Israel. Confronted by enemies on three sides and separated from the West by a sea on the remaining side, Israel was again cut off from the rest of the world—but for El Al.

El Al's initial three morning flights on 5 June departed as scheduled, but to reduce risks, El Al quickly decided to operate in Israel only at night. Inbound aircraft that day and the next were delayed until nightfall, and departures were forbidden after daybreak. On the night of 5 June, all aircraft in El Al's fleet returned to Lod Airport and were turned around that same night. The turnarounds were made in near-record times, both to get the aircraft out before dawn and because of the tight schedule flown for government requirements. For takeoffs and landings, the runway lights were switched on and normal procedures followed. Otherwise there was a complete blackout.

The Avia Hotel a few miles from the airport was used as a terminal building so as not to expose the passengers to danger in case of air raids on the airport or shelling from Jordan. Several 155-mm guns shelled the airport from beyond the hills on the Jordanian border on the night of 6 June, but caused little damage.

After 36 hours, when it became clear that Israeli air superiority had been established and daylight attacks on the airport were unlikely, morning and afternoon flights were resumed, although still on a modified wartime schedule.

With the outbreak of the war, passenger traffic from Israel came to a virtual halt, while in the opposite direction, load factors soared under pressure by Israelis, foreign volunteers and

El Al's Tel Aviv office building in the 1960s (constructed in 1963). (El Al Israel Airlines collection)

newsmen trying to get into the country. During the entire week of the war, El Al remained the sole airline operating between Israel and other countries.

Meanwhile, aircraft of El Al's domestic subsidiary, Arkia, were also mobilized. Its 50-seat Handley Page Heralds, first acquired in 1964, were converted to flying ambulances. On the outbound leg to the Sinai, the aircraft flew water in jerry cans to Israeli troops in the parched desert, landing at Egyptian air bases as these were captured. The return flights were made with wounded soldiers, both Israeli and Egyptian.

Many of the pilots of El Al and Arkia were air force reservists, and they were drafted to fly combat missions for the Israeli air force in jet strike aircraft. El Al lost four pilots and pilot trainees in action, including one captain, and Arkia also lost one of its pilots.

The miracle of the lox that flies.

Although Israel suffered many casualties, they were small compared to those sustained by the Arab forces. Within a handful of days Egypt, Jordan and Syria were pleading for a cease-fire, and after six days it was all over. Israel found itself in control of not only all the territory it held before the war, but also of the Sinai Peninsula and Gaza Strip to the southwest, the West Bank and East Jerusalem areas formerly occupied by Jordan, and the Golan Heights to the northeast which the Syrians had previously used as a high plateau from which to shell Israeli settlements situated below in the Jordan Valley.

With Jerusalem in Israel's hands and once again a united city, El Al launched an intensive campaign, in cooperation with the Ministry of Tourism, to attract more visitors to Israel. Travel agents and writers were invited to see for themselves that Israel was a tourist attraction of high caliber. About two months later the tourist stream from abroad began, and it even continued throughout the year. The phrase "off-season", meaning the

October to March period, almost vanished from the Israeli vocabulary as hotels found themselves filled winter as well as summer, and tourist figures reached an all-time high.

At the same time, El Al's domestic affiliate Arkia started new service to areas acquired in the war. This included Kalandia (Atarot) airport in Jerusalem as well as service to the Sinai, including flights to Ophira, Sharm-el-Sheikh and St. Catherine (Mt. Sinai).

Another significant result of the 1967 War was the resumption of direct air service to Africa. After the 1956 Sinai Campaign, as a consequence of Egyptian threats, El Al was forced to abandon its direct run south via the Red Sea and Nairobi to Johannesburg, South Africa; and during 1962-67 it was flying to Johannesburg via Teheran by way of one of the world's most circuitous air routes. If El Al could safely fly to Nairobi directly across the Sinai and down the Red Sea, its aircraft could reach Nairobi in four and a half hours and Johannesburg in slightly more than eight hours,

Israel is also a popular destination for numerous Christian groups desiring to make pilgrimages to the Holy Land. Shown is a group of Christian clergy from Europe upon arrival at Lod Airport, in the late 1960s.

Lod Airport decorated upon Israel's 20th anniversary. (Courtesy of Palphot Ltd., Herzlia, Israel, postcard no. 8729)

eliminating the 16-hour endurance test via Teheran and saving 3,860km (2,400mi) of flying.

On 12 June 1967, just one day after the end of the Six Day War, El Al tested the direct route with a special flight to Nairobi. It went unmolested, meaning that El Al could now offer the most direct and shortest route from the West to the eastern and southern segments of Africa, placing Israel again in the crossroads between three continents. On 7 November 1968, using Boeing 720Bs and later 707-320Bs, El Al started regular direct flights to Nairobi and Johannesburg. This service continues today notwithstanding the return of the Sinai to Egypt following the Egyptian-Israeli peace treaty signed in March 1979.

Under New Management

The new wave of tourists planning trips to Israel to see the Western Wall and other sights of now-united Jerusalem gave rise to new battles on the issue of charter versus scheduled flights. Ben-Arzi (who had moved from President to Chairman of the Board in 1966 following a heart attack) and Col. Shlomo Lahat (who succeeded him as President) insisted that charters remain banned and refused any compromise. The Ministry of Tourism lobbied to permit charters, but El Al won the battle (although with a few exceptions, mainly for Scandinavian flights). However, the strain of the political fight, as well as other personal reasons, led both Ben-Arzi and Lahat to resign their positions.

El Al's Board of Directors then elevated to the Presidency the man who had been so instrumental

in El Al's successful commercial development— Mordechai Ben-Ari. With expanding tourism to Israel and a modern jet fleet, Ben-Ari correctly looked forward to leading El Al through a succession of profitable years. Under his able leadership El Al would also smoothly enter the age of mass travel with the 747 jumbo jet. However, little did he know upon assuming the Presidency that El Al would first have to cope with a new challenge—the most dangerous of all.

Terrorism Rears Its Ugly Head

El Al flight LY426, operated by El Al's first Boeing 707 (4X-ATA), seemed perfectly routine as it took off from Rome's Fiumicino Airport on 23 July 1968 for its return leg to Tel Aviv. Veteran Captain Oded Abarbanel was in command, one of the original native-born Israeli pilots. The aircraft leveled off while still in Italy's airspace. Suddenly, three passengers, actually Arab members of the Popular Front for the Liberation of Palestine (PFLP), jumped from their seats brandishing grenades and revolvers, forced their way into the cockpit, shot and wounded First Officer Maoz Poraz, and seized control of the aircraft. Grabbing the radio microphone from the captain, they agitatedly told Rome then Algiers air traffic control that the aircraft was now renamed "Al Jiddah 707" and was being diverted to Algiers. This, then, was the first terrorist act directed against El Al.

While there had been prior hijackings on other airlines, particularly to Cuba, nothing significant of the kind had occurred in the Middle East, and it caught El Al and the aviation world completely by surprise. Little could be done once the plane was

Terrorism struck as Arab guerrillas attacked El Al's Boeing 720B (4X-ABB) with grenades and machine gun fire at Zürich's Kloten Airport on 18 February 1969. Forty bullets hit the cockpit, killing Yoram Peres, a trainee pilot. The patched bullet holes can be seen in the photograph. (El Al Israel Airlines)

Part of the damage to El Al's 707 (4X-ATR) inflicted by Arab terrorists in an attack at Athens Airport, 26 December 1968. Despite numerous Arab guerrilla attacks from 1968 into the 1970s, El Al broke the back of the terrorists through the strictest security measures in the industry and the strong determination of its personnel. (El Al Israel Airlines collection)

taken over, and it landed in Algiers. Israeli and international protests poured into Algeria, and many diplomatic initiatives ensued to release the hostages. Slowly but surely, groups of hostages, starting with the non-Israelis, were released. The El Al crew, however, was kept under arrest in Algeria the longest. It was 40 days before the last of them, the male crew members, were freed on 1 September 1968. Nor would the Algerians release the aircraft directly to El Al. Eventually a French crew flew the plane from Algiers to Rome, where an El Al crew took over and returned it to Israel.

El Al management and the Israeli Government warned that this could be a harbinger of things to come, not only for Israel but all nations. However, after the release of all the crew, world outrage subsided. While the specter of unlawful interference with civil air transport loomed everywhere, the hijacking of 4X-ATA still seemed minor.

Attack at Athens

The Arab terrorists, however, soon took a far more deadly turn. Less than four months after the Algerian hijacking ended, on 26 December 1968, an El Al 707 (4X-ATR) was on the ramp at Athens, flanked by foreign aircraft and being serviced prior to its scheduled flight to Paris and New York. On board was a crew of ten, plus 37 passengers.

Meanwhile, a group of passengers was filing out of the airport transit lounge to an aircraft of another airline about 45m (50yd) from the El Al plane. Suddenly two young men broke away from the group and ran directly to the El Al aircraft. One brandished a submachine gun, a Soviet-made Kalishnikov, and a bag of hand grenades. Firing as he ran, he pumped bullets into the aluminum skin of the plane until he was only a few feet away, piercing the nose and forward fuselage. A passenger sitting at the window, a Haifa maritime engineer on loan to the United Nations, was killed instantly.

Miraculously the crew and other passengers were not hit. Athens police finally overpowered the two terrorists, and the El Al passengers were evacuated by emergency chutes and fled to the terminal building.

The PFLP proudly took responsibility for the attack, and Lebanese newspapers praised the attackers as heroes. Israel responded two days later with a lightning helicopter-borne reprisal raid, destroying 14 aircraft of Arab airlines at Beirut International Airport, the jumping-off point for the terrorists. While the United Nations condemned Israel for using "excessive force", Israel had made its point. It would not allow El Al aircraft to be attacked and riddled with bullets while Arab airlines continued to fly with impunity.

The terrorists, broadcasting from Beirut and Damascus, made no secret of their plans to destroy the viability of El Al. Their systematic program called for the creation of a web of fear that would frighten passengers away from the airline. Sudden, murderous attacks would undermine the morale of the airline, they reasoned, and cause serious physical damage to the aircraft and facilities of El Al.

But the terrorists miscalculated as to the toughness of El Al and its President, Mordechai Ben-Ari. The airline swiftly organized an around-the-clock security alert and also appealed, through the Israeli Government, to all nations enjoying reciprocal landing rights with Israel to give maximum protection to El Al aircraft when they were under the jurisdiction of those governments. Through international civil aviation organizations it urged world-wide legislation against criminal attacks on civil airliners. El Al introduced other security measures as well, but for the time being these were kept secret.

Zürich Airport Assault

On 18 February 1969, El Al flight LY432, a Boeing 720B (4X-ABB), with a crew of 11 and 17 passengers, was taxiing to the runway for takeoff from Zürich's Kloten airport after a scheduled stop on the Amsterdam—Tel Aviv route. Four Arab terrorists were waiting near a fence at the edge of the taxiway. As the aircraft approached, they suddenly opened fire with several Kalishnikov submachine guns and started hurling grenades. About 40 shots tore through the cockpit, killing Yoram Peres, a trainee pilot. Swiss police moved quickly to the scene, but not before Mordechai Rahamim, a supposed passenger on the plane, opened the aircraft door and started shooting back at the terrorists, killing one before being taken into custody himself. In Amman, Jordan, the PFLP again took responsibility for the action.

Rahamim proved to be none other than an El Al security guard. El Al had initiated the practice of having armed security personnel on every flight. The airline was going to protect itself by whatever means available, and would not just be a sitting target.

The other passengers and crew were fortunately unhurt. All eventually continued to Israel with El Al, and the aircraft was back in Israel six days after the incident. Not only did the terrorist attacks not damage El Al, the airline actually continued to experience increased bookings both in Israel and in other parts of the world.

Prime Minister Golda Meir, who flew on El Al flights since its earliest days in 1949, arriving at Lod Airport aboard a 707 jet in the late 1960s. (El Al Israel Airlines collection)

New Types of Terrorism

Frustrated at their unsuccessful attempts against El Al, the Arab terrorists turned their attention to U.S. airlines. On 29 August 1969 guerrillas hijacked a Trans World Airlines (TWA) aircraft shortly after takeoff from Rome on a Los Angeles—Tel Aviv flight. The plane was diverted to Damascus, where the passengers were taken off and the aircraft severely damaged in a bomb explosion (although subsequently repaired). Two Israeli passengers on board were incarcerated until 5 December 1969.

The terrorists then switched to attacks on El Al offices. On 8 September 1969 they used two Arab teen-agers to hurl two hand grenades into El Al's Brussels office, injuring four persons. On 27 September Arab youngsters lobbed grenades into El Al's Athens office, injuring four members of a Greek family and killing one of their children. Attacks also occurred on El Al's offices in Istanbul and Teheran, but damage was inconsequential.

By 1970 police were patrolling El Al offices on a round-the-clock basis and airport authorities all over the world started providing extra protection for El Al aircraft on their ramps.

Trying yet another horrific approach, on 10 February 1970 at Munich Airport, Arab terrorists attacked a bus carrying El Al passengers, using automatic fire and grenades. Aryeh Katzenstein, a former paratrooper from Haifa, shielded the rest of the passengers from a grenade thrown through a window by absorbing the explosion with his own body. He died instantly. Uri Cohen, the captain of the flight, engaged one of the armed Arabs with his bare hands when the terrorist pulled the pin of a grenade and was about to throw it among the crowd of passengers and bystanders near the bus. Cohen was hurt in the struggle when the grenade exploded, but his action probably saved many lives. Meanwhile, Hannah Meron, one of the passengers and a leading Israeli actress, was badly injured and lost a leg in the attack.

Again the terrorist attacks failed in their purpose to disrupt El Al and its passenger traffic. Instead, El Al starting developing a global reputation as one of the safest and most security-conscious of all air carriers. Both Jews and non-Jews demonstrated a strong feeling of solidarity with Israel's national carrier, and also appreciated the fact that El Al's careful security measures had become the envy of the industry.

Despite the terrorism, El Al had some of its most productive years. In 1968 El Al had a profit of $2.2 million, and the following year, in the face of an international tourist decline and economic difficulties affecting almost all airlines, El Al still earned a net profit of nearly $2 million. Terror attacks led to very few passenger cancellations and virtually no interruption of regular services.

Top: *An El Al Boeing 720B at Teheran-Mehrabad Airport, Iran, in the late 1960s. The 720Bs were well-suited to the "hot and high" climate and elevation at Teheran.* (El Al Israel Airlines collection) **Above, left:** *The arrival of El Al's first scheduled passenger flight to Addis Ababa, Ethiopia, in April 1970 was celebrated complete with a lion recalling Ethiopia's "Lion of Judah" symbol. However, a break in diplomatic relations between Ethiopia and Israel following the 1973 Yom Kippur war led to suspension of this route.* (El Al Israel Airlines collection) **Above, right:** *New modern El Al busses joined its aircraft-to-terminal ground services in 1971.* (El Al Israel Airlines collection)

6 September 1970

On this infamous date in civil aviation history, Arab terrorists launched their most ambitious attack ever against Israel and travelers to the United States. Four simultaneous hijackings were attempted: against El Al Flight 219 (Boeing 707 4X-ATB) from Amsterdam to New York; Pan American 093 (a Boeing 747) from Amsterdam to New York via London; Trans World Airlines (TWA) 741 (a Boeing 707) from Tel Aviv via Frankfurt to New York; and Swissair 100 from Zürich to New York. When it was all over, the Pan Am, TWA and Swissair aircraft, plus a Vickers VC10 of British Overseas Airways Corporation, which was hijacked three days later operating a flight to London from Bombay, lay in smoldering ruins, blown up by PFLP guerrillas at Cairo, Egypt, and Dawson Field, Jordan. The only one of the four flights to reach its destination safely, albeit late, was El Al 219.

About 30 minutes after takeoff from Amsterdam, when LY 219 was over the North Sea, Arab terrorist Leila Khaled (who had been involved in the TWA incident in August 1969) and her male companion, Patrick Arguello, brandishing revolvers and grenades, rushed to the cockpit in an attempt to take over the aircraft. They found the cockpit door locked and specially reinforced just for such contingencies. The terrorists then pinned a stewardess next to the cockpit door, threatening to kill her unless it was opened.

The El Al flight crew saw what was happening through the cockpit door's one-way peephole. Captain Uri Bar-Lev decided there was only one way to save the aircraft and passengers and put the 707 into a steep dive, dropping nearly 4,300m (14,000ft). This raised havoc with anyone standing and not strapped into a seat and the hijackers were thrown off balance. Khaled staggered, and a passenger and an El Al steward pinned her down. One of her grenades rolled to the floor but miraculously did not go off. Arguello shot El Al steward Shlomo Vider, then was himself killed by gunfire from an El Al security officer who had reached the forward section of the cabin. Bar-Lev then diverted to London-Heathrow, and although this meant the turning over of Khaled to the British and her eventual release under pressure (after the hijacking of the London-bound VC10), his action helped save Vider's life.

As in the previous terrorist attempts, the mass hijackings of September 1970 merely served to reinforce El Al's reputation for security. El Al continued to attract ever-increasing numbers of tourists, while discouraging renewed terrorist attempts. Over the years the importance and sophistication of El Al security has continued to grow (see Chapter 8).

Other Developments

More Aircraft and Cargo

In January 1969 El Al took delivery of a third Boeing 707-320B and, more significantly, within another year it acquired two Boeing 707-320Cs (4X-ATX and -ATY) convertible between passenger and all-cargo configurations. Each -320C could carry 37,800kg (42 tons) of cargo in bulk or 34,200kg (38 tons) using pallets. These acquisitions expanded El Al's fleet to ten aircraft—eight 707s and two 720Bs.

The -320Cs allowed El Al to take advantage of the rapid rise in demand for air cargo, and it started regular all-cargo flights to the U.S. via many points in Europe. The first all-cargo jet flight to New York from Tel Aviv operated, via Paris, on 28 September 1969. A schedule of four weekly cargo flights to Europe and the U.S. was initiated. This expansion, together with flexible air cargo rates negotiated for specific commodities, stimulated the growth of exports from Israel of agricultural products, textiles, fashion garments, fruits and flowers, sheep and baby chicks. El Al's air cargo traffic in 1969/70 reflected a doubling of volume in just three years.

An unusual hybrid color scheme resulting from El Al leasing a 707 from British Midland Airways during a few weeks in August-September 1972. The British Midland livery is retained, but with El Al titles. (Jean-M. Magendie)

New Routes

In April 1968 El Al inaugurated scheduled service to Geneva, Switzerland, and Nice, France (the latter being replaced by Marseilles in March 1971). Four months later, in August 1968, El Al added Bucharest, Romania, to its network. Pending construction of airport facilities suitable for 707s at Bucharest, El Al initially flew to Constanta on the shore of the Black Sea.

Bucharest was a particularly important destination for El Al and Israel as it was their only window at the time to the Communist Eastern European world.

In April 1970 El Al also started service to Addis Ababa, Ethiopia. This route, however, was terminated by the Ethiopian government under Arab pressure shortly after the October 1973 Yom Kippur War.

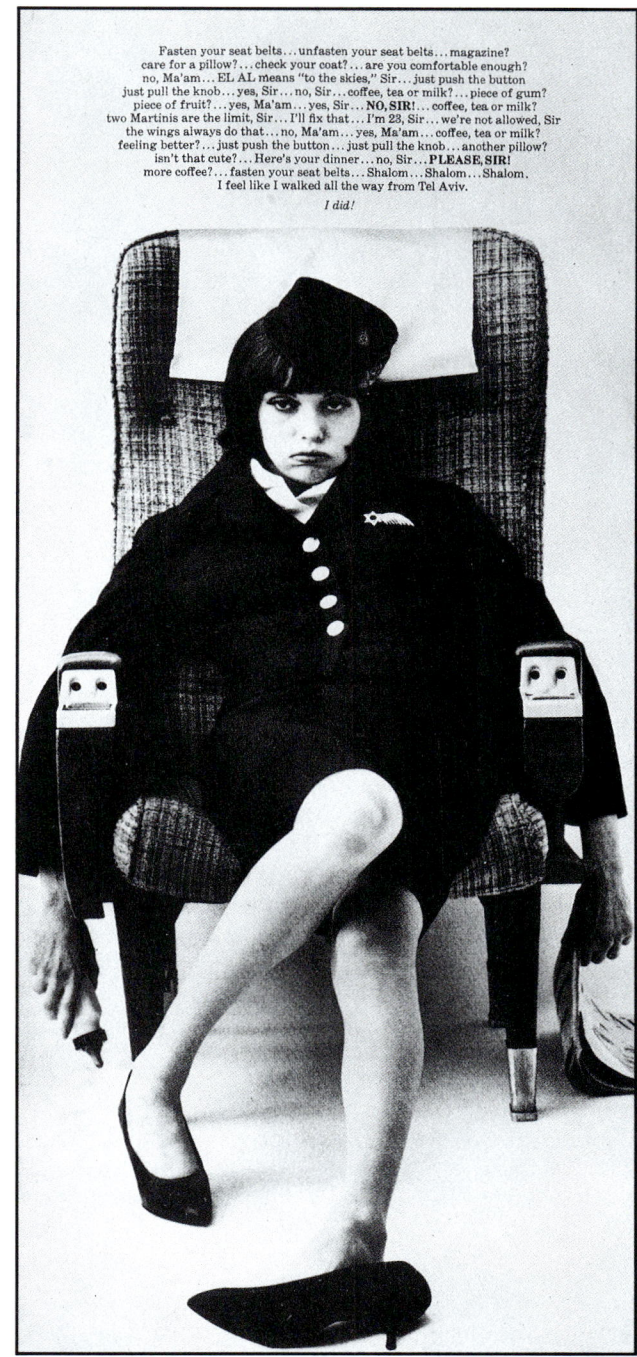

The exuberance of passengers on El Al's New York to Tel Aviv nonstop, and their proverbial willingness to walk the aisles and talk to friends all through the flight, led to many an exhausted El Al stewardess (1960s). (Marvin Goldman collection)

Above: *Aviva Glazer, Manager of Simulator Training for El Al Boeing 707 crews for many years, shown in the training cockpit of a 707.* (El Al Israel Airlines collection)

Right: *El Al celebrated its 20th anniversary in 1968-69 with a "flower plane" symbol, as seen in this airline-issue postcard. One daisy forms each of the four jet engines.* (Marvin Goldman collection)

Right, below: *Flight attendant Zahava Shilon models the orange designer uniforms introduced by El Al in 1969.* (Marvin Goldman collection)

The Pinnacle of 707 Service

By 1970 average utilization of the El Al fleet of ten Boeing 707/720s was an exceptionally high 12 hours per day. Considering that El Al was then operating only about 306 days per year due to the constraints of flying on the Jewish Sabbath and holy days, this translates into an actual utilization of nearly 15 hours per day. All ten aircraft were used during the April-October high season. During October to March, the fleet would consist of nine aircraft, while the tenth would undergo a major overhaul.

The number of employees grew to nearly 4,000 by the end of 1970, including 64 captains and flight crews, and about 90% of the staff total were Israeli nationals. Pilots were typically recruited directly out of one of the finest training centers in the world—the Israeli Air Force. The average age at which pilots would make captain fell to 30, among the youngest in the industry.

By early 1971 the 707s and 720Bs had served El Al faithfully and safely for almost ten years. They became the proud symbol of an airline that continued to gain acceptance as one of the most efficient operations in the civil aviation industry. Soon, however, these aircraft, like their predecessors, would have to relinquish their position of eminence. Already industry leader Pan Am and other carriers had entered a new technological era—that of the Boeing 747 "jumbo jet". El Al would not be far behind.

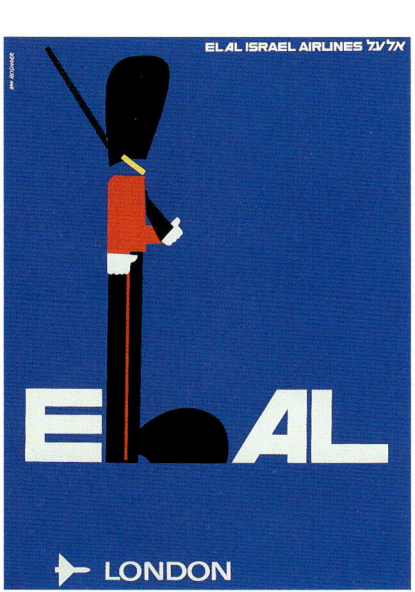

Posters from a destination series by noted Israeli artist/designer Dan Reisinger. In each poster, one of El Al's letters is transformed into a famous symbol of the destination. All date from the 1960s except "Israel" which was issued in 1973. (Marvin Goldman collection via Dan Reisinger)

EL AL *RAINBOEING THE SKIES*

El Al's beautiful "Rainboeing the Skies" poster, designed by Dan Reisinger about 1970, melds a "rainbow" with El Al's all-Boeing fleet. (Marvin Goldman collection)

CHAPTER SIX
The Jumbo Ark: Boeing 747s

"The way of an eagle in the air"

(Proverbs 30:19)

Design of the Boeing 747, first of the jetliners to coin the term wide-body, began in the early 1960s. Market research indicated that if passenger and cargo traffic continued to grow at its existing rate, there would be a need for much larger capacity aircraft. Production of the 747, inevitably nicknamed "jumbo jet" by the popular press, started in early 1967 at a huge new Boeing factory near Everett, Washington.

El Al's first 747 on the production line at the Boeing plant at Everett, Washington, 1970. (El Al Israel Airlines collection)

El Al watched the development of the 747 closely, as it hoped the 350 to 400-seat airliner would be ideal for its main long-haul route between Tel Aviv and New York. The very first 747s, the -100 series, were passed up by El Al, in part because the early engines could not meet the desired range and load capabilities. Instead, El Al opted for the improved -200B series with more powerful engines and increased operating weights.

El Al required that its 747s could fly nonstop the prime New York to Tel Aviv route, a distance of 9,270km (5,760mi), with a full payload and fitted its first two aircraft with Pratt & Whitney JT9D-7 engines of 20,250kg (45,000lb) thrust each, considerably more powerful (and reliable) than the earlier JT9D-3 powerplants of the Dash 100 series.

Lod Airport's existing runways proved adequate for the 747s, as its wing-flap system and 16-wheel, four-main truck landing gear allowed the 747s to operate from runways normally used by 707s.

The 747 represented the largest investment Israel had ever made for a single piece of equipment. The price tag of $31-35 million each (including training and spares) was staggering for the small economy of the State. Yet El Al was able to finance the acquisitions entirely out of revenue, with the assistance of long-term, low-interest loans from the Export-Import Bank of the United States.

But the cost of the aircraft themselves was only the beginning. The Boeing 747 was twice as big as any previous airliner, with a length of over 70m (231ft), a wing span of 59m (195ft), and a tail height of 19m (63ft)—equal to a six-story building. The gross weight of El Al's initial 747-200s was an enormous 348,750kg (over 387 tons). The maximum passenger capacity of over 400 also was a quantum jump over any previous airliner. New ancillary equipment and maintenance and training facilities were necessary to service the 747 and its passengers, and a new hangar was built with a roof area covering one hectare (2½ acres), the largest structure of its kind in the Middle East at the time. New cargo facilities also had to be built. In all the initial investment in aircraft and facilities exceeded $200 million.

Almost every work group in the Company had to be re-educated; pilots had to be specially trained and certified for the 747 and most of the mechanics and technicians had to be indoctrinated in the new technology. They took advantage of knowledge gained in the industry since the introduction of the first 747 in scheduled service by Pan American in January 1970.

El Al President Mordechai Ben-Ari (right) viewing a 747 with Boeing Vice President M. T. Stampler at Boeing's factory at Everett, Washington, late 1960s. (El Al Israel Airlines)

Delivery of El Al's first 747 (4X-AXA) by Boeing at Everett, Washington, on 26 May 1971. (Boeing Airplane Co.)

A New Look

With the advent of the 747, El Al introduced a striking new paint scheme—one that proved so popular it has continued into the 1990s. A light blue stripe flows from head to tail on a white background, while a darker blue stripe starts at the front wing area and sweeps upward onto the tail, capped by the Israeli flag with the inset six-pointed Star of David.

Inside the 747, a new interior design featured themes of cheerfulness and light. Since the 747s were to be used for long flights between Tel Aviv and the U.S., designer Danny Reisinger and the El Al design team aimed for a bright atmosphere with extensive use of color. The scheme was based on the image of the sun—orange, pink, red, silver and white—in keeping with El Al's wish to welcome passengers to the warm Mediterranean sun colors of Israel. Seats, ceilings and walls were decorated in several different hues, staggered throughout the aircraft.

To provide a feeling of intimacy and personalized service, the main cabin of the 747 was divided into five self-contained sections. Each sector featured its own food galleys (appropriately divided into meat and dairy areas to comply with kosher dietary law requirements), service areas, and entrance/exit doors for convenient and fast seating.

The 747 also featured an upper deck, immediately behind the cockpit. Originally conceived as an impressive first-class lounge, El Al and many airlines have instead configured it for the seating of first-class or business-class passengers. Since

Touchdown of El Al's first 747 at Lod Airport, 2 June 1971, upon completing its delivery flight from Boeing's plant at Everett, Washington. This was the only El Al 747 that originally had just three windows on each side of the upper deck, and a few years later additional windows were installed. (Boeing Airplane Co.)

1981, El Al's 747 first-class section is fitted entirely with "sleeperette" seats and is luxuriously limited to just ten passengers.

Also with the advent of the 747, El Al initiated in-flight entertainment, showing a wide range of the latest films. Passengers may further select any of eight audio programs, including not only the usual range of music, but Israeli and Jewish songs, Bible readings, and comedy as well.

Enter the 747

On 26 May 1971 Boeing formally delivered to El Al its first 747 (4X-AXA). On 2 June the jumbo ark, commanded by Gad Katz, Reuven Narunsky and Danny Rosin, arrived over the shoreline of Tel Aviv and landed at Lod Airport. The next day, in one of El Al's proudest moments, Prime Minister Golda Meir, Transport Minister Shimon Peres, and El Al Chairman Moshe Carmel and President Mordechai Ben-Ari, greeted a large gathering of dignitaries and El Al employees at an airport welcoming ceremony for the 747.

On 8 June 1971, the first 747 entered scheduled flight operations on the Tel Aviv—New York route, with a stopover in London in both directions. The second 747 (4X-AXB) was delivered to El Al on 22 November 1971 and promptly entered trans-Atlantic service, with a stopover each way in Paris.

With the introduction of these two wide-body jets, El Al increased its total seat capacity by over 50%. It also marked the completion of El Al's aircraft acquisition and development program initiated in 1968. In the four-year period, El Al had acquired three additional Boeing 707s (including two -320C models that could be used for mixed passenger-cargo or all cargo) and its first two 747s. Its total fleet now consisted of 12 modern all-Boeing aircraft—eight 707s, two 720s and two 747s.

El Al's first 747, newly arrived at Lod Airport and ready for a gala reception, on 3 June 1971. (Israel Government Press)

Operationally, El Al developed procedures to maintain its exceptional turn-around time of aircraft on the ground, even with the 747 which could carry nearly triple the passengers of the 707s. For example, at New York's JFK Airport, in a typical single three-hour turn-around, El Al would deplane 400 passengers, remove about 1,000 pieces of luggage and 18,000kg (20 tons) of freight, clean and replace 400 blankets, pillows and headrests, vacuum carpet covering the equivalent of 13 large living rooms, wash 14 lavatories, load eight galleys with food for 800 meals, fuel the aircraft with over 190,000 liters (50,000 gallons) of fuel, load about the same amount of baggage and cargo that had just been offloaded, and enplane 400 new passengers.

Many observers had doubted El Al's capacity to achieve such an ambitious program of aircraft acquisition in so short a time. They claimed El Al had overextended itself, especially in view of the technical demands, the tense situation in Israel and on its borders, and terrorist attacks on civil aviation in general and El Al in particular. Yet, under the leadership of Mordechai Ben-Ari, El Al attained unprecedented success.

El Al 747 crew members welcoming, left to right, Prime Minister Golda Meir, El Al President Mordechai Ben-Ari, Transport Minister Shimon Peres, and El Al Chairman Moshe Carmel, on 3 June 1971. (Israel Government Press Office)

With the introduction of the two 747s, El Al's passenger traffic soared. The 1971-72 fiscal year recorded nearly 700,000 passengers, a 40% increase over the previous year. Load factors also stayed at or near the highest among North Atlantic carriers. In the first year of 747 operations, trans-Atlantic load factors reached 89.6% during peak travel periods, with an annual average of 79.4%, well above the industry average of 51%. Of 106 carriers in the International Air Transport

Amsterdam), and by April 1972 frequency had reached four flights a week. Another new route started in March 1971 to Marseilles, France, which soon thereafter supplanted the existing service to Nice.

El Al also moved into related tourist areas. Having formed Teshet, a wholly-owned subsidiary, in 1968 to enter the airline catering business, El Al proceeded to utilize Teshet to acquire a 24% interest in the Nairobi Hilton and to provide management and marketing for the Laromme

Association (IATA), El Al, with its small fleet of 12 aircraft, was number 16 in terms of production (total revenue passenger kilometers flown divided by the number of employees). El Al became an airline to emulate. Major airlines sent representatives to check out El Al's superior security precautions, and El Al's commercial policies were carefully studied by air carriers of developing countries.

More Expansion

The success of the first two 747s, and El Al's continuous profitable operations, led the Government of Israel to approve the purchase of a third 747. This aircraft (4X-AXC) was the first of the -200B series with increased gross operating weights and was delivered to El Al on 18 April 1973 and brought El Al's fleet to a total of 13 aircraft—three 747s and ten 707/720s.

While El Al had been operating nonstop flights from New York to Tel Aviv for many years, it had never before operated scheduled nonstop flights in the opposite direction. Now with the introduction of a third 747 into scheduled service, on 29 April 1973 regular nonstop service from Tel Aviv to New York was started. As this westward travel involved flying against the prevailing winds, it amounted to a 13-hour nonstop flight—then the longest in the world. At first, with the most powerful 747 engines available at the time, the Pratt & Whitney JT9D-7AWs, only 360 of the 400 seats could be occupied and no cargo carried. However, with the introduction of more powerful Pratt & Whitney Dash 7F engines in 1975, full passenger and cargo loads could be carried on the flight.

Meanwhile, El Al expanded its routes by opening a second North American gateway at Montreal, Canada, on 28 March 1971 (via

Hotel in Jerusalem and the Laromme Hotel (later known as the Carlton) in Tel Aviv.

The year 1973 was the 25th Anniversary of the State of Israel, further tourist expansion was hoped for, and the emblem of the notable event was painted on El Al's aircraft in celebration. Paralleling the optimism, El Al entered negotiations to obtain additional U.S. gateways. Extension of routes to the East, as well as a new route to Buenos Aires, Argentina, were being considered. All these plans, however, ended suddenly. In October 1973 Israel found itself unexpectedly thrust into another war for its very survival.

The Yom Kippur War

On 6 October 1973 the combined forces of Egypt and Syria attacked Israel in the early afternoon of the Jewish fast of Yom Kippur (Day of Atonement), the holiest day of the Jewish year. Egyptian fighters struck at Israeli air bases in the Sinai, while heavy guns and mortars pummeled the

Welcoming passengers onto one of El Al's first 747 flights, 1971.

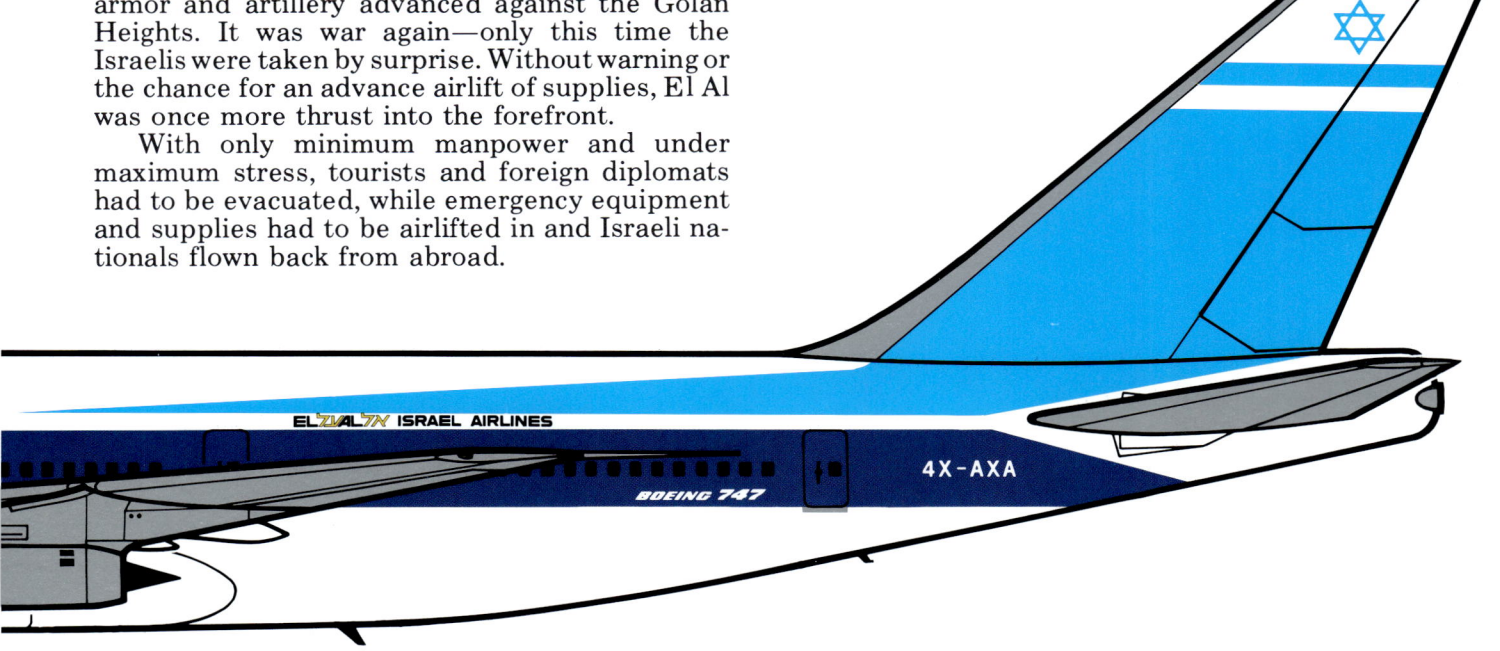

Israeli defense positions on the Suez Canal; Syrian armor and artillery advanced against the Golan Heights. It was war again—only this time the Israelis were taken by surprise. Without warning or the chance for an advance airlift of supplies, El Al was once more thrust into the forefront.

With only minimum manpower and under maximum stress, tourists and foreign diplomats had to be evacuated, while emergency equipment and supplies had to be airlifted in and Israeli nationals flown back from abroad.

Upon the outbreak of the fierce battles, all foreign carriers stopped flying to Israel, and Lod Airport was closed to all unnecessary civilian traffic. Meanwhile several thousand outbound passengers filled the passenger terminal. Helicopters landed with wounded from the front lines who were then rushed to hospitals. Not all those wishing to leave could be accommodated the first day on El Al aircraft, and many had to return to Tel Aviv hotels in order to leave the following day when some normalization returned to departures.

While passenger traffic was cut back, El Al rapidly began ferrying Israeli nationals home from overseas and airlifting emergency supplies, medicines and vital materials. El Al again became the only air link between Israel and the outside world.

On the second day of the war, the interiors of El Al's 707s were gutted and an emergency cargo "skytrain" operation began. The El Al pilots virtually lived in their planes; aircraft were unloaded and reloaded as rapidly as possible. Boeing personnel in Seattle made new weight and balance calculations to raise the 707's cargo capacity to the limit, finally blessing an increase in maximum cargo weight from 42,300 to 57,150kg (94,000 to 127,000lb). Pilots logged 180 hours of flying time in two weeks, an average of over 12 hours per day. Friendship and support greeted the El Al crews wherever they landed. Incredibly, there were no aircraft accidents during the two-week operation.

On the ground, most of the regular young cargo handlers were fighting on the front. Other ground staff had to do the work, despite their age and physical condition, and worked double shifts and slept in offices when time permitted.

While the skytrain operation continued, a U.S. Air Force supply shuttle by its Military Airlift Command started on 14 October. Giant Lockheed C-5A Galaxy aircraft, supported by C-141 Starlifter and C-130 Hercules freighters, arrived in numbers at Lod Airport bringing additional desperately-needed equipment and materiel.

Despite the call-up of all personnel under 40 years of age, and with only a quarter of the normal staff on duty to keep the aircraft flying, El Al managed to maintain regular air links and communications with the world. With a greatly reduced fleet, El Al carried over 22,000 passengers in that hectic period.

Nearly three weeks of battle passed before a shaky cease fire was initiated. Israel had won the war, but paid a high price for victory. Over 2,500 Israelis were killed and over 3,000 wounded in action, a painful number for a small nation. Sixteen of those killed, including nine pilots, were El Al employees.

El Al's first 747 in its giant hangar, No. 3, at Lod Airport, early 1970s. (El Al Israel Airlines collection)

War's Aftermath

The 1973 war severely damaged Israel's tourist industry. The number of visitors plunged, and El Al and its domestic subsidiary Arkia immediately experienced a sharp drop in traffic. Meanwhile, El Al's aircraft had to be completely refurbished, since the interiors had been all but destroyed in the airlift. Personnel levels returned to normal only slowly, as those in the armed services were not immediately released from duty.

Ethiopia, bowing quickly to Arab pressure, denied El Al landing rights in Addis Ababa and, within one month after the war, all of El Al's operations there were shut down.

In December 1973 the pioneer Israeli leader David Ben-Gurion died at age 87, and the realization that his passing marked the end of an era further dampened the nation's mood. Soon thereafter, the Israeli Government changed the name of Lod Airport to Ben-Gurion Airport in his memory.

Israel began to feel the severe economic aftershocks of the war by early the following year. The financial costs of the war had been tremendous, and now the Arab States were discovering their oil weapon and starting to use it. Fuel prices rose to unprecedented heights, afflicting Israel and El Al alike.

By mid-1974 flight operations had returned to normal. However, the psychological effects of the war and the strained economy and new mood in Israel took their toll on El Al's employees. Discontent and inefficiency grew. Wildcat work stoppages frequently disrupted flights. Not until February 1975 was a new work contract and pay agreement signed which brought a fragile labor truce with the workforce.

In July 1974 the Cypriot-Turkish conflict erupted, and foreign airlines canceled flights to Israel and other Middle East destinations. For the second time in nine months, El Al became the only air link between Israel and the western world. Israelis again appreciated the vital importance of their national carrier, as El Al added more flights and worked overtime to accommodate stranded and interline passengers from other airlines.

Serving breakfast with fresh hot bagels and lox (smoked salmon) aboard one of El Al's 747s, early 1970s.

Interior of an El Al Boeing 747 in the early 1970s. Originally El Al's 747s were configured with two-four-three across seating per row, as in this photo, rather than the later and now more usual three-four-three. (El Al Israel Airlines collection)

Air Cargo Expands

El Al's three new Boeing 747s could each handle 13,500kg (15 tons) of freight besides their passengers. By supplementing the two 707-320C convertible cargo aircraft, the 747s contributed to further expansion of El Al's air freight. New cargo facilities were built at Ben-Gurion Airport and at Heathrow Airport, London. As a result, in fiscal year 1971/72, cargo operations increased to over 22 million kg (25,000 tons).

The sharply increasing demand for cargo led to the acquisition of El Al's first 747-200C convertible passenger/cargo "Combi" (4X-AXD) in December 1975 and its first pure-cargo 747-100F (-AXZ) in June 1977. The latter aircraft had previously served with Continental Airlines and the Imperial Iranian Air Force, and it was refurbished by Boeing prior to delivery to El Al.

El Al then purchased three additional new 747s from Boeing before calling a halt to its aircraft acquisition program for the 'Seventies: a second 747-200C "Combi" (4X-AXF) received in June 1978, a pure-cargo 747-200F (-AXG) delivered in March 1979, and a fourth all-passenger 747-200B (-AXH) added in December 1979.

The two Combi 747s and the pure-cargo 747-200F feature an enormous freight capacity of 113,400kg (125 tons), and the nose of each aircraft swivels upward for commodious front-loading. As the pure-cargo 747-100F (-AXZ) is a conversion from an early passenger aircraft, it carries a maximum of 89,100 kg (99 tons) and does not have a nose entrance. Loading is completed through a side cargo door installed in the left side of the rear fuselage (the -200F also has this feature). El Al's 747 fleet now totaled eight, with its overall aircraft number rising to a new high of 18. Besides the added capacity, El Al benefited greatly from the convertible features of its passenger/cargo aircraft which allowed it to constantly select the best mix of passenger and cargo to meet its needs at any given time.

The profitable Israeli export cargo market and the desire of the Agricultural Board in Israel (Agrexco) to share in it led to the formation, in 1975, of the Israeli all-freight carrier, Cargo Air Lines (C.A.L.). Although C.A.L. is not owned by El Al, C.A.L.'s operating authority from the Israeli Government obligates it to utilize 747 freighters leased from El Al. C.A.L. may lease equipment from others only when El Al is unable to supply aircraft. (For details on C.A.L., see Chapter 7).

Above: *El Al's first pure cargo Boeing 747, 4X-AXG, at Everett/Paine Field in the State of Washington, March 1979. (El Al Israel Airlines collection)*

Lower left: *One of El Al's two convertible passenger/cargo 747s in freight configuration swallowing cargo through its flip-open nose at Amsterdam's Schiphol Airport. El Al called its 747 freighters "Samson" due to their herculean capacity. (Marvin Goldman collection)*

Lower right: *Loading Israeli produce for export in a 747, in the 1970s. The cargo gets a welcome sign, too. (Israel Government Press Office)*

Labor Unrest Surges Again

The fragile labor truce based on the February 1975 new contract ended abruptly seven months later. The issue involved the Government imposing an income tax on overtime work. The El Al workshops responded by refusing to work extra hours, raising havoc with the airline's key morning departure schedule.

Eventually the workers gave in to the new taxes, but when the benefits of certain management groups were increased shortly thereafter, the unions staged a crippling 19-day strike. By the time the labor dispute ended on 3 November 1975, 300 flights and 30,000 passengers had been affected. Work stoppages continued to plague the airline sporadically in the years ahead, severely damaging El Al's reputation.

Another devastating wildcat strike occurred in 1978. The work committees, backed by the rank and file of employees, pressured management to complete negotiations on a new labor contract by 1 April 1978. They chose the busiest and most profitable season, the Passover/Easter period, as their deadline. Without a contract by the deadline, the workers struck for 21 paralyzing days. Eventually an agreement was signed, but everyone lost, as many passengers and travel agents refused to book flights on El Al due to continued concern over possible labor disruptions, and it took months to coax traffic back to normal.

Improved Technology

In 1975 El Al started an upgrade program to a more powerful "Dash 7F" engine for its 747s, phasing in the new powerplants over a three-year period. With these engines, the 747s could carry a full passenger and cargo load on its longest nonstop westbound route, from Tel Aviv to New York, significantly boosting the fleet's productivity. Subsequently, the 747 fleet has been refitted with Dash 7J engines, featuring further improvements.

In January 1976 El Al placed into operation its first computerized reservations system, called "Carmel". El Al also started to perform 747 maintenance work at its Ben-Gurion Airport base in order to reduce costs and upgrade its long-term maintenance capabilities.

New Destinations

For a brief period during 1974-77, El Al operated flights between Europe and Atarot Airport in Jerusalem. The European countries, however, did not allow El Al to fly nonstop to Jerusalem because Atarot is located in what was East Jerusalem, Jordan, prior to the 1967 Six Day War. El Al aircraft therefore landed first in Tel Aviv, and after a quick change of crew they took off immediately for a seven-minute flight to Atarot. The service was eventually dropped for commercial reasons.

On 9 November 1976 a new route to Mexico City was opened with Boeing 707 aircraft via stops in Amsterdam and Montreal. This became El Al's longest route—13,050km (7,830 mi). In 1979 the Mexico City service was re-routed via Rome and New York, but the destination failed to achieve profitability, and in October the same year the city was dropped from the network. More successfully, service to Lisbon was launched in September 1977 and continues to date. In 1978 a new bilateral U.S.-Israel aviation treaty was signed, and El Al won landing rights to four additional U.S. cities. On 1 April 1979 flights were inaugurated to Miami and Chicago, in addition to its existing New York services.

The most dramatic new destination of all, however, proved to be Cairo. Following Egyptian President Anwar Sadat's historic visit to Jerusalem in November 1977, Israel's Prime Minister Menachem Begin prepared to reciprocate, and an advance Israeli governmental delegation was dispatched to Egypt in December.

The Israeli all-cargo airline, Cargo Air Lines ("C.A.L."), is obligated by the Israeli Government to lease all of its aircraft from El Al when available. At times El Al will lease a freighter from another carrier and then sublease it to C.A.L. Here is the ultimate hybrid, a Flying Tiger Line 747 (N801FT), in basic Flying Tiger colors, but with El Al colors on the tail and C.A.L. titles on the forward fuselage, at Munich Airport, April 1978. (Jacques Guillem collection)

An El Al 707 (4X-ATY) was polished up and the word *Shalom* painted on the aircraft's nose in Hebrew and Arabic. Special flag holders were mounted by the windows of the cockpit to allow the plane to taxi to the Cairo terminal with the flags of Israel and Egypt fluttering in the breeze. Eventually, the talks between Begin and Sadat yielded an Israeli-Egyptian peace treaty, and on 3 March 1980 El Al started regular scheduled service to Cairo, its first and only service to date to an Arab country.

The Siege of Teheran

For years El Al had maintained important operations in Iran. Teheran was its most easterly destination and also one of its most profitable, accounting for heavy passenger and freight traffic. El Al's offices in Teheran boasted five floors of prime space in the center of the city with a staff of 20, plus 12 more employees at the airport to handle the daily passenger and cargo flights. The 747 freighters carried tons of fruit, vegetables and industrial and construction equipment in addition to millions of eggs and baby chicks.

In 1978 political events in Iran heated up as Islamic fundamentalists and other revolutionaries, encouraged by the Ayatollah Khomeini, fought to oust the Shah of Iran and his government. By December, thousands of Jews and Moslems waited in line to buy tickets on El Al to flee Teheran. El Al increased its schedule to three flights a day, and at one point added 747s to meet the demand. On 24 December, mobs of hostile Iranians gathered outside the El Al offices, and Iranian soldiers were called in to guard the personnel. The office manager started issuing tickets on an emergency basis out of his home. The main office was finally attacked and the staff escaped to the roof until Iranian soldiers arrived and disbursed the mob. Fuel supplies dwindled at the airport, and aircraft had to take off from Tel Aviv with full tanks in order to ensure round-trips to Teheran without refueling there. Control tower operations were frequently cut off, requiring captains to decide on the spot whether a visual landing approach was possible. At times the weather was so bad, that no landing could be made and the aircraft had to divert back to Israel.

By the end of January 1979, the situation deteriorated to the point where radio communication with the control tower was nonexistent and each flight had to arrive and depart totally unassisted. Yet El Al continued its flights to Teheran until 10 February 1979, nine days after Khomeini returned to Iran. It was reported that the El Al building in Teheran was burned and officially confiscated and the last allusion was in August 1980 when Khomeini announced that the property of Israel's airline was being turned over to Syria's national airline as a reward for anti-Israel activities.

Above: *An El Al 747 (4X-AXB) showing the "fifth pod" slung under the wing whereby an additional engine can be transported for overhaul or for replacement purposes. Originally, El Al had to transport its jet engines for overhaul outside the country, but now El Al performs all required work on the engines of its 747s and other aircraft. (BIAF—Israel Aviation & Space Magazine collection)*

Below: *Immigrant Soviet Jews, arriving at Lod Airport in 1973 via El Al from their transit in Vienna after fleeing the Soviet Union. (El Al Israel Airlines collection)*

Welcome, and Farewell

In 1975, the competition from charters heated up anew. Responding to the threat in a sudden move, President Mordechai Ben-Ari set up a new subsidiary in 1977 to combat the effect of charter activities on El Al's operations. It was called El Al Charter Services Ltd. and later became known as Sun d'Or. Details on Sun d'Or are contained in Chapter 7.

Two years later, in 1979, Arkia's equal 50% owners, El Al and the Israeli Histadrut labor organization, decided to sell Arkia to private investors. Arkia had been serving as Israel's principal domestic airline as well as a charter operator to European destinations. The sale was completed in March 1980, with 75% of Arkia's stock being purchased by a private company called Kanaf Arkia and the remaining 25% purchased by Arkia's employees. For a summary of Arkia's history, see Appendix I.

Fuel Costs Spiral Upward

At the end of the 1970s ten of El Al's all Boeing fleet of 18 aircraft were 707s/720Bs (the balance being 747s). With the sharp rise in fuel prices during the 1970s and new noise restrictions imposed by many European airports, the gas-guzzling and relatively noisy 707s and 720s were now becoming a significant liability. El Al was then having only about 7½ hours/day utilization from its 707s, partly because of noise restrictions at major European airports. It could have only one 707 round-trip per day to Western European cities without running into landing or takeoff restrictions. In contrast the daily utilization rate of the 747s was at the more typical El Al high of 10 hours.

To compound the problem, El Al could not decide on a suitable aircraft to replace the 707s and 720s. It considered proposals from Airbus Industrie, McDonnell Douglas and Lockheed. At one point it took options on the Airbus A300, but delayed exercising them because of new financing proposals received from Lockheed for the L-1011 TriStar, and eventually it allowed the options to lapse. Then the delivery times and size of the aircraft proposed by McDonnell Douglas and Lockheed did not quite fit El Al's plans for expansion into shorter-range markets, so those proposals fell through as well.

As the 1970s passed their mid-point, El Al's operational costs started to rise much faster than revenues from increased passengers and cargo. Fuel costs continued to surge. Air fares were increased too little, too late, to recover inflated costs. Meanwhile, its labor force swelled in numbers, reaching over 6,000 in 1978 and 1979. Productivity lagged, and work stoppages only made matters worse. In 1975, for the first time

since 1963, El Al sustained a net loss, and the balance of the 'Seventies ended with significant losses.

Management Changes

In November 1977, hoping once and for all to solve labor troubles which in the previous six years had led to over 60 work stoppages and "work-to-rule" slowdowns, the Ministry of Transport decided to introduce new management. Ben-Ari was moved up from President to Chairman, and Mordechai ("Motti") Hod, a former commander of the Israeli Air Force and one of the founders of Cargo Air Lines, was appointed President. Assisting Hod was Raphael "Rafi" Harlev, formerly deputy chief commander of the Israel Air Force.

Hod could not have become President at a worse time. The spiral of rising labor and fuel costs coupled with downward pressure on air fares on El Al's premier North Atlantic route due to fierce competition assured continued losses unless drastic changes were made. Hod tried to do the necessary, such as implementing staff reductions, closing nonprofitable routes, and selling off the aging 707s, but he was frustrated at every turn. The 1978/79 fiscal year loss reached $24 million. By July 1979, with no progress on these fronts, Hod resigned. Ben-Ari reluctantly accepted Hod's decision and appointed Rafi Harlev as Acting President.

On 13 November 1979 the Government, as the main shareholder of El Al, decided to reorganize the Board of Directors and charge it with the task of revitalizing the airline. Eight new directors were appointed, half of whom were drawn from the public (not from the Government or the airline). Board Chairman Mordechai Ben-Ari resigned after 29 years of service with El Al, including ten in the role of President or Chairman. He had contributed greatly to the growth and prominence of El Al, and his talents and ingenuity in market development and tariff structures created permanent reminders of his contribution to civil aviation. Appointed to replace Ben-Ari was Avraham "Buma" Shavit, an industrialist and President of Israel's Manufacturers Association.

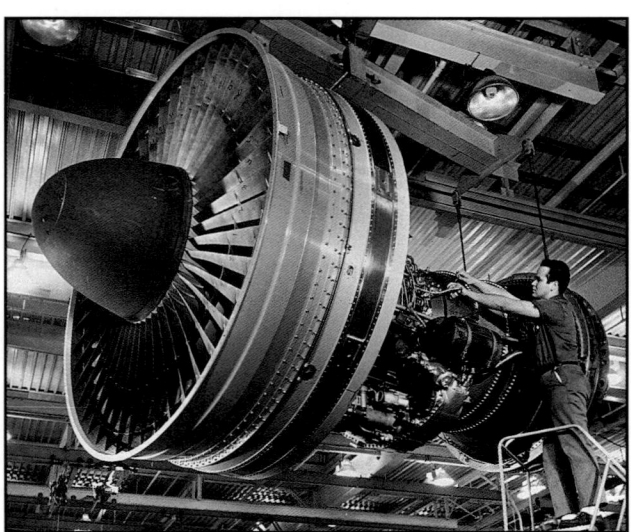

Maintenance of a giant Pratt & Whitney JT9D engine at El Al's base at Lod Airport, 1970s. Over the years, El Al has acquired upgraded JT9D engines for its 747 fleet which offer increased thrust and improved fuel consumption. (El Al Israel Airlines collection)

El Al's fourth 747 (4X-AXD), the first of the convertible passenger/cargo type. Received in 1976, it greatly increased El Al's flexibility in scheduling its passenger and cargo needs. (Boeing Airplane Co.)

Spiral to Shutdown

Mandate for New Management

Hard times were gripping the airline industry, and particularly El Al, when Buma Shavit was recruited from outside the industry in November 1979 to be El Al's new Chairman. Not only was El Al operating at a loss, its losses were growing at a runaway pace, reaching $98 million for the 1979/80 fiscal year. Fuel accounted for one-third of operating expenses and its cost was still escalating. Ticket prices hardly covered operating costs, as fierce competition held fares down, while a world-wide recession and economic uncertainties kept passengers home. Despite El Al's burden of fuel-inefficient 707 aircraft, no Government approval of new aircraft was in the offing. On-time departures became a thing of the past.

Employee-management relations were in shambles, with not even an effective dialogue going on. Many management decisions were made, or at least approved, by committees of employees. There were eight workers committees, each representing a different group, and each committee had to approve plans before they could be implemented. Even though there were more employees than ever, over 6,000, service was a shadow of its former self. Against this backdrop Shavit's mandate was to revitalize or shut down.

The new management set out its goals, including reduction of personnel; the sale of older aircraft and acquisition of modern fuel-efficient ones; cost-cutting schemes especially in the areas of fuel savings and closure of non-profitable routes and offices; flight rescheduling; opening of new markets; and expansion of cargo operations. Actually, these aims were not very different than those of the previous management, but the hard question was whether the new leaders could cajole all concerned to pull together to carry them out.

Shavit worked 12-hour days and fought off press attacks and the belief of the public and the government that the new actions would be vain. He first focused on employee relations. Addressing employees in a general meeting at the head office, he emphasized the importance of a renewed commitment by everyone to achieve on-time service and making the airline the best. The 1980s would mean "A New El Al for a New Decade".

Astonishingly, a new air of optimism and cooperation set in. Timely departures increased and service improved. On 25 December 1979 a historic agreement was reached with the pilots, providing for 20% pay cuts and an end to the artificial income tax exemptions that dated back to the founding of El Al. A similar pact was soon reached with the flight attendants. Temporary workers were dismissed, and an early retirement program and hiring freeze were instituted. This successfully reduced the swollen ranks of employees and managers, yielding a 15% decrease within a year. Meanwhile, a long-time veteran El Al employee, Itzhak Shander, was appointed Acting President on 1 April 1980. In July 1980 a welcome new two-year labor agreement was signed, including a no strike clause.

New Aircraft At Last

Progress was finally made in modernizing the aircraft fleet. One of the early 707s, and the two 720Bs, were sold in 1980. Two twin-engine Boeing 737s (4X-ABL and -ABM) were leased from Belgian airline Trans European Airways for short-haul routes, entering service in October the same year. El Al also acquired options to purchase two new 737s from Boeing for delivery in 1982.

Even more significantly, options were taken in 1979 and 1980 respectively to purchase two wide-body twin-engine Boeing 767-200 aircraft and two more 767-200s of the extended range type, all for delivery in 1983/84. The new 767s and 737s promised savings of millions of dollars of operating costs over their 707/720 predecessors.

Service Changes

In 1979 El Al successfully introduced departure times after midnight (usually 0100) for many of its westbound nonstop 747 flights from Tel Aviv to New York. The flights were well-received as a full night's sleep could be had during the 12/13-hour flight which would arrive at JFK Airport about 0600 in the morning New York time. El Al also benefited because the early morning departure hour provided cool temperatures, offering its 747s better performance to allow them to carry more passengers and freight than would be possible in the heat of the day. The acceptable maximum takeoff weights for these flights are very carefully computed so as to allow maximum payload while retaining the necessary margin of safety. Today, El Al's westbound Tel Aviv to New York flights remain the longest scheduled flights by 747s other than those of the SP (Special Performance) and Dash 400 types.

Service to Cairo, introduced in March 1980, proved quite successful and was increased to five times a week by 1982. In October 1981 El Al inaugurated service from Ben-Gurion to Eilat, Israel's Red Sea tourist destination, but only as an extension of its service originating in the U.S. and Europe. Purely domestic Israeli service to Eilat was still reserved for Arkia. Boston was added in June 1982, but flights to Chicago were halted in April 1980, and several marginal sales offices in the U.S. and Europe were closed, in an effort to restore profitability.

El Al refurbished its first-class "King David" service, and at the beginning of 1980 it introduced business class service for the first time. Known as "King Solomon" class, it provided more space between seats and improved food, beverage service and other amenities compared to coach class.

With everyone now pulling together in the airline, El Al returned to its historic efficiency levels. On-time performance during the second half of the 79/80 fiscal year reached 83% compared to an abysmally low 50% during the previous comparable period. For all of 1980 El Al logged the highest on-time performance record of any international airline.

Travel agent support was won over anew, and passengers returned. High marks were received for service and safety. The London *Daily Mail* newspaper conducted a secret survey of in-flight services of trans-Atlantic carriers, and El Al placed first. The King Solomon business class service was ranked by a leading magazine as one of the top seven in the world. Pride in the national carrier blossomed again.

Opposite: *Examples of some of El Al's most popular advertisements during the 1970s.* (Marvin Goldman collection) **Below:** *On 3 March 1980, following the Sinai peace accord between Egypt and Israel, El Al inaugurated scheduled service to Cairo, Egypt—its first to an Arab country. This first flight cover shows a painting by Israeli aviation artist Danny Shalom of El Al's Boeing 707 4X-ATY decorated for the flight with the word "peace" in Arabic and Hebrew and the Egyptian and Israeli flags.* (Marvin Goldman collection)

Inaugural flight Tel Aviv-Cairo رحلة ال عال الجوية تل ابيب - القاهرة טיסת בכורה תל אביב-קהיר

In October 1980 El Al started operating its first Boeing 737 twin-jet aircraft (4X-ABL and -ABM) through a lease from Trans European Airways (TEA) of Belgium. Shown is 4X-ABL, named Ilana after one of the children of TEA's owner, at Paris (Orly Airport). The "To Eilat With Love" titles proclaim the introduction in fall 1981 of El Al's extension of service from Tel Aviv to Eilat for passengers on El Al flights originating in Europe. (Jacques Guillem)

The first of El Al's two purchased 737-200s (4X-ABN) on a test flight over the State of Washington, in 1982. (Marvin Goldman collection)

The second of El Al's two 737s leased from TEA, named Jonathan after another of the children of TEA's owner, at Ben-Gurion Airport, 8 October 1980. The leased 737s were returned to TEA upon El Al receiving delivery of its two new 737s purchased from Boeing. (Israel Government Press Office)

The End of the Honeymoon

On 15 October 1980 a special report on El Al was released, commissioned by the airline's new management and prepared by the international consulting firm, McKinsey. The report followed their full-scale audit and evaluation of the company's operations and one of McKinsey's recommendations was to cut an additional 700 employees. Suddenly the euphoria in management/labor relations ended. A furor erupted among employees, and the debate found its way into the Israeli press. The workers committees strongly fought additional cuts, but the Government insisted on implementing all the report's recommendations, saying only then would the Government be willing to serve as a guarantor for the $250 million loan needed by the airline to purchase its desired new Boeing 767 and 737 aircraft.

Finally, on 23 December 1980 a new labor agreement was reached. The workers committees waived salary increases that would save $23 million and a compromise was reached on the issue of dismissing 700 workers, so that many would be given early retirement benefits and the balance given mandatory vacation periods of one to three months. But the bitterness persisted.

Soon sporadic work stoppages and slowdowns reared their heads again. Annual losses were still running in excess of $30 million. The tourism market, already in a slump internationally, was further hurt by the Lebanese war, Israel's *Operation Peace for Galilee*, of July 1982. Speculation about shutting down the airline was rife, and calls arose from many quarters to cut back on flights and nonessential routes.

In September 1982 the El Al flight stewards called a strike, and the Government decided this was the last straw. On 12 September it placed El Al in financial receivership and shut down the airline's passenger operations. No one knew whether El Al would ever rise again.

A portion of El Al's fleet grounded at Ben-Gurion Airport. (El Al Israel Airlines collection)

One of El Al's colorful ticket jackets of the 1980s, showing typical street signs in Israel. (Marvin Goldman collection)

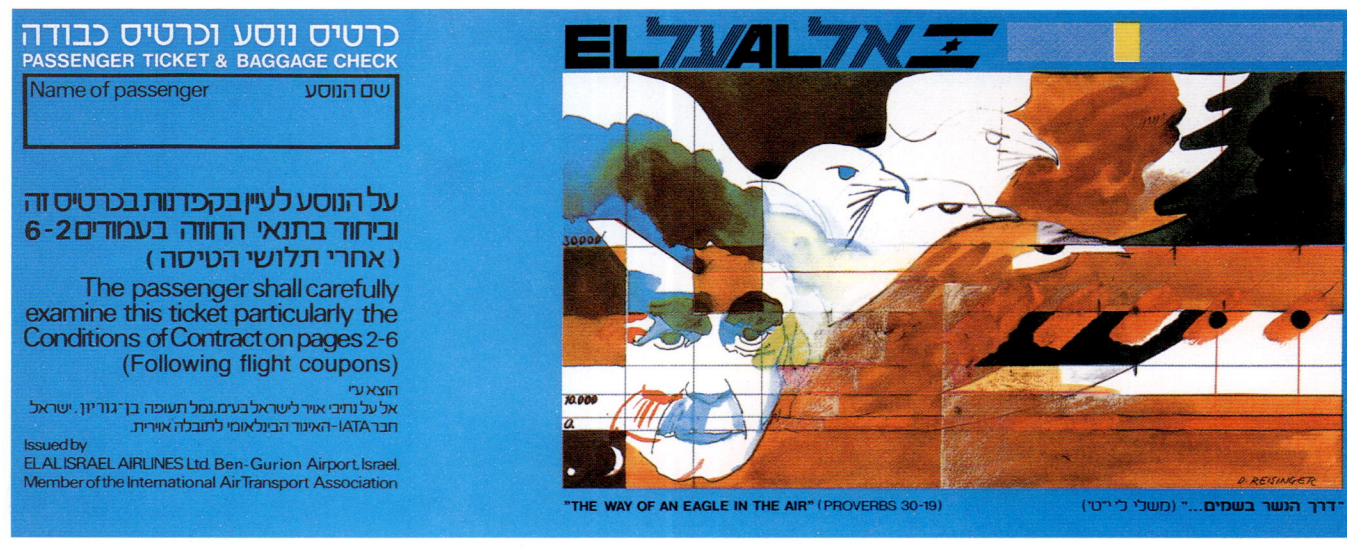

The front of two El Al tickets from the 1980s, featuring part of a series of illustrations by designer Dan Reisinger. (Marvin Goldman)

CHAPTER SEVEN

The Star of David Soars Anew

"Be strong and of good courage" . . .
"and the rainbow shall be seen in the clouds"

(Joshua 1:6; Genesis 9:14).

The plunging of El Al into temporary receivership on 12 September 1982 halted all of its passenger operations. Those holding tickets were transferred to other scheduled carriers or special planes chartered by El Al. The majority of employees were placed on leave of absence. Only some profitable freight operations continued.

Many predicted that this marked the end of El Al and that if Israel were ever to have a national carrier again, it would have to be an entirely new airline.

Boeing 767 aircraft were allowed to be operated by the intended cockpit crew of two instead of three. Salary fringe benefits were reduced, and a scheme was developed whereby the Company's payroll would be reduced by an additional 1,000 employees, of whom 650 were permanent, upon the payment of greater than normal severance pay.

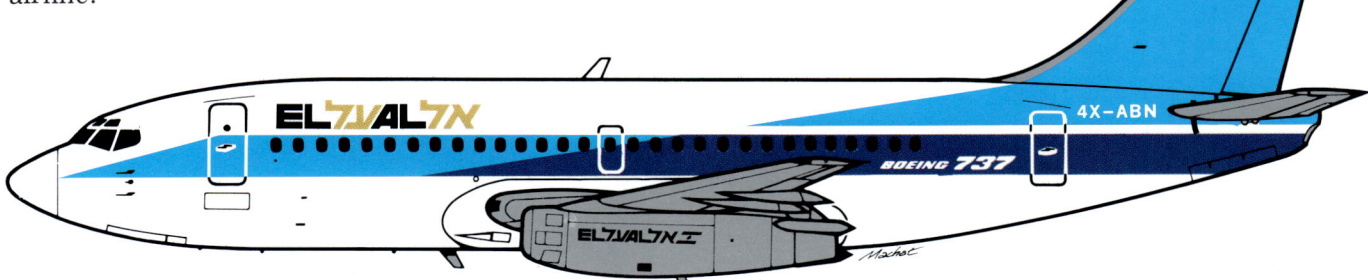

The receivership left the El Al Board of Directors in a legal limbo, without power to act. On 3 December 1982, an application was filed with the Jerusalem District Court to liquidate El Al, and two days later the Court appointed an attorney, Amram Blum, the Official Receiver of the State of Israel to act as "Provisional Liquidator", vesting in him the total power to operate the airline. At the same time, Rafi Harlev, former deputy chief commander of the Israeli Air Force and already an El Al officer for a few years, was installed as the new President of El Al to run day-to-day operations. Nevertheless, all management powers, including the power to hire and fire, remained with the Provisional Liquidator and ultimately with the Court.

Against this ominous backdrop, El Al's personnel, in a new spirit of cooperation, joined forces to see if the airline could be saved again. A single workers committee covering all air and ground sectors, with one representative from each of the former eight committees, was named the sole bargaining agent for the employees, and a new labor agreement was hammered out. Management regained its authority over the company including the determination of work norms. Strikes and sanctions were forbidden. The expected new

Meanwhile, the Government accepted delivery of El Al's first purchased Boeing 737 (4X-ABN) on 30 September 1982 and agreed to place this aircraft and a second purchased 737 (4X-ABO) at El Al's disposal. No amount would be charged by the Government for the use of the aircraft, but El Al would bear their current maintenance and insurance costs.

The four Boeing 767s on order would also be purchased by the Government, at an aggregate cost exceeding $200 million. El Al would act as sole representative of the Government for the implementation of the agreements to acquire the 767s—two of which would be delivered in 1983 and the remaining two in 1984.

Back to the Skies

With new labor agreements worked out, and with Government support for the new aircraft plus Government guaranteed loans to permit a return to passenger operations, El Al resumed passenger service on 12 January 1983. The shutdown had lasted four months.

For El Al's fiscal year ended 30 April 1983, the airline reported its biggest loss in history—$123.3 million. This consisted of an operating loss of

Takeoff of El Al's first Boeing 767 (4X-EAA) from Boeing Field, Seattle, Washington, for Tel Aviv on 14 July 1983. With this aircraft the State of Israel started allocating the letter "E" as the first letter for all future registrations of El Al aircraft. (Boeing Airplane Co.)

$45.2 million, a loss of $46 million from the four-month suspension of operations, and $32.1 in extraordinary expenses for severance pay (in excess of the usual 100%) paid to employees who left the Company.

Nevertheless, there was cause for optimism. Although service resumed only on a limited basis, the airline was surprised to see passengers return much more quickly than expected. Load factors for the six months after the shutdown reached 81% system-wide and 88% on the trans-Atlantic routes, and revenues were 10% higher than anticipated. By early September 1983 El Al was operating 95 flights per week to 26 destinations, including a new route to Madrid, Spain, and a resumption of its new service to Boston.

Management started a campaign to win back the confidence and cooperation of the work force, which had been reduced to below 4,000 "permanent" employees. Workers from each department were selected weekly to meet with President Harlev and other senior management to discuss their problems and make suggestions. The high efficiency, which El Al had amply demonstrated in earlier years, returned.

By 1985 El Al was ranked number seven among the world's international airlines in productivity, with 1,730,000 scheduled revenue passenger kilometers (RPKs) per employee (total kilometers flown by all passengers in scheduled revenue service divided by total employees). On the cargo side El Al ranked third among all airlines in freight ton-kilometers (157,300 FTKs) per employee.

Fleet Modernization

Three new Boeing aircraft joined El Al's fleet in 1983, its second 737 and its first two 767-200s. The twin-engine 737s were fitted with 111 seats and operated on El Al's shorter flights to Europe, replacing the two 737s leased the preceding year from Trans European Airways.

The 767s (4X-EAA and EAB) introduced the latest technology in flight deck avionics. In addition, their two Pratt & Whitney JT9D-7R4D engines provided a quantum leap in efficiency and fuel economy. Twin aisles added wide-body comfort for passengers on routes formerly served only by narrow-body one-aisle aircraft. El Al happily retired its two oldest 707s, which had been much more expensive to operate. Typically, an El Al 767 is fitted with 18 business class and 206 economy class seats. The first El Al 767 entered service 24 July 1983, from Tel Aviv to Frankfurt—making El Al the first operator of the 767 on a scheduled flight in Europe.

El Al introduced several cargo innovations on its 767s. It devised a system for increasing lower-deck cargo capacity from the nominal 8,900kg (9.9 tons) to 14,850kg (16.5 tons), without reducing passenger load. This was accomplished by changing from standard 767 cargo containers to pallets, which increased the volume capacity of the cargo holds by 60%, as well as by other pallet and cargo loading improvements.

Extended Range 767-200s

In 1984 El Al took delivery of two more 767s (4X-EAC and -EAD). These were of the -200 Extended Range (ER) type, with a range of 9,025km compared to the regular 767's 6,870km (5,610mi vs. 4,270mi), achieved with a more powerful engine, the Pratt & Whitney JT9D-7R4E. The first El Al commercial flight of this Extended Range 767 was on 30 March 1984, from Tel Aviv to Vienna, ironically a route that did not require the extra performance.

El Al boldly decided to attempt to use its Extended Range 767s on trans-Atlantic service. This would be a new experiment with the twin jets as all airlines were then using four-engine or three-engine aircraft on the long crossing over the North Atlantic Ocean. El Al specially modified its 767

Above: *El Al's first 767 cruises above the clouds over the State of Washington on a test flight in June 1983.* (Boeing Airplane Co.)
Below: *El Al Boeing 767 cockpit with Avner Slapak, Chief Pilot 767 Fleet (left), and Boaz Harpaz, First Officer. One of the most modern commercial cockpits, the 767 flight deck is more spacious than any previous Boeing airliner cockpit, has better outside visibility, and assists the two-pilot crew to operate the aircraft with maximum safety and fuel efficiency. It features digital electronic equipment, cathode ray tubes (like television pictures) to communicate flight and systems information in alpha-numerics and color, re-designed control wheels for better instrument panel visibility, zone air-conditioning and lower noise levels.* (El Al Israel Airlines collection)

Extended Range aircraft to meet the necessary standards for continuous trans-Atlantic operation. This included installation of extra electrical generators, 120-minute-capacity fire extinguishers for the cargo holds and subsystem cooling sensors.

On 26 March 1984, using a 767ER (4X-EAC) on a nonstop flight from Montreal to Tel Aviv, El Al became the first scheduled airline to cross the North Atlantic on a revenue flight with a two-engine aircraft under the U.S. Federal Aviation Administration (FAA) 60-minute rule. This rule provided that twin-engine aircraft could not fly on a route that is more than 60 minutes (assuming operation on one engine) from the nearest airport.

In early February 1985 El Al began using the 767ERs on some of its regular trans-Atlantic services from Tel Aviv to Los Angeles via Amsterdam and Chicago. This was soon followed by several 767ER flights on the Tel Aviv—Amsterdam—Montreal and Tel Aviv—Amsterdam—New York—Miami routes. The flights were primarily to test the operational and economic aspects of trans-Atlantic 767 service and obtain a sampling of passenger reaction. The 767 proved very popular as passengers appreciated its roomy and pleasant cabin, and El Al has continued operating 767s (along with its 747s) on trans-Atlantic service to date. Although service was begun under the FAA's 60-minute rule, El Al quickly built up enough trouble-free experience to be able to extend its over-water route to 120 minutes from the nearest airport, provided that at least half the flight is no more than 90 minutes from the nearest airport.

With the arrival of the 767-200ERs, El Al's fleet reached a total of 20, including eight 747s, four 767s, two 737s and six 707s. Two to three of its all-passenger 707s, however, were usually under lease during this time to Arkia.

In 1984 El Al acquired two Extended Range 767s allowing the type to be used on trans-Atlantic flights. On 26 March 1984, using one of these 767ERs on a nonstop flight from Montreal to Tel Aviv, El Al became the first scheduled airline to cross the North Atlantic on a revenue flight in a two-engined aircraft under the U.S. FAA rule requiring a route not more than 60 minutes flying time (on one engine) from the nearest airport. Shown is 767ER 4X-EAC at Tel Aviv's Ben-Gurion Airport in 1988. (El Al Israel Airlines collection)

Return to Profitability

The profitability of the commercial aviation industry as a whole improved markedly during this period, and El Al shared in that rally. Fuel prices decreased and inflation slowed, and international economic growth resumed. As a result, substantial increases in passenger and cargo traffic were experienced, with particularly strong improvement on the North Atlantic route. While travel to Europe and the Middle East in 1986 was adversely affected by terrorist activity in Europe, El Al did not suffer unduly as passengers flocked to the airline because of its well-deserved reputation for stringent security.

El Al's losses were brought under control. The fiscal year ending 31 March 1984 resulted in a much lower loss of $14.3 million. Losses in 1985 and 1986 were lower still. Finally, for the fiscal year ending 31 March 1987, El Al happily reported a $15.2 million profit, its first in 13 years. For calendar 1987 El Al announced a profit of $18.2 million, and in calendar 1988, despite a fall-off of tourism to Israel, its profit rose further to $18.8 million.

New pilot and flight attendant uniforms introduced by El Al in fall 1984. On the left is Capt. Amitai Levin. (El Al Israel Airlines collection)

El Al's first Boeing 757 under construction at Boeing's Renton plant, Seattle, Washington, in 1987. (Marvin Goldman)

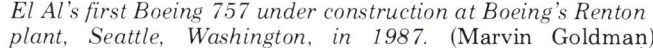

Boeing 757s

Through the 1980s El Al continued operating several of its aging but well-maintained 707s, their economic life having been extended due to reduced fuel prices. Nevertheless, with noise limitations about to be imposed in additional airports in Europe, which would prevent the use of the 707s unless costly noise-reduction modifications to the engines were made, and with the demand for more modern aircraft, in October 1986 an order was placed with Boeing for efficient twin-jet 757s for use on European routes. The first El Al 757 (4X-EBL) was delivered from Seattle to Tel Aviv on 20 November 1987, and it entered commercial service on 20 December from Tel Aviv to Brussels. It was soon joined by two additional 757s, in December 1987 (-EBM) and in July 1988 (-EBR).

El Al's 757s are usually configured with 189-191 seats (16-24 business class and the balance tourist), compared to an El Al 707 with a typical seating capacity of 175. The 757s are able to operate to all of El Al's European destinations, with a full passenger load and 2,700kg (3 tons) of freight. Like most customers, El Al selected Rolls-Royce engines (RB.211-535E4s) for its 757s, resulting in one of the quietest and most fuel-efficient airliners available. On an 800km (500mi) flight, the 757 burns nearly 50% less fuel than a 707. El Al also benefits from the common systems built into the new 757s and its 767 airliners. Flight deck avionics and controls are virtually identical in the two aircraft types—greatly simplifying training and crew cross-qualification for the fleet.

With the arrival of the 757s, El Al was able to reduce further its usage of 707s. By the end of 1989 all the 707s were sold except 4X-ATX on lease to Arkia and Sun d'Or and 4X-ATY utilized for cargo. The passenger aircraft has had its engines "hush-kitted" for noise reduction allowing it to operate from all the European charter destinations of Arkia and Sun d'Or. It also remains available to El Al for emergency use if needed.

In 1988 El Al purchased a passenger 747-200B from QANTAS, the Australian airline, bringing its 747 fleet to a total of nine.

The Network Expands

El Al finally opened its long-awaited route to Los Angeles, both for passenger and pure-cargo flights, on 17 June 1984 and simultaneously it restored service to Chicago. The route from Tel Aviv to Los Angeles (via Amsterdam and Chicago) became El Al's longest. Soon thereafter a direct route to Los Angeles via New York was initiated.

Less than a year later, on 22 April 1985, a new route was inaugurated to Manchester, England. Since April 1981 a weekly flight had been operated to Manchester by Sun d'Or, El Al's charter subsidiary. Due to rising demand, however, El Al decided to launch scheduled service on a twice-weekly basis. On 2 April 1986 service was started to Toronto, El Al's second Canadian gateway, as a continuation of service to Montreal; and on 13 March 1989 scheduled service began to Stockholm, Sweden, El Al's second Scandinavian destination, as a continuation of its Copenhagen route.

Flights to Eilat, Israel, continued to expand, with service from Ben-Gurion increased to a daily flight, an extension of services originating in the U.S. and Europe. Arriving passengers would change at Ben-Gurion to 737s because Eilat Airport could not handle 747s. Arrangements were also made to allow El Al to use the Israeli Air Base at Uvda, 70km (43mi) north of Eilat, which can accept larger jet aircraft without concern about Eilat's noise level restrictions.

In winter 1989-90 El Al started an extensive schedule of direct flights between several European cities and Eilat, without the intermediate Tel Aviv stop. While there had been some nonstop flights from London (Heathrow) to Eilat in preceding years, now El Al flies from Amsterdam, Brussels, Frankfurt, Helsinki (a new scheduled destination), London, Paris, Stockholm, Vienna, and Zürich direct to the sunny resort.

With the spirit of *glasnost* taking hold in the Soviet Union, Eastern Europe started opening up to El Al in 1988. Previously, its only air link to Eastern Europe had been with Bucharest, Romania. In 1988 an agreement was signed with LOT, the Polish airline, establishing a direct air link between Israel and Poland. Special El Al/Sun d'Or flights started from Israel to Warsaw on 21 June. This was the first service on a sustained basis between Poland and the Holy Land since prior to World War II when LOT used to be one of the scheduled air carriers to Palestine. Scheduled El Al service to Warsaw started on 28 March 1989 on a weekly basis using Boeing 757s and 767s. The new right to overfly Polish air space also allowed El Al to fly a more direct route to Copenhagen, reducing flight time by 35 minutes.

Meanwhile, special flights to Budapest, Hungary, started on 12 November 1988, with regular scheduled service inaugurated on 27 March the following year. By fall 1989 traffic to Budapest grew to the point that 747s were introduced on the route. On 11 April 1989, El Al started special flights to Zagreb, Yugoslavia.

The most dramatic of El Al's new destinations is Moscow, considered of prime national and business importance. In January 1989 El Al and Aeroflot officials met for the first time, secretly in Vienna at the invitation of the Soviets, to discuss methods of cooperation. Five months later El Al received permission for its first ever direct flight to the Soviet Union, and a specially chartered 757 flew at the end of June to Yerevan, Armenia, where it picked up 61 badly injured victims of the devastating Armenian earthquake and brought them to Israel for special medical treatment with the approval of the Soviets. In December 1989 El Al signed an agreement with Aeroflot which would grant landing rights in Moscow and Aeroflot reciprocal authority in Tel Aviv. The agreement is subject to Soviet government approval. Upon receipt of such approval, El Al intends to initiate Israel's first scheduled air link to the Soviet Union with weekly service from Tel Aviv to Moscow. In the meantime several El Al and Aeroflot charter flights have flown on the route.

Soaring above Mt. Rainier, Washington, is El Al's first Boeing 757, 4X-EBL, on a test flight in November 1987. The 757 provides El Al with a very fuel-efficient aircraft for its service between Israel and European destinations. (Boeing Airplane Co.)

BOEING 757

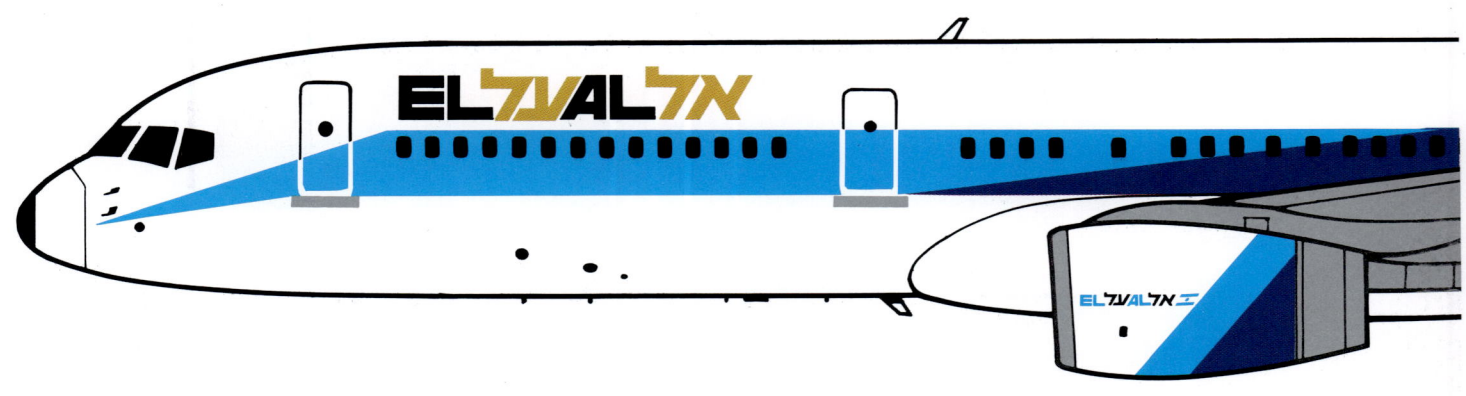

BOEING 767

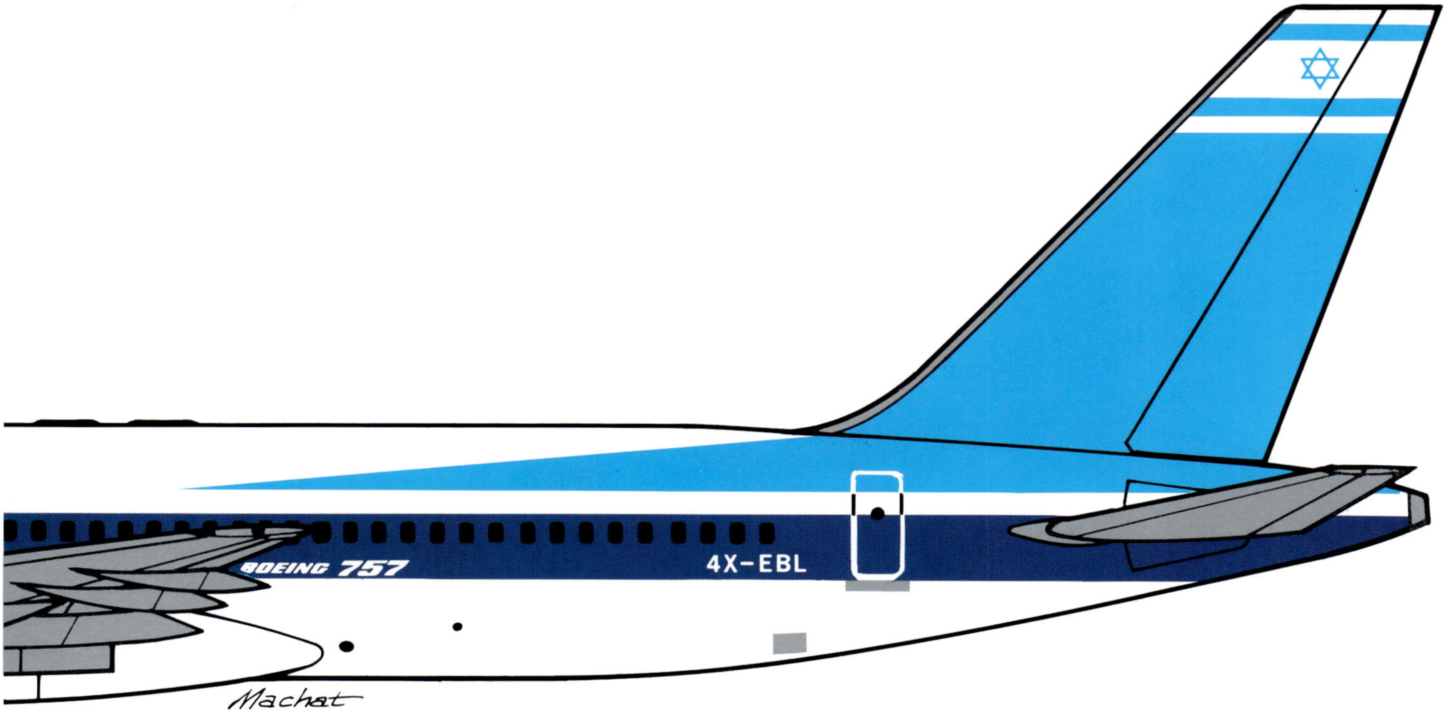
BOEING 757
4X-EBL
Machat

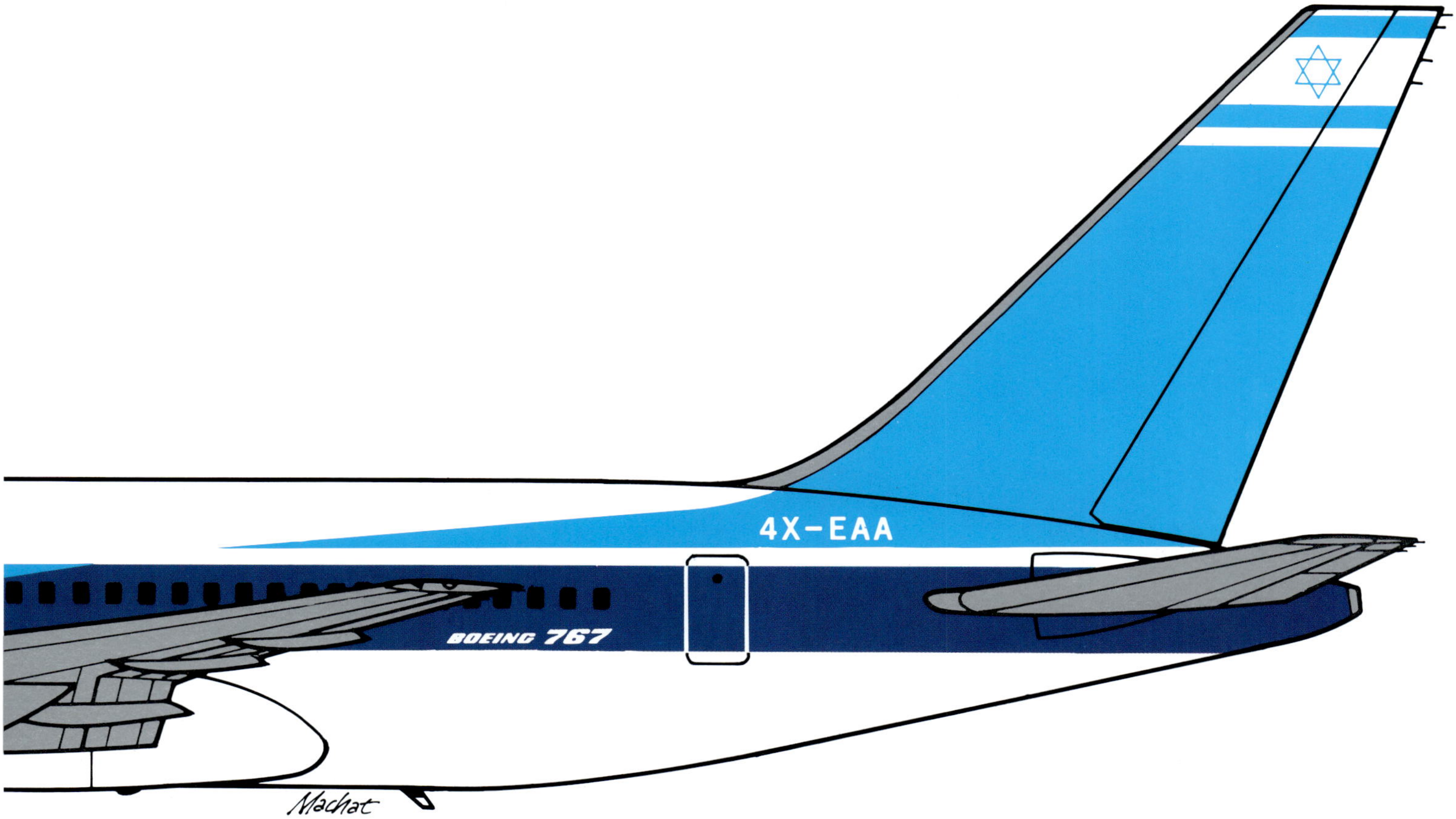
4X-EAA
BOEING 767
Machat

Sun d'Or

Sun d'Or International Airlines is a charter passenger airline wholly-owned by El Al. It was incorporated on 2 October 1977 under the original name of El Al Charter Services to penetrate the non-scheduled market and reduce El Al's losses stemming from the Israeli Government policy of permitting charter flights to Israel. To distinguish more clearly between El Al's scheduled flights and charter operations, and to develop its own identity, the new subsidiary adopted the Sun d'Or name in 1981. Flight numbers, however, have always used El Al's "LY" prefix. Sun d'Or utilizes a variety of aircraft leased from El Al. Although it once operated an El Al 707 (4X-ATR) painted in special Sun d'Or colors and titles, its leased aircraft are now ordinarily painted in standard El Al colors but with the El Al titles and flag of Israel removed.

Sun d'Or's operations are closely coordinated with El Al's as to business goals and economic policies. Its mandate is to maintain market share and minimize damage from competing charters, and to operate charter routes to and from Israel on a profitable basis.

In April 1977 Sun d'Or (under the name El Al Charter Services and prior to incorporation) operated its first flight, employing a leased BAC One-Eleven between Tel Aviv and Rome. Later that year it operated a charter to Dublin, Ireland, this being the first Israeli flight to that city. Since then Sun d'Or has operated charters to numerous destinations including, for example, Cologne, Düsseldorf, Hamburg, Munich and Stuttgart, Germany; Bordeaux, Montpellier and Paris, France; Barcelona, Madrid and Malaga, Spain; Copenhagen, Denmark; Malmö, Sweden; and Helsinki, Finland; and vacation destinations such as Corfu, Rhodes, Nice, and the Canary Islands. Sun d'Or has also served to open routes to new cities that would later become regularly scheduled El Al destinations, such as Boston, Chicago, Madrid and Manchester. As a policy decision instituted in 1981, Sun d'Or ordinarily no longer flies to any city that is a scheduled destination of El Al.

To compete with nonscheduled flights invading the Israeli market, El Al established a wholly-owned subsidiary, Sun d'Or International Airlines (originally named El Al Charter Services) in 1977. Sun d'Or operates charter flights between Israel and many European destinations, using aircraft leased from El Al, mainly Boeing 707s. Today Sun d'Or cooperates with Arkia's charter operations, so they can both enjoy marketing economies and schedule coordination. At Ben-Gurion Airport, 707 4X-ATR (above) is shown in a Sun d'Or livery utilized only during 1981-82, and 4X-ATY (below) is shown in a later Sun d'Or color scheme. Presently, Sun d'Or aircraft operate in El Al colors but with titles removed. (Yaacov Katz Photo via El Al)

On 1 May 1985 Sun d'Or entered into a joint operating agreement with Arkia, in an effort to garner a larger share of the charter market for Israel, which until then had only been about 10%. The airlines operate several weekly flights to destinations in France, Germany, England and Switzerland, plus some flights to the Greek and other Mediterranean islands. Each airline has exclusive rights on certain routes and common rights on others, based on alternating days and sharing of aircraft.

Sun d'Or has contributed both to El Al's profitability and to Israeli tourism. Even when El Al was shut down for four months in late 1982, Sun d'Or continued operating, thus reducing the damage. Since its inception, Sun d'Or has carried over one million passengers, and 70% have been tourists to Israel.

Cargo Air Lines (C.A.L.)

Cargo Air Lines was registered as an Israeli carrier of international cargo in July 1976. It is owned by the Agricultural Board of Israel (Agrexco) and by private Israeli interests, and its formation coincided with a time of rapid and profitable growth in El Al's cargo operations. Agrexco had appealed to the Israeli Government to permit the establishment of its own cargo airline to share in the profitable air transport of Israeli exports, but El Al vigorously protested the need for two cargo airlines in one small country. Finally, the Government opted to placate both sides by allowing C.A.L. to engage in cargo operations, but on the condition that it utilize El Al aircraft and crews. Accordingly, C.A.L. is obligated to lease all its aircraft from El Al and can resort to other aircraft only if El Al cannot meet its needs.

C.A.L.'s first flight was on 2 November 1976, from Tel Aviv to Cologne, operated by a 747 freighter leased from El Al. Since then it has promoted and participated in the great expansion of air cargo to and from Israel. Today, 747 freighters in the basic El Al color scheme, but with "C.A.L." lettering rather than "El Al", can frequently be seen in freight operations at international airports in Europe, Canada and the United States.

Above: *Israeli baby chicks being loaded for export into the interior of one of El Al's 747 cargo aircraft.* (El Al Israel Airlines)

Below: *El Al's convertible passenger/cargo 747 4X-AXF in an all-cargo configuration on lease to Cargo Air Lines (C.A.L.), at Amsterdam Schiphol Airport, January 1985.* (Bob Neumeier)

Boeing 707 at Ben-Gurion Airport utilized as a training center by El Al. The fuselage, part of the wing, and tail of this aircraft are actually the remnant of El Al's first 707, 4X-ATA. The cockpit comes from a 707-430 scrapped by Israel Aircraft Industries (last registered in Equatorial Guinea as 3C-ABH) since the original section was removed and shipped to New York City where it became an exhibit on the U.S.S. Intrepid aircraft carrier museum in Manhattan's New York harbor. (Moshe Stern collection)

One of El Al's last two remaining Boeing 707s, the convertible passenger/cargo 4X-ATX, in El Al livery but with titles removed, at Amsterdam's Schiphol Airport in March 1974. In recent years this aircraft has been utilized by El Al (passenger and cargo), Sun d'Or (passenger) and Cargo Air Lines (cargo), as needed. (Bob Neumeier)

North American Airlines

In 1989 El Al entered into a cooperation agreement with a new United States carrier, North American Airlines (NAA). It also acquired an option to purchase a 24.9% ownership interest in NAA, and the actual purchase is pending Israeli government approval. The airline is majority-owned by Dan McKinnon, a previous head of the now defunct U.S. Civil Aeronautics Board. The main purpose of NAA is to operate one or more Boeing 757s on feeder flights for El Al. NAA's flights connect with El Al aircraft flying between Tel Aviv and El Al gateway cities in North America, such as New York and Montreal. This saves El Al the cost of operating its 747s between, for example, New York and Los Angeles without full loads (since El Al does not have so-called Fifth Freedom rights in the United States, that is, it cannot carry passengers who depart from a U.S.

city and whose end destination is also in the U.S.). In turn this frees the 747s for more productive service elsewhere on El Al's route network. El Al guarantees taking a minimum number of seats from NAA.

The first NAA flight in cooperation with El Al took place on 22 January 1990 between New York and Los Angeles. The airline started with twice-weekly coast-to-coast flights, and anticipates more frequent operation in the future. NAA has U.S. crews, except that at least one El Al flight attendant is on board. El Al provides all the ground handling, dispatch and catering services at New York (JFK Airport) and Los Angeles. El Al is also looking into the possibility of using NAA's rights to expand its freight services on Europe—U.S. routes.

A Boeing 757 of North American Airlines, which links directly to El Al flights in the United States and Canada, at Los Angeles in March 1990. (Jukka Kauppinen)

Above: *In honor of El Al's 40th anniversary, the Israel Postal Authority designed this Souvenir Leaf. Inset are Israel's postal souvenir sheet issued to honor El Al's bar mitzvah (thirteenth) year in 1962 and Israel's stamp commemorating the 40th anniversary of the State.*

Left: *El Al's 40th anniversary logo, designed by graphic artist Yisrael Krug and widely used on its advertising material during 1988-89. The "4" was inspired by the tail design of El Al's aircraft.*

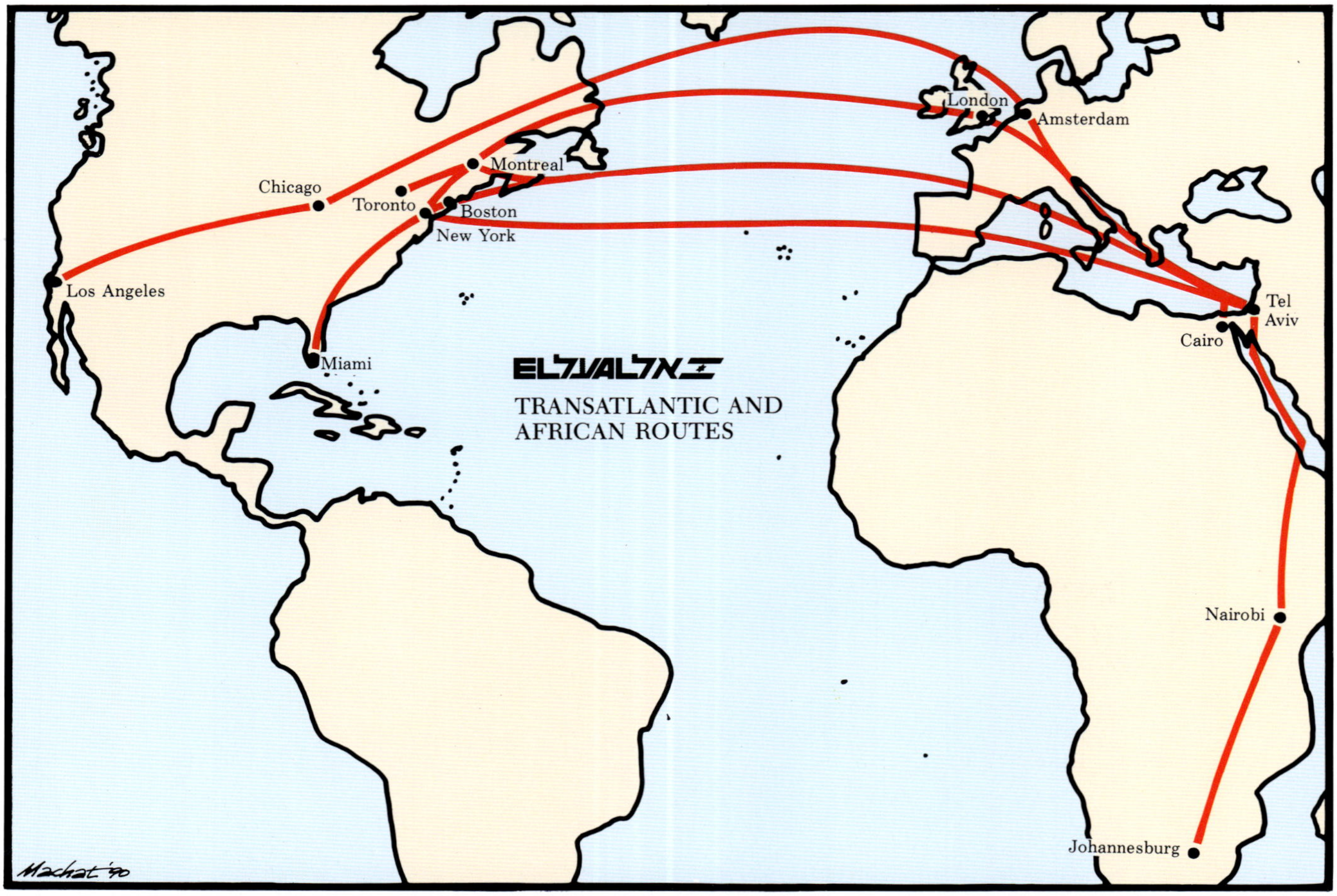

EL AL

TRANSATLANTIC AND
AFRICAN ROUTES

Chicago · Montreal · Toronto · Boston · New York · Los Angeles · Miami · London · Amsterdam · Tel Aviv · Cairo · Nairobi · Johannesburg

EL AL

EUROPEAN ROUTES

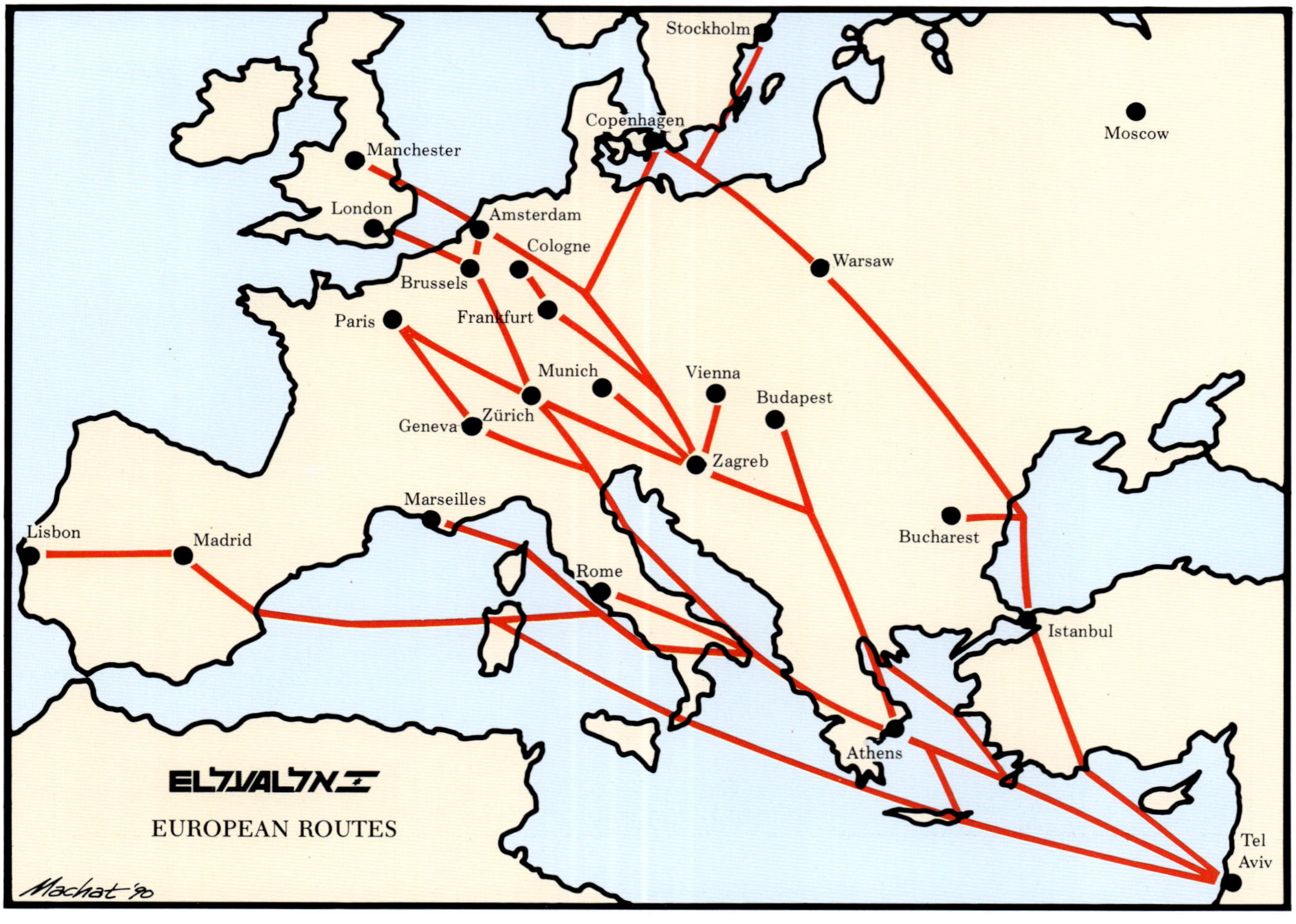

Stockholm · Copenhagen · Moscow · Manchester · London · Amsterdam · Cologne · Warsaw · Brussels · Frankfurt · Paris · Munich · Vienna · Budapest · Geneva · Zürich · Zagreb · Lisbon · Madrid · Marseilles · Bucharest · Rome · Istanbul · Athens · Tel Aviv

Machat '90

יעדים וזמן טיסהממוצע
DESTINATIONS AND
AVERAGE FLYING TIME

EL AL אל על

MIAMI 13 HRS.
NEW YORK 10 HRS. 20 MINS.
LOS ANGELES 15 HRS. 35 MINS.
CHICAGO 11 HRS. 40 MINS.
BOSTON 10 HRS.
TORONTO 11 HRS.
MONTREAL 9 HRS. 45 MINS.
LONDON 4 HRS. 35 MINS.
MANCHESTER 4 HRS. 55 MINS.
MADRID 4 HRS. 35 MINS.
LISBON 5 HRS. 5 MINS.
MARSEILLE 3 HRS. 45 MINS.
PARIS 4 HRS. 20 MINS.
BRUSSELLS 4 HRS. 15 MINS.
AMSTERDAM 4 HRS. 20 MINS.
STOCKHOLM 5 HRS. 30 MINS.
COPENHAGEN 4 HRS. 20 MINS.
GENEVA 3 HRS. 50 MINS.
ZURICH 3 HRS. 50 MINS.
COLOGNE 4 HRS. 55 MINS.
FRANKFURT 3 HRS. 55 MINS.
MUNICH 3 HRS. 35 MINS.
WARSAW 3 HRS. 35 MINS.
VIENNA 3 HRS. 20 MINS.
ROME 3 HRS. 5 MINS.
ZAGREB 3 HRS.
BUDAPEST 3 HRS.
ATHENS 1 HR. 50 MINS.
ISTANBUL 1 HR. 50 MINS.
BUCHAREST 2 HRS. 25 MINS.
JOHANNESBURG 8 HRS. 50 MINS.
NAIROBI 5 HRS.
CAIRO 1 HR. 20 MINS.
EILAT 35 MINS.

TEL AVIV

CHAPTER EIGHT

El Al Into the 1990s

"Lift up your eyes to the skies"
(Isaiah 51:6)

I n the decade of the 'Nineties, as El Al moves towards its 50th anniversary in 1998, most of its long-standing policies can be expected to continue. Profitability will be stressed. This will require continued emphasis on high aircraft utilization and technical efficiency—made even more important by the reduced number of days that El Al can operate due to Jewish sabbaths and holidays. On the other hand, security will never be compromised in the name of profits, as El Al intends at all costs to retain its outstanding record for secure operations.

El Al's future policies will also continue to factor in the contingent need to serve the State of Israel in the event of war or other emergency. As the "chosen instrument" of the State in civil aviation, El Al is singularly relied upon to keep Israel's air transport lanes open whenever other airlines may cut off service.

In addition to passenger and route expansion, El Al can be expected to further advance its already strong position in air cargo. At the same time, El Al plans to embark on a $1.5 billion fleet modernization and acquisition program in the 1990s. To meet the major financing requirements of this program as well as to maintain a sound future direction, El Al looks forward to the end of its receivership status and to the possible sale to the public of a portion of the Government's ownership interest in the airline.

The anticipated economic unification of Europe in 1992 also affects El Al's strategic planning as European routes and market share are very important to its profitability. Concern over the possibility that the European Community might try to strengthen European airlines at the expense of those from other countries has stimulated El Al into exploring the desirability of an affiliation with a European airline. It also serves as a reminder that El Al must make financially sound decisions in order to meet the challenge of the expected increased competition from European airlines.

Profitability

El Al enters the new decade with a string of four consecutive profitable years following the difficult period of 1977-1986. The remarkable turnaround reflects the new era of rehabilitation that started in 1983 when El Al took to the skies again after its four-month shutdown of passenger operations. El Al resumed operating on strict economic considerations, as if it were a private company.

The number of full-time or "permanent" employees in recent years has been maintained at 3,600, with temporary employees increasing its ranks to a little over 4,000. This is a marked reduction from the 1978/79 period when total employees had ballooned to over 6,000. Efficiency in meeting seasonal variations in passenger demand is met by the flexible hiring of so-called "temporary" employees, and in fact the majority of flight attendants are in this category. This has not lowered quality, however. For example, the demand for flight attendant positions is so high that El Al has far more applicants than it can handle and can always select highly qualified candidates.

The year 1988 provides a good example of how El Al's policies managed to convert a period of almost certain losses into a profitable one. Passenger traffic to Israel that year fell substantially below expectations, whereas air cargo grew significantly, and El Al was able to quickly adjust to the situation. By maintaining the minimum number of full-time or "permanent" employees, and by continuing its flexible fleet program whereby the configuration of its aircraft can be readily adjusted between passengers and cargo, El Al was better positioned to cope with the reduced passenger load. El Al attained a profit by hiring less temporary workers, adjusting the choice of aircraft on different routes, temporarily leasing out one of its own aircraft, and cutting down on aircraft leased from others.

Since restarting passenger operations in 1983, El Al has enjoyed a period of relative peace in labor-management relations. Cooperation at all levels of the airline has been a big key to El Al's recent success. In turn, the resultant profits have allowed the airline to give its employees bonuses starting in 1987. The extent to which this mutual collaboration continues in the '90s, and the soundness of decisions on new aircraft acquisitions, will be big factors in El Al's profitability in the decade ahead.

El Al Boeing 747, 767 and two 757s at Tel Aviv's Ben-Gurion Airport, 1989, stars to the sky. (El Al Israel Airlines collection)

The 306-Day-a-Year Airline

A recent El Al advertisement, quoting from the Bible "on the seventh day thou shalt rest", shows a clear blue sky, and no El Al aircraft anywhere in sight! It's a reminder that El Al observes the traditional Judaic principle that the period from sundown Friday to sundown Saturday is a day of rest, with all work forbidden. The refrainment from work also applies during several Jewish holy days, including Rosh Hashanah (the Jewish New Year), Yom Kippur (Day of Atonement), and the three major festivals of Pesach (Passover), Shavuot and Succot. As such, El Al carries no passengers on the Jewish sabbath or on any of these Jewish holidays. This policy has been in effect during most of the airline's existence, including the entire period since it restarted passenger operations in 1983.

As a result, El Al's scheduled service operates only about 306 days a year. This places it at a competitive disadvantage with other airlines. Notwithstanding, El Al's average daily utilization of aircraft (even considering days when it does not fly) is consistently higher than the industry average. This remarkable achievement comes from tight scheduling, superb maintenance performed during the night, and maximum efficiency.

Another religious influence on El Al, observed since its founding, is that all food served is strictly kosher in accordance with Jewish dietary laws. In fact, El Al owns its own catering companies, Borenstein and Tamam, to provide its kosher meals. Certain foods, such as shellfish and specific kinds of meat are entirely prohibited and not served at all. Nor may meat and dairy products be combined. As a result, El Al maintains two separate lower galleys aboard each aircraft, one for dairy products and the other for meat, together with separate utensils for each, at a cost in weight of about 1,350kg (1½ tons) per aircraft.

Since a high percentage of El Al's passengers are observant Jews, its flights have a number of other special elements. At daybreak on night flights, one will frequently see Jewish men donning *tallit* (prayer shawl) and *tfillin* (phylacteries; small leather cases containing Biblical passages) and saying the daily morning prayer. Seating assignments can sometimes be a juggling act for check-in personnel, as ultra-orthodox men may refuse to sit next to women who they believe are not modestly dressed. In-flight movies also are selected with special care so as not to offend religious sentiments.

Night maintenance on an El Al 747 at Ben-Gurion Airport, 1989. (El Al Israel Airlines collection)

Technical Efficiency

To compete as a "306-Day Airline" with the world's airline giants, El Al has to utilize each aircraft to the maximum during the days it does operate. It actually achieves this goal through tight scheduling and a particularly efficient maintenance program.

El Al performs all of its own maintenance, at its home base of Ben-Gurion Airport (Tel Aviv). Most maintenance is done at night, allowing aircraft to take off from Tel Aviv on scheduled flights in the early morning. At dawn each day, Ben-Gurion Airport is already a beehive of activity, but El Al has alleviated passenger congestion by pioneering previous-day passenger and luggage check-in at several locations. Stops at foreign airports are kept to a minimum—an average of 90 minutes— through fast turnaround procedures. Most aircraft then return to Ben-Gurion for overnight maintenance before taking off again for the next morning's early flight. Some major maintenance is done in phases during the overnight periods, and other major maintenance which cannot be completed overnight is performed during periods of slower traffic. In this way El Al has been able to maintain in recent years an average peak season utilization of up to ten hours a day for its fleet.

El Al's Training Center at Lod Airport, attended by over 200 employees each day, is one of the finest in the industry. From pilots to flight attendants to reservation agents, all receive scheduled periodic training at the Center with the latest advanced technological equipment. El Al's efficiency has translated in recent years into high marks for on-time arrivals (nearly 90% at Ben-Gurion Airport), seat occupancy (averaging 74%), and productivity per employee. According to the International Air Transport Association (IATA), El Al is now among the world's three most efficient airlines (measured by the number of kilometers in which revenue scheduled passengers and tons of freight are flown, divided by the number of employees) and one of the leaders in the quality of its in-flight services.

Moreover, virtually all of El Al's pilots and technicians originally learn their profession in one of the world's most demanding training grounds— the Israeli Air Force. These professionals provide the airline with skills that are among the finest available anywhere.

Security First

In response to terrorist attacks, El Al has developed the most intensive and respected airline security system in the world. The airline does not volunteer any information about its security measures—this in itself helps the program—but certain elements of its security have become public knowledge over the years.

Security at El Al starts by having the best-trained personnel available. The security workers of El Al are among the highest paid employees of the airline. They undergo intensive technical and psychological training by leading experts in the field, and their physical and mental health must be excellent.

Typical airline security measures such as metal detectors and routing hand luggage through X-ray machines are only the beginning of a security check at El Al. Most passengers checking in must undergo detailed questioning. This helps make the passengers "security conscious", an advantage in itself. It also ferrets out whether anyone may have given parcels to the passenger before takeoff which, unknown to the passenger, might contain explosives. Questions are often repeated by different security staff to be sure that the answers are not merely routinely given. Through an El Al profile system, those passengers falling into certain categories during the questioning process are subject to body searches and scrutiny in greater depth.

Security guards are trained to spot potential terrorists or other persons having hostile intentions. Often such persons are more nervous than other passengers. These and other "signs" can be picked up by those specially trained to spot suspicious travelers. Security is not a matter of routine. Rather, security personnel place themselves into the minds of terrorists to see what they might do before they do it.

All carry-on baggage is closely examined by hand. In addition, checked-in luggage is carefully matched to each passenger. El Al wants to be sure that every passenger bag on an aircraft is identified by one of the passengers as belonging to him or her, so that no unidentified baggage is carried aboard. If a bag remains unidentified, the aircraft will not take off unless a positive identification is made or the bag is left behind.

Research has shown that passenger baggage is not merely X-rayed, but is subjected to special secret checks by El Al personnel for potential explosives. It is believed that baggage is passed through modern low-pressure barometric chambers to check for the presence of detonators set to go off when a plane reaches a certain altitude. It is also believed that new thermal neutron activation devices are also used to determine whether explosives are present, and that other improved devices can "sniff" minute quantities of gas (such as nitrogen) given off by chemicals in explosives. Infrared sensors are also used.

Each El Al aircraft parked at an airport is closely guarded by security personnel and other surveillance methods. In some countries, local troops surround the aircraft while parked. As an aircraft taxis out to the runway for takeoff (or upon landing and taxiing in), armored cars or other vehicles with armed guards accompany the aircraft and patrol the surrounding areas.

Reports indicate that aboard each El Al aircraft armed security guards accompany every flight. These guards are said to be veterans of elite Israeli Defense Forces combat units and are thoroughly trained in anti-terrorist combat. Their dress and actions aboard the aircraft are designed to avoid notice, and passengers rarely can tell who the guards are.

El Al aircraft themselves also feature special modifications to guard against terrorism. For example, bullet-proof cockpit doors are fitted and, like most airlines today, the door remains locked throughout the flight. The deck plates between passenger and cargo compartments are structurally strengthened as an added precaution in the unlikely event that an explosive device passes the thorough baggage and cargo checks.

All the above measures are costly. El Al spends more than twice as much money as other airlines in protecting its passengers and aircraft. Yet the added personnel and equipment costs, and the added fuel costs from structural additions to the aircraft, are well worth the investment. For example, on 17 April 1986 a specially trained El Al security guard discovered a carefully concealed bomb at London's Heathrow Airport in a bag carried by a woman about to board El Al Flight 016, a 747 due to depart for Tel Aviv with 340 passengers. The bomb had been planted in the woman's hand baggage by her supposed boyfriend, actually an Arab terrorist who was later apprehended and jailed in England.

While no security system can be 100% foolproof under all conditions, one can be sure that to the extent further improvements in airline security occur during the decade of the 1990s, El Al will continue to be in the forefront.

"Samson" Cargo to Grow Even Stronger

While most people think of El Al in terms of its passenger services, the importance of cargo has been continuously increasing for some time. Not so well known is that El Al today is one of the ten leading airlines in scheduled freight tons carried internationally, and is the third largest airline in cargo tonnage across the North Atlantic. One-fourth of its annual revenues comes from cargo.

El Al presently has 34 cargo destinations on four continents. At its home base at Tel Aviv's Ben-Gurion Airport, El Al carries nearly two-thirds of the total incoming and outgoing air freight. The main cargo center outside Israel is in Amsterdam, where most El Al cargo entering and leaving Europe is loaded and unloaded. Smaller European cargo centers exist in Frankfurt and London. The second major cargo base is at Kennedy Airport in New York City, with smaller distribution centers in Chicago, Los Angeles and Miami. With a very precise system of collecting and delivering cargo, El Al freighters stop at the above cities several times a week, with at least one stop at Kennedy each day. Additional cities served with regular all-cargo flights include Brussels, Cologne and Montreal. El Al also provides a door-to-door containerized service which employs an overland trucking feeder and distribution system linking the foregoing European cities to other European centers and connecting its United States destinations to other major U.S. cities. A computerized tracking and space control system, called "Comas", monitors all airborne cargo equipment.

Currently, El Al operates two 747 freighters (a -200F and a -100F) exclusively for cargo and two convertible 747-200Cs available for all-cargo use whenever necessary. The -200 series freighters can each handle up to 113,400kg (125 tons) of cargo. At times, one or more of the 747s is on lease to the Israeli all-freight carrier, Cargo Air Lines, which by its charter is obligated to lease all of its aircraft from El Al whenever available.

El Al's plans for the 1990s call for further expansion of cargo services and the possible addition of another 747 freighter.

Routes

El Al's present route system spreads out like spokes from the central hub at its Tel Aviv base at Ben-Gurion Airport, where it maintains a 50% market share of passenger traffic. The spokes all lead, however, to the west and northwest, serving El Al's destinations in Europe and North America, except for two African routes, one to Cairo and another south to Nairobi and Johannesburg. El Al's potential routes to the east have been thwarted to date by unfriendly Arab states and Iran and by a lack of close relations with Far Eastern countries.

As of early 1990 El Al serves 34 destinations with scheduled passenger service. These include seven in North America (Montreal, Toronto, New York, Boston, Chicago, Los Angeles and Miami); 18 in Western Europe (London and Manchester; Paris and Marseilles; Madrid; Lisbon; Brussels; Amsterdam; Copenhagen; Stockholm; Geneva and Zürich; Cologne, Frankfurt and Munich; Vienna; Rome; Athens); three in Eastern Europe (Bucharest; Budapest; and Warsaw); Istanbul in Turkey; three in Africa (Cairo; Nairobi; and Johannesburg); and two in Israel (Tel Aviv and Eilat). Other European cities are served by El Al's charter subsidiary, Sun d'Or International Airlines, on non-scheduled flights. Helsinki, Moscow, and Zagreb, Yugoslavia, have been served recently by charter and special flights, and El Al hopes to establish scheduled service to these cities.

Further expansion is expected in Eastern Europe in the near future, including the eventual establishment of scheduled service to Sofia, Bulgaria; Prague, Czechoslovakia; and Berlin.

A major objective of El Al is to open a route to the Far East. Negotiations are in progress with the government of Thailand to open scheduled service to Bangkok. This service would operate either via Nairobi or Mombasa, Kenya (a circuitous route since El Al cannot presently fly directly east from Tel Aviv over Arab countries or Iran) or, if the new air agreement with the Soviet Union is implemented, El Al might be able to inaugurate non-stop service to Bangkok by flying over Soviet airspace, only a nine hour flight. On the assumption that the Bangkok route becomes a reality, El Al is exploring the establishment of the Thai capital as a hub to serve other possible destinations in the Far East, including Seoul, Korea; Tokyo, Japan; and Singapore; as well as Australia.

Arrival of Jewish immigrants from the Soviet Union on El Al's first charter flight from Moscow, at Ben-Gurion Airport, 1 January 1990. The sign (in Cyrillic) welcomes the new arrivals. As part of Operation Exodus, *El Al is transporting as many as possible of the Soviet Jews immigrating to Israel. Budapest and Bucharest have been the main air transit pickup points for El Al, as the airline hopes for permission from the Soviet Union for additional direct flights to and from Moscow.* (El Al Israel Airlines collection)

El Al's $1.5 Billion Investment Program

The beginning of 1990 marked the 23rd consecutive year that El Al has an all-Boeing fleet. Its 20 aircraft include nine 747s (five all-passenger, two passenger/cargo convertibles and two all cargo); four 767s; three 757s; two 737s; and two 707s (the 707s are either leased to Arkia/Sun d'Or or used for special charters, cargo, or back-up.

During the seasonal high travel periods for El Al, such as the Passover holiday period and the summer, El Al leases aircraft from other carriers. For example, in Passover and summer 1989 it leased two 757s from the European carriers Monarch and Air Holland to replace 767s utilized with increasing frequency to the United States and Canada. El Al also occasionally leases aircraft together with their foreign crews, such as a DC-10 from Martinair of Holland in 1989. The aircraft comes with a Martinair crew, but with El Al catering and one El Al purser on board to assist Hebrew-speaking passengers. In addition, starting in 1990, North American Airlines is utilized as a feeder airline (using a 757) at New York and Montreal for flights to Los Angeles and Miami (see Chapter 7).

El Al recognizes, however, that its present fleet is not well-positioned for the 1990s. Its 747s are aging, and larger-capacity 747-400s with more fuel-efficient engines and a cockpit designed for two (as opposed to three) crew members, are now available. Its 737s are also of the older, less-efficient variety. Only its 767s and 757s are modern aircraft.

Three additional 757s are on order from Boeing with delivery expected in late 1990, early 1991, and 1992 respectively. More significantly, in spring 1990, El Al advised Boeing of its decision to order two 747-400s for delivery in 1993 and 1994, and to take options on two more. The long-range 747-400s could be utilized to inaugurate nonstop Tel Aviv—Los Angeles service. Consideration is also being given to the acquisition of additional 757s as well as to the proposed 777 (a twin-engine

aircraft designed to fill the niche between the 767-300 and 747-400). Although El Al has been pleased with its close relationship with Boeing over the years, orders for aircraft from other manufacturers, such as the McDonnell Douglas MD-11 and the Airbus Industrie A340, are also possible. Decisions also have to be made as to whether the 767s and 737s owned by the Israeli Government and used by El Al will be given or sold to the airline.

Unquestionably, the aircraft requirements of El Al during the 1990s will require it to make its largest capital investment decisions since the late 1960s and early 1970s when it entered the jumbo jet era. El Al's strategic plan calls for it to invest $1.5 billion during the 1990s to modernize and expand its fleet and to acquire other necessary equipment. It hopes to make this investment entirely from its own capital, without government help. Another important element of El Al's investment program is its installation of a new computer reservations system in spring 1990, called "Carmel 2". Based on technology acquired from Swissair, it was customized to its specific needs. Carmel 2's immediate response time enables travelers to select from optimum travel routes and flight schedules throughout the world as well as instantaneous hotel and car rental reservations. Pre-reserved seat selection and on-the-spot printing of travel itineraries, as well as air tickets and boarding passes, are possible. This allows El Al to match the competition of other leading airlines in this area.

To meet expected passenger growth at Ben-Gurion Airport, the airport authority itself is undertaking a major investment. A new air terminal, expected to cost $40-45 million, is to be built some 200 meters (650ft) west of the existing terminal. Passengers will check in at the existing terminal and then be transferred on "people movers" to the new building, avoiding the present need for busing to aircraft. Completion of the new terminal is expected by about 1995. The airport authority also plans to construct a taxiway parallel to the main runway which presently carries 90% of all traffic. The new taxiway is to be ready by 1992.

123

Above: *An artist impression of an El Al Boeing 747-400.* **Below:** *The two-crew cockpit of a 747-400 is dominated by six large CRT (cathode ray tube) displays.* (Boeing Commercial Airplanes)

End of Receivership and Start of Privatization

In early 1989 El Al opened negotiations with government officials to end its temporary receivership status (in effect since late 1982) and to restore the airline to the management of its own board of directors, rather than having the official court-appointed receiver as the ultimate manager. Since El Al has now enjoyed four consecutive profitable years, the outlook for an early end to the receivership is promising.

Meanwhile, in August 1989 the Israeli Government announced the decision to move towards ending El Al's receivership and to partially privatize El Al. The first stage of the privatization plan would be to sell about 25% of El Al's shares of stock to investors in Israel and to the airline's employees. An additional 25% would then be offered for sale on foreign stock exchanges.

El Al enters the last decade of the Twentieth Century with the optimism that it can operate successfully under its own management control. The requirements of huge capital investment in the 1990s, and the need for continued high productivity and good employee relations, will test the airline to its fullest.

Historically, El Al has survived unanticipated adversity remarkably well. It should again be able to successfully confront future challenges and keep flying the star, "el al"—"to the skies".

One of El Al's 747s arriving home at Ben-Gurion Airport. Following overnight maintenance by El Al, it will be ready for another early morning departure, carrying the star to the skies. (El Al Israel Airlines collection)

ARKIA – FORTY YEARS FROM TAKE-OFF

APPENDIX I
Arkia Israeli Airlines

"And the wise will shine as the brightness of the skies ('ha-ra-ki-a')"

(Daniel 12:3)

U pon the declaration of Israel's independence in May 1948, its first Minister of Transport, David Remez, thought not only of the formation of an international airline—which became El Al —but also of the establishment of a domestic airline. This new airline would link cities within Israel, and in particular it would open air service to the then-primitive development town of Eilat, located at Israel's southern tip on the beautiful Gulf of Eilat leading to the Red Sea.

A small light plane "airline" called Aviron, owned by Israel's labor federation *Histadrut* and other Jewish organizations, already existed in 1948. However, its few aircraft were swallowed up by the War of Independence, and Remez decided to dissolve Aviron and start fresh with a new domestic airline. Accordingly, in late 1949 Arkia was founded with 50% ownership by El Al and 50% by Kanfot, a holding company of the *Histadrut*.

The original name of the new airline was "Eilata", meaning "to Eilat". However, as David Remez preferred names drawn from the Bible, it was changed in September 1950 to "Arkia", which translates as "I will soar" or more specifically as "I will go up to the *rakia*"—the Biblical Hebrew word "rakia" meaning a special portion of the sky high above, or the canopy of heaven. In short, both "el al" and "arkia" are Hebrew expressions that loosely translate as "to the skies".

Remez assigned responsibility for managing the new company to Yaacov Hozman, formerly head of the major Israeli bus cooperative called *Egged*. Hozman, like his counterparts Pincus and Ryvkind of El Al, had no prior aviation experience but turned to his new task with messianic zeal. He remained as Arkia's head until his death in 1965, and his energy and drive made Arkia a very successful operation.

Arkia's first mission was to inaugurate air service between Tel Aviv and Eilat. This took awhile because, at first, Arkia had no aircraft and there was not even a reliable landing strip at Eilat. At the beginning of 1950, however, a reasonably suitable runway paved out of rock and sand, and a primitive terminal, were built at Eilat. Only a few pioneers lived in Eilat at the time. It was largely barren with only a few living quarters, the adjacent Gulf of Eilat, and deserts and multi-hued mountains in the distance. The hot and dry climate often gave rise to dust and sand storms that would choke the runway and reduce visibility to near zero.

Earliest Flights

Arkia's official inaugural flight from Tel Aviv to Eilat was on 28 February 1950, utilizing a Curtiss C-46 (4X-ACT) turned over to Arkia by El Al, with an El Al crew under the command of Zvi Tohar. This C-46, together with two twin-engine eight-seat de Havilland D.H.89 Dragon Rapide aircraft (4X-ACN and ACU) obtained from the Israeli Air Force, initially comprised Arkia's entire "fleet". Flight time between Tel Aviv and Eilat was typically a little over one hour, whereas a road journey was impractical because only a primitive, often impassable, dirt road to Eilat existed at the time. Soon Arkia was bringing in food, water and machinery to Eilat's settlers and construction workers. It also delivered all newspapers and mail, and was the only practical means of evacuating the sick to medical facilities in Tel Aviv. Arkia's activities thereby became the social center of life in Eilat. Flight frequency soon rose to at least two a week in each direction, and in Arkia's first year of operations to Eilat it operated 450 flights and carried 13,000 passengers.

In 1951 the unpaved road to Eilat was improved. Complete reliance on air service dropped, and starting May 1952 Arkia ordinarily utilized one or two of the Dragon Rapides in place of the much larger C-46. With the slow but steady expansion of Eilat in the early 1950s, however, Arkia's traffic started to grow, and by 1954 the Rapides were flying twice daily from Tel Aviv. In February 1955 Arkia resumed C-46 operations by utilizing 4X-ALC received from El Al, fitted with 36 relatively comfortable seats. The aircraft operated in El Al colors but with the Arkia emblem near the cockpit. Meanwhile, the Rapides were used to inaugurate non-scheduled service to Mahanaim Airport near Rosh Pinna in the Galilee in Northern Israel, using a military runway abandoned by the British, and to Sdom near the Dead Sea in the South.

Early 1950s Arkia baggage sticker promoting the tourist attractions of Eilat. (Marvin Goldman collection)

Enter the Venerable DC-3

By 1956, with further modest increases in passenger traffic, Arkia turned to the reliable Douglas DC-3 for service and ceased using the C-46 and Rapides. Acquiring four C-47s from the Israeli Air Force and converting them to civilian DC-3s, it placed two in service in 1956 (4X-ACW and ADA) and another two in 1957 (4X-AEO and AES). The latter additions reflected the increased interest in Eilat arising from the 1956 Sinai War. Flights to Eilat were now on a regular thrice-weekly basis. The number of passengers doubled to 23,000 in 1956, and nearly tripled again to 65,000 the following year.

In 1958 Rosh Pinna became Arkia's second scheduled destination, with service flown once daily by DC-3s and soon thereafter by smaller Beech 18 aircraft. The acquisition of the Beech 18s in 1958 was designed to inaugurate additional non-scheduled flights into unprepared airstrips and to initiate air-taxi operations.

The same year Arkia formed a partnership with the owner of the French aero-engine company Tur-boméca, under the name Arkia-Aliza, to establish commercial helicopter service in Israel. This proved to be the first operation of helicopters in commercial service not only in Israel but in the entire Middle East. Three jet-powered Sud-Est

Alouette II helicopters were employed, but their fuel consumption and other high operating costs caused the service to be abandoned in 1961.

In 1961 Arkia obtained from the Israeli Department of Civil Aviation an international non-scheduled operator's certificate. It then proceeded to operate charters for El Al to Europe, with Arkia's DC-3s becoming frequent visitors to Athens, Rome, Frankfurt, Amsterdam, Paris and London. However, the Douglas twins proved to be uncompetitive by international standards for these flights, and operations were discontinued after only a few charters.

Tourism Surges

The year 1964 marked a turning point for Arkia as the first luxury hotels in Eilat opened. During the Passover holiday in 1964 Eilat was flooded with over 50,000 visitors. To meet demand Arkia acquired the first two of what became a fleet of five Handley Page Herald two-engine turboprop aircraft, each seating 50. These aircraft also reduced the flight time from Tel Aviv to Eilat from one hour or more to 45 minutes. With the arrival of a third Herald in 1965, annual passenger volume rose to 177,000 on all routes by the following year.

Arkia's initial role was to serve the then-remote development town of Eilat located at Israel's southern tip on the Gulf of Eilat which leads into the Red Sea. This March 1956 photo shows Eilat's airstrip, with the first large tourist hotel under construction in the background. A leased Arkia DC-3 may be seen at left in the registration (G-ANAF) and colors of the British lessor, BKS Air Transport. Two Israeli Air Force camouflaged Douglas C-47s are at the right. (Israel Government Press Office)

An Arkia DC-3 at Eilat in the late 1950s. This aircraft (4X-AEO) was formerly registered 4X-ATA and served briefly in 1951 with El Al (as its sole DC-3) to open its service to Istanbul. (Courtesy of Palphot publishers, Herzliya, Israel, postcard no. 5298)

In January 1966 a new asphalt paved runway was built at Massada near the Dead Sea to replace the former primitive landing strip. This allowed Arkia to establish non-scheduled service with DC-3s and even with the new Heralds. Massada has the distinction of having the lowest airport in the world, some 395 meters (1,300ft) below sea level.

Arkia resumed international service in March 1967 with flights between Lod and Nicosia, Cyprus, utilizing the new Heralds. This move resulted from El Al's sale that month of its last Britannia, leaving El Al only with Boeing 707/720s which were not suitable for the short-range, low-capacity route. Arkia's service to Cyprus continued until suspended in 1974 as a result of the Greek-Turkish conflict.

In 1964 the first large hotels in Eilat opened, leading to an upsurge in tourism, and Arkia received delivery of its first larger aircraft—Rolls-Royce Dart turboprop-powered Handley Page Heralds. Shown is Dart-Herald 4X-AHR at Eilat in April 1967. (Israel Government Press Office)

Arkia Viscount turboprop aircraft in the 1970s at Tel Aviv. The Viscounts boosted Arkia's capacity to move increasing numbers of tourists betwen Tel Aviv, Eilat and the Sinai. (Airliners America/ATP-Dean Slaybaugh)

Expansion to the Sinai

During the Six Day War of June 1967, Arkia's aircraft like those of El Al were requisitioned for the war effort. Arkia airlifted water and supplies to the front, returning with wounded from the Sinai. As a result of the War, Israel found itself in possession of the entire Sinai Peninsula as well as East Jerusalem. Arkia then extended its routes to Ophira and Sharm-el-Sheikh in the southern Sinai and to Santa Caterina airfield near Mt. Sinai. It also started service to Atarot (Kalandia) Airport in East Jerusalem which became incorporated by Israel into a single united city of Jerusalem.

With the new tourist attractions of the Sinai and with tourism to Eilat also growing, Arkia experienced a rapid increase in demand. Traffic surged to 313,000 passengers in 1968 and to 471,000 in 1969. To meet its needs, Arkia purchased from other airlines six Vickers Viscount four-engine turboprop aircraft between 1969 and 1974. Arkia benefited from the standardization of Rolls-Royce Dart powerplants and other features common to both the Viscounts and Heralds. On the other hand, since Tel Aviv's Sde Dov Airport could not accommodate a fully-laden Viscount, Arkia had to split its Tel Aviv operations between its home base at Sde Dov and Lod Airport.

In December 1972 Arkia and a light-plane operation called Kanaf Air Services agreed to form Kanaf-Arkia Airlines, each holding a 50% interest. Kanaf's aircraft were transferred to Kanaf-Arkia, thereby placing at Arkia's disposal a fleet of aircraft with up to ten-seat capacity for air taxi services. The aircraft included Cessna 172s, Grand Commanders, and Britten-Norman Islanders. Kanaf-Arkia furnished regular service to secondary airstrips such as Haifa, Beersheva, Rosh Pinna, Mitze Ramon, Ein Yahav and Massada, as well as to Ophira and Santa Caterina in the Sinai. In 1974 Kanaf-Arkia started to replace the Islanders with Piper Navajo Chieftains.

Affiliation With El Al Ends

In 1977 Arkia management made the momentous decision to acquire two BAC One-Eleven Series 500 pure-jet aircraft, with a view to expanding service and inaugurating international charters. This step proved to be disastrous, however. Passenger numbers did not rise as fast as anticipated: the Sinai was returned to Egypt with the resultant curtailment of Arkia's routes there; the jets did not operate with sufficient load factors and, even more importantly, their operational costs—due to surging fuel prices—were much too high. Losses started to mount out of control. By the end of 1979, El Al and the *Histadrut* labor federation, Arkia's joint owners, decided to dispose of the One-Elevens and to sell Arkia to private investors.

Following the 1967 Six Day War, Arkia started flying to airstrips in the Sinai Peninsula. Vickers Viscount 4X-AVB was photographed at Santa Caterina near Mt. Sinai on 21 August 1974. (Israel Government Press Office)

An Arkia pure-jet BAC One-Eleven "Super Jet 500" at Tel Aviv's Ben-Gurion Airport in September 1977. Arkia utilized two of these air-craft during 1977-80. (Israel Government Press Office)

Fleet of Arkia's then-existing light-plane subsidiary, Kanaf Arkia, about 1976, at Sde Dov Airport in North Tel Aviv. The two aircraft in front, and the fourth from the camera, are Navajo Chieftains; the third is a Swearingen Metro; and those in the rear are BN-2A Islanders. (Ron Ardah photo via Dan Yaari of Arkia)

The New Arkia

In March 1980 a new Arkia became airborne. A private owner, Kanaf Arkia (not to be confused with Arkia's prior light-plane subsidiary also named Kanaf Arkia), acquired 75% of Arkia's stock, with the remaining 25% owned by Arkia's employees. The new owners decided that the time was ripe to make another attempt to develop an international charter operation with jet aircraft. They proved to be right. Arkia acquired three new Boeing 737-200 aircraft from 1981, later replacing these with 187-seat 707s leased from El Al. Jet fuel prices eased, the charters were successful, and Arkia returned to profitability. Meanwhile, the domestic flights with smaller aircraft were shifted in 1981 from Ben-Gurion Airport to Sde Dov in Tel Aviv which proved more readily accessible to passengers. Another sound decision was the acquisition of de Havilland Canada DHC-7 (Dash 7) four-engine turboprop aircraft to service Arkia's inland routes. The 52-seat Dash 7s have proved to be ideal for shuttle service flights between Tel Aviv's Sde Dov airport and Eilat, Jerusalem and Haifa.

Since 1985 Arkia and El Al's charter subsidiary Sun d'Or have jointly cooperated in their international charter services. This has led to many operating economies in the utilization of crews, aircraft and equipment.

Passenger traffic on the new Arkia has steadily grown. Eilat has developed into an international resort of the first rank. In fiscal year 1987-88 Arkia carried a record 113,000 passengers on its international flights\and 335,000 on domestic flights—all with the same outstanding safety record it has maintained over its entire history.

Alongside Israel's national carrier El Al on the one hand, and several light-plane domestic operations of other Israeli carriers (such as Canari, Nesher, Shahaf and Snunit) on the other, Arkia maintains an excellent reputation and a major role in Israeli civil aviation.

Top: *Since early 1984 Arkia has leased Boeing 707s from El Al for its charter service between European cities and Israel. While 4X-ATB (at Munich in March 1984) is in Arkia colors, in subsequent years Arkia has utilized El Al 707s in El Al colors with the titles removed.* (Peter Miche)

Center: *In 1981 Arkia introduced new De Havilland Canada DHC-7 four-engine turboprops for its flights within Israel. The "Dash 7" is particularly well-suited for Arkia's main Tel Aviv—Eilat run.* (Arkia Israeli Airlines collection)

Below: *An Arkia Dash 7 landing in 1986 at the now-burgeoning tourist resort of Eilat.* (Arkia Israeli Airlines collection)

APPENDIX II: El Al Key Dates

1948

14 May	State of Israel declares its independence.
18 August	State of Israel decides to establish a national civil airline.
29-30 September	First Israeli-registered civil aircraft, 4X-ACA, a Douglas C-54 (DC-4) borrowed from the Air Force and painted with the name "El Al", brings Chaim Weizmann from Geneva, Switzerland, to Israel to be sworn in as Israel's first President.
October	First Israeli landing rights obtained in a foreign country (France). Non-scheduled special flights made to Paris.
15 November	El Al is incorporated, with its shareholders being the Israeli Government and Jewish-owned organizations in Israel.

1949

January	Start of *Operation Magic Carpet*, airlift of Yemenite Jews to Israel.
26 February, 15 March	El Al purchases its first two DC-4 aircraft, 4X-ACD and 4X-ACC respectively, from American Airlines.
15 July	State of Israel issues to El Al a formal Certificate to Commence Business.
31 July	First scheduled flight, Tel Aviv to Paris (DC-4, 4X-ACD).
16-17 August	Special flight to bring body of Theodor Herzl, founder of political Zionism, from Vienna, Austria, to Israel for reburial (Tel Aviv—Vienna—Tel Aviv, DC-4, 4X-ACD).
18 December	First scheduled service to Rome, Italy, and Zürich, Switzerland (DC-4, 4X-ACD).
22 December	First scheduled service to London (Tel Aviv—Rome—London, DC-4, 4X-ACC).
Late 1949	Arkia formed, with 50% El Al ownership, to provide domestic Israeli service between Tel Aviv and Eilat.

1950

26 January	Freight operations between Israel and several European cities launched with Curtiss C-46s.
6 February	DC-4, 4X-ACD, lost in a crash on take-off at Lod Airport. No serious injuries.
May	Start of *Operation Ali Baba*, airlift of Iraqi Jews to Israel.
18 June	First charter passenger trans-Atlantic flight (Tel Aviv—Rome—Paris—Shannon—Gander—New York, DC-4s, 4X-ADB and ADC).
5 July	First scheduled service to Vienna.
Fall	Universal Airways acquired, a South African company which conducted Johannesburg—Tel Aviv DC-3 service.
29 October	First service to Johannesburg.
22 December	Arrival of first El Al Lockheed 49 Constellation in Israel, 4X-AKB.

1951

Early 1951	First scheduled service to Athens, Greece, and Nicosia, Cyprus.
1 March	First scheduled service to Istanbul, Turkey (via Nicosia, DC-3, 4X-ATA).
29 April	First scheduled service to New York (Tel Aviv—Athens—London—Shannon—New York, Lockheed Constellation). Becomes the first carrier outside of Europe and North America to start scheduled trans-Atlantic service.
24 November	DC-4, 4X-ADB, on an all-cargo flight, crashes on approach to Zürich, killing six of the seven crew members.

1955

22 June	Becomes the first non-British airline to place a firm order for the Bristol Britannia aircraft.
27 July	Constellation 4X-AKC shot down by Bulgarian MiGs over Bulgaria near Greek border, with no survivors.

1956

5 March	First scheduled service to Amsterdam, Netherlands (Constellation).
8 March	First scheduled service to Brussels, Belgium (Constellation).
29 October	Sinai War.
November	Efraim Ben Arzi becomes President of El Al, replacing Aryeh Pincus.

1957

8 December	An El Al Britannia, on a proving flight from New York to London, sets a new speed record of 8hr 3min.
18-19 Dec.	El Al's Britannia 4X-AGC, on a proving flight, flies nonstop, New York to Tel Aviv, 9,270km (5,760mi)—the longest ever flight by a commercial airliner—with a flight time of 14hr 46min at an average speed of 645km/h (401mph).
22 December	First Britannia scheduled service (Tel Aviv—London—New York 4X-AGB).

1958

8 January	An El Al Britannia, on a scheduled flight from New York to London, sets a new speed record of 7hr 44 min.
24 February	First scheduled service to Cologne, West Germany.
10-11 March	El Al Britannia 4X-AGA sets a new speed record from London to New York, 9hr 23min.
25 March	First scheduled service to Munich, West Germany.

1959

August	First scheduled service to Teheran, Iran (discontinued 10 February 1979).

1961

8 January	First Boeing 707 service, between Tel Aviv and New York with an aircraft leased from VARIG.
7 May	El Al takes delivery of its first purchased 707, 4X-ATA.

15 June	On the return segment of the maiden scheduled flight of 4X-ATA, El Al establishes three world records: (1) fastest flight from New York to Tel Aviv, 9hr 33min; (2) first nonstop service between New York and Tel Aviv; and (3) world's longest nonstop commercial flight (9,270km/5,760mi).
15 October	Last Constellation retired from service.

1962

	El Al's 13th (Bar Mitzvah) year. Carries one millionth passenger.
26 March	First Boeing 720B joins the fleet.
11 June	First scheduled service to Frankfurt, West Germany.

1964

30 June	First scheduled service to Rhodes, Greece (discontinued late 1960s).
11 October	First scheduled service to Copenhagen, Denmark.

1967

February	Last Britannia (4X-AGC) sold. El Al becomes an all pure-jet airline, first in the Middle East.
May-June	Operations disrupted by emergency preparations to meet Egyptian threats of war and by the Six Day War of 5-10 June. El Al becomes the only carrier linking Israel to the outside world.
Summer	Mordechai Ben-Ari becomes President of El Al.

1968

	20th Anniversary Year.
1 April	First scheduled service to Geneva, Switzerland.
5 April	First scheduled service to Nice, France.
7 May	First scheduled service to Romania (originally to Constanta, switched to Bucharest shortly thereafter).
22 July	El Al's 707, 4X-ATA, is skyjacked by PFLP terrorists and diverted to Algeria.

26 December	Terrorist attack on El Al's 707, 4X-ATR, on the ground at Athens, Greece.

1969

18 February	Terrorist attack on El Al's 720B, 4X-ABB, on taxiway at Zürich.
15 May	First 707-320C convertible passenger/cargo aircraft acquired, 4X-ATX.

1970

10 February	Terrorist attack on El Al bus at Munich Airport, Germany
April	First scheduled service to Addis Ababa (discontinued in late 1973).
6 September	Attempted skyjack of 707 4X-ATB, by Khaled and others, and simultaneous skyjackings of Pan Am, Swissair and TWA aircraft. Only the El Al aircraft survives.

1971

28 March	First scheduled service to Montreal, Canada (via Amsterdam).
31 March	First scheduled service to Marseille (replacing Nice).
2 June	First 747-200B, 4X-AXA, arrives in Tel Aviv.
8 June	747 enters passenger service on route Tel Aviv—London—New York.
22 November	Second 747, 4X-AXB, enters passenger service on route Tel Aviv—Paris—New York.

1973

	25th Anniversary Year.
29 April	Starts first scheduled nonstop service from Tel Aviv to New York, becoming the longest duration nonstop civil air route at the time.
6 October	Yom Kippur War breaks out. Fleet requisitioned for massive airlifts. El Al again becomes only carrier connecting Israel with the outside world.

1974

15 January	Lod Airport renamed Ben-Gurion Airport in memory of Israeli pioneer leader David Ben-Gurion.

1975

31 December	El Al takes delivery of its first convertible passenger/cargo 747-200C "Combi", 4X-AXD.

1976

16 January	El Al's first computerized reservations system, Carmel, placed into operation.
July	Registration of Cargo Air Lines (C.A.L.), an Israeli all-cargo airline obligated to lease its aircraft from El Al whenever available.
9 November	First scheduled service to Mexico City (discontinued in 1979).

1977

September	First scheduled service to Lisbon, Portugal.
2 October	Formation of El Al's wholly-owned charter subsidiary, Sun d'Or (originally named El Al Charter Services).
	Intermittent labor slowdowns and strikes during 1977-82.

1978

	30th Anniversary Year.

1979

1 April	First scheduled service to Chicago and Miami, U.S.A.

1980

3 March	First scheduled service to Cairo, Egypt.
March	Sale of Arkia to a private company and Arkia's employees.
1 October	Two 737-200s leased from TEA.

1981

October	First scheduled service to Eilat, as an extension of service originating in Europe.

1982

June	First scheduled service to Boston, U.S.A.
12 September	Due to labor problems and other difficulties, El Al is placed in financial receivership, and its passenger operations are shut down for four months.

1983

12 January	Passenger flights resume, following new labor agreements and renewed Government support. Workforce reduced 20%.
18 January	First purchased Boeing 737, 4X-ABN, delivered.
18 July	First Boeing 767-200, 4X-EAA, delivered.
August	First scheduled service to Madrid, Spain.

1984

26 March	First 767-200ER (Extended Range) received. On its initial flight to Israel it becomes the first twin-engine aircraft to cross the North Atlantic in scheduled commercial passenger service.
17 June	First scheduled service to Los Angeles, U.S.A. Renewal of scheduled service to Chicago.

1985

22 April	First scheduled service to Manchester, U.K.
1 May	Joint operating agreement signed between Sun d'Or and Arkia for charter services and use of aircraft.

1986

2 April	First scheduled service to Toronto, Canada, as an extension of service to Montreal.

1987

26 November	First Boeing 757-200, 4X-EBL, delivered.

1988

40th Anniversary Year.

May	Longest nonstop flight in El Al's history, Los Angeles to Tel Aviv— 11,260km (7,000mi) in 13hr 41min.

1989

13 March	First scheduled service to Stockholm, Sweden.
27 March	First scheduled service to Budapest, Hungary.
28 March	First scheduled service to Warsaw, Poland.
August	Israeli Government announces plans to privatize El Al through partial public ownership of its shares of stock.
October	Expansion of direct scheduled flights between Eilat and Europe without intermediate Tel Aviv stop.

1990

1 January	First charter flight to Moscow, U.S.S.R., to airlift Soviet Jews to Israel in *Operation Exodus*.
22 January	First flight by North American Airlines (New York—Los Angeles—New York) pursuant to cooperation agreement with El Al.

El Al Chief Executive Officers

Date	El Al President*	El Al Chairman of the Board
1949	Aryeh Pincus	Avraham Ruttenberg
Nov 1956	Efraim Ben-Arzi	Moshe Carmel
1 Jan 1966	Shlomo Lahat	Efraim Ben-Arzi
Summer 1967	Mordechai Ben-Ari	Moshe Carmel
Nov 1977	Mordechai "Motti" Hod	Mordechai Ben-Ari
3 July 1979	Raphael "Rafi" Harlev, Acting President	Mordechai Ben-Ari
13 Nov 1979	Raphael Harlev, Acting President	Avraham "Buma" Shavit
1 April 1980	Itzhak Shander, Acting President	Avraham Shavit
12 Sep 1982- 12 Jan 1983	(Operations suspended; Official Receiver and Provisional Liquidator, Amram Blum, appointed, 3 Dec. 1982)	
5 Dec 1982	Raphael Harlev	No Chairman, Board subject to Official Receiver.

Position known as "Managing Director" until 1960s.

El Al Active Aircraft at 31 December Each Year

	DC-4	C-46	Con. 49	Brt.	707 420 Pax	720 B	707 320 Pax	707 320 Cvt	747 200 Pax	747 200 Cvt	747 F Cgo	737 200	767 200	757 200	Total
1949	2	0	0												2
1950	4	3	2												9
1951	2	3	3												8
1952	0	6	3												9
1953		6	4												10
1954		6	4												10
1955		1	4												5
1956		0	4	0											4
1957			4	3											7
1958			4	4											8
1959			4	4											8
1960			4	4	0										8
1961			3	4	2	0									9
1962			0	2	3	2									7
1963				2	3	2									7
1964				2	3	2									7
1965				2	3	2	0								7
1966				1	3	2	1								7
1967				0	3	2	2								7
1968					3	2	2	0							7
1969					3	2	3	1							9
1970					3	2	3	2	0						10
1971					3	2	3	2	2						12
1972					3	2	3	2	2						12
1973					3	2	3	2	2						12
1974					3	2	3	2	3	0					13
1975					3	2	3	2	3	1					14
1976					3	2	3	2	3	1	0				14
1977					3	2	3	2	3	1	1				15
1978					3	2	3	2	3	2	1				16
1979					3	2	3	2	4	2	2	0			18
1980					2	0	3	2	4	2	2	2			17
1981					2		3	2	4	2	2	2			17
1982					2		4	2	4	2	2	2	0		18
1983					2		4	2	4	2	2	2	3		21
1984					1		4	2	4	2	2	2	4		21
1985					1		4	2	4	2	2	2	4		21
1986					0		4	2	4	2	2	2	4	0	20
1987							4	2	4	2	2	2	4	2	22
1988							1	2	5	2	2	2	4	3	21
1989							0	2	5	2	2	2	4	3	20

Notes: 1. During 1951 El Al utilized a DC-3 on a few flights.
2. During 1953-57 El Al utilized an Airspeed AS.65 Consul as a training aircraft.
3. During 1984-89, two to four 707s were leased at various times to one or more of Arkia, Sun d'Or, and Cargo Air Lines. Other aircraft have occasionally been leased to El Al for brief periods (see Appendix III).
4. Pax = Passenger; Cvt = Convertible; Cgo = Cargo.

Selected El Al Statistics

Fiscal Year	Passengers	Net Income (Loss) US$	Load Factor %	Scheduled Flights	Cargo (tons)	Employees
1949	2,154	(435,000)			300	130
1950	4,699	265,000	60.0		700	375
1951	15,000	722,000			800	592
1952	21,904	12,000	60.7	774	800	1,006
1953	28,801	(492,000)	62.2	910	900	1,003
1954	30,277	(1,137,000)	61.7	910	800	1,036
1955	34,462	(1,989,000)	64.4	906	500	1,082
1956	36,671	(1,367,000)	60.9	889	600	1,136
1957	38,004	(733,000)	61.9	863	600	1,084
1958	46,384	(684,000)	63.4	984	700	1,394
1959	69,879	(1,136,000)	55.8	1,278	1,000	1,517
1960	95,533	12,000	61.2	1,637	1,000	1,527
1961	116,502	871,000	60.9	2,019	2,000	1,644
1962	171,068	616,000	58.5	2,705	3,000	2,008
1963	206,655	(946,000)	54.0	2,859	6,000	2,160
1964	231,376	1,096,000	54.3	2,780	6,000	2,248
1965	231,793	243,000	57.0	2,845	7,000	2,368
1966	298,206	602,000	61.7	3,201	8,000	2,572
1967	314,404	338,000	60.2	3,355	9,000	2,776
1968	364,360	2,220,000	63.7	3,797	11,000	3,136
1969	464,915	1,900,000	64.9	4,913	13,000	
1970	469.001	1,400,000	62.4	5,701	18,000	3,883
1971	520,770	300,000	67.0	6,057	21,000	
1972	678,920	3,000	68.2	6,958	25,000	
1973	689,564	243,000	63.3	6,965	30,000	
1974	756,887	137,000	66.2	7,010	33,000	4,850
1975	759,943	(79,000)	68.3		33,000	5,128
1976	767,745	(1,200,000)	65.2		34,000	4,845
1977	964,507	300,000	67.3		35,000	5,260
1978	1,089,910	10,000	69.0		49,000	6,121
1979	1,126,510	(23,900,000)	70.7	7,302	48,000	6,038
1980	1,250,602	(98,700,000)	69.7	7,350	61,000	5,458
1981	1,178,350	(47,400,000)	69.1	6,687	66,000	4,987
1982	1,254,703	(32,600,000)	72.2	7,253	68,000	5,007
1983	1,017,000	(123,300,000)	73.0	5,371	66,000	4,830
1984	1,311,000	(14,300,000)	73.0	6,972	93,000	4,123
1985	1,515,000	(9,700,000)	76.3	8,147	111,000	4,116
1986	1,419,033	(6,700,000)	73.1	8,464	125,000	4,110
1987	1,546,436	15,200,000	75.1	8,566	139,000	4,140
1987	1,707,000	18,200,000	76.6		146,000	4,174
1988	1,553,000	18,800,000	73.0	8,197	153,000	4,088
1989	1,741,000	24,600,000	75.9	9,113	165,000	4,125

Note: During 1949-56 El Al's fiscal year ended each 31 December. From 1957 through 31 March 1987 El Al's fiscal year ended each 31 March. In late 1987 El Al reverted to a fiscal year ending each 31 December. The second row of "1987" above covers calendar 1987 except profit is for 1 April to 31 December 1987. "Employees" are fiscal year-end data in all years. Varying statistics may be found in different publications, and the above should be viewed as approximations.

APPENDIX III: El Al Aircraft Fleet List

Note: Leased aircraft are listed only for longer-term leases or when the aircraft is of special interest.

Abbreviations

The following abbreviations and acronyms appear in this appendix:

AAXICO	American Air Export and Import Company
AFB	Air Force Base (U.S.)
AK	Alaska
AL	Alabama
AVIANCA	Aerovias Nacionales de Colombia, SA
AZ	Arizona
BOAC	British Overseas Airways Corp.
CA	California
CofA	Certificate of Airworthiness
COPA	Compania Panameña de Aviacion, SA
DCA	Israeli Department of Civil Aviation
FBI	Federal Bureau of Investigation
FL	Florida
HI	Hawaii
IDF	Israel Defense Forces
LANICA	Líneas Aéreas de Nicaragua
LN	Line Number (assigned by manufacturer)
MGTOW	Maximum Gross Take-Off Weight
MSN	Manufacturer's Serial Number
NJ	New Jersey

NTU	Not Taken Up
NY	New York
OH	Ohio
OK	Oklahoma
QANTAS	Queensland and Northern Territory Aerial Services
RAF	Royal Air Force
REAL	Redes Estaduais Aéreas Ltda
RFC	Reconstruction Finance Corp. (agency of U.S. government responsible for disposal of war surplus property and equipment within U.S.A.; this task passed to the War Assets Administration shortly after March 1946)
SAAF	South African Air Force
SBAC	Society of British Aircraft Constructors
TACA	Transportes Aéreos Centro Americanos
TX	Texas
USAF	U.S. Air Force
USAAF	U.S. Army Air Force
VASP	Viacao Aérea São Paulo, SA

DOUGLAS DC-4

Note: All El Al DC-4s were originally built as military C-54 transports.

4X-ACC C-54A-15-DC MSN: 10410/LN DC141
Delivered to USAAF 26 Sep 44 as 42-72305, then to American Airlines 1946 as NC90433.

Purchased by El Al via The Flying Tiger Line as an intermediary, and delivered to El Al at Tulsa, OK, 15 Mar 49. Flown from Tulsa to Idlewild, NY, for overhauled by Willis/Rose. Registered in Israel as 4X-ACC, 25 Mar 49. Named *Rechovoth* by El Al in honor of the city of President Chaim Weizmann's residence in Israel. Flown 29 Mar–2 Apr 49 by El Al's Capt. Maurice Kouffman, together with Pan Am crew, on El Al's first survey flight over New York (Idlewild)—Gander—Shannon—Paris—Tel Aviv route, thereby becoming the first aircraft purchased by El Al to land in Israel. Flown 9-26 Apr 49 Tel Aviv—Rome—Amsterdam—Paris—Santa Maria, Azores (where impounded 7 days by Portuguese authorities)—Gander—New York. Flown 31 Jul 49 New York (Idlewild)—Columbus, OH,—Santa Monica, CA, to Douglas Aircraft factory for checking and confirmation of airworthiness. Flown 17 Aug 49 from Santa Monica to Idlewild and then to Israel where it entered regular scheduled service for El Al. Registration canceled 15 Jan 52 as sold by El Al to The Flying Tiger Line Jan 52.

Crashed 1,600km (1,000mi) west of Honolulu, HI, 23 Sep 55.

4X-ACD C-54A-10-DC MSN: 10339/LN DC70
Delivered to USAAF 30 Jun 44, 42-72234. To American Airlines in 1946 as NC90439 *Flagship Hartford*.

Purchased by El Al via The Flying Tiger Line as an intermediary, and delivered to El Al at Tulsa, OK, 26 Feb 49. Flown from Tulsa to Idlewild, NY, for overhaul by Willis/Rose. Registered as 4X-ACD, 10 May 49. Flown 29-31 May 49 on a U.S.A. public relations tour, New York (Idlewild)—Indianapolis—Oklahoma City—New York. First arrived Tel Aviv 11 Jul 49. Named *Herzl* Operated El Al's first scheduled flight, 31 Jul 49, Tel Aviv—Rome—Paris. Operated special flight 16-17 Aug 49, Tel Aviv—Vienna—Tel Aviv, to bring remains of Herzl, founder of Zionism, to Israel. Crashed on take-off from Tel Aviv, 6 Feb 50, at 0100 local time, under unusual snow and icing conditions; burnt out, but all aboard escaped safely.

4X-ADB C-54B-1-DC MSN: 10512/LN DC243
Delivered to USAAF 6 Jan 45, 42-72407. Returned to Douglas 5 Nov 45 and converted to DC-4 (no. 5) at El Segundo, CA. To Western Air Lines 21 May 46 as NC86581. To United Air Lines in 1947 as *Mainliner Grand Canyon*.

Purchased by The Flying Tiger Line on behalf of El Al 27 Apr 50. First arrived in Tel Aviv, 28 May 50. Registered

4X-ACC at Tel Aviv in 1951 in second livery with rectangles painted around the windows to resemble a DC-6. (El Al)

4X-ACD at Tel Aviv in original livery, 1949. (Zionist Archives & Library, New York).

4X-ADB at Gander, Newfoundland, July 1950 (Hilda Krumbein collection, Rehovot)

4X-ADC at New York (Idlewild, now JFK), 1951. (Joyce Perlman Baron collection)

4X-ACF (J.M.G. Gradidge)

4X-ACG at Ekron Air Base, Israel, 5 May 1949. (Noam Hartoch collection)

4X-ACT at Eilat, 1950. (Israel Government Press Office)

4X-ALA at Tel Aviv. (BIAF—Israel Aviation & Space Magazine)

in name of El Al as 4X-ADB 31 May 50. Operated the initial segments of El Al's first passenger trans-Atlantic flight, a charter from Tel Aviv to New York, 18 Jun 50, via Rome—Paris—Shannon—Gander, arriving 19 June. Also operated the initial segments of El Al's first round-trip passenger trans-Atlantic flight, a charter on route Tel Aviv—Rome—Shannon—Gander—New York (Idlewild), 25 Jun 50, with return to Tel Aviv. Re-registered as **4X-ADN** (see below), 4 Feb 51, but retained 4X-ADB markings. Crashed and burnt out while on a cargo flight, on descent into Zürich, 24 Nov 51. Six crew members, including Capt. Ted Gibson, died, and one survived.

4X-ADC C-54B-10-DO MSN: 18367/LN DO141
Delivered to USAAF 25 Sep 44, 43-17167. Returned to Douglas 11 Jan 46 and converted to DC-4 (no. 47) at Santa Monica, CA. To United Air Lines 31 May 46 as NC30058 *Mainliner Hudson River*.

Purchased by El Al 17 May 50. Registered in Israel as 4X-ADC 26 Jun 50. Operated at times with Cuban registration CU-T-465. Israeli registration canceled 7 Apr 52 and sold to The Flying Tiger Line.

Re-registered as N30058, 25 Apr 52 (Cuban registration canceled 28 Apr 52). Sold to Pan American Airways 1957 and leased to Ariana Afghan Airlines as YA-BAG, Jun 57. Crashed at Beirut, Lebanon, 21 Nov 59.

4X-ADN C-54A-15-DC MSN: 10416/LN DC147
Delivered to USAAF 29 Sep 44, 42-72311. To Trans-Caribbean Airways as NC56011. Sub-leased to Mercury Aviation Services (Pty.) Ltd., Johannesburg, and re-gistered ZS-BYA, 2 Feb 48 for single trip to South Africa. Returned to NC56011 later in Feb 48.

Purchased by El Al, and registered as 4X-ADN 11 Jun 50. Flown in Aden airlift under markings of Near East Air Transport (eg, on 26 Aug 50). Registration changed to **4X-AMD** 4 Feb 51. Sold to Trans-Caribbean Airways Jun 51, Israeli registration canceled 24 Jun 51, and reverted to N56011.

Sold to Kaman Aircraft Corp., U.S. registration canceled 8 Apr 55 and final fate unknown.

DC-4 Operated by El Al Prior to its Incorporation

4X-ACA C-54B-15-DO MSN: 18395/LN DO169
Delivered to USAAF 21 Nov 44, 43-17195. Sold to U.S. Overseas Airlines and registered NC58021.

Acquired by the Israeli Air Force's Air Transport Command through the Haganah defense arm 15 May 48 with serial 1801. Participated in airlift of arms from Czechoslovakia to Israel, May-Sep 48. Registered as 4X-ACA on 27 Sep 48 in the name of El Al in the Official Aircraft Registry book of the Ministry of Transportation of the State of Israel. This was the first entry in such Registry after the establishment of the State on 14 May 48. Painted in first "El Al" livery Sep 48 (even though El Al was not incorporated until 15 Nov 48 and did not start scheduled passenger service until 31 Jul 49), and utilized for the flight on 29-30 Sep 48 that brought Chaim Weizmann from Geneva to Israel to be the first President of Israel and for a special civilian flight to Paris, Oct 48. Returned to the Israeli Air Force's Air Transport Command Oct 48.

On 2 Jan 49, enroute from Czechoslovakia to Israel while in military service on *Operation Velveta 2*, developed engine problems and crashed on the beach at Tel Aviv while attempting to land. Aircraft severely damaged and later scrapped. Canceled from civil register 26 Jun 49 (see photo page 24).

DC-4 Leased to El Al

4X-ACB (N90441) C-54A-15-DC MSN: 10348/LN DC79
Delivered to USAAF 15 Jul 44, 42-72243. To American Airlines in 1946 as NC90441 *Flagship Rainbow One*.

Acquired by the Israeli Air Transport Command through the Haganah defense arm 15 May 48, and bore Israeli Air Force serial 1802. Participated in airlift of arms from Czechoslovakia to Israel. Registered 4X-ACB to El Al 5 Dec 48. Sold by El Al to California Aircraft Corp., and Israeli registration canceled, 22 Feb 49.

Re-registered in U.S. as N90441, then to Twentieth Century Aircraft and Hemisphere Air Transport. Operated with crew of Near East Air Transport on airlift operations to Israel in 1950. Leased to El Al for passenger operations on European routes, Feb-Apr 50.

Sold to REAL, Brazil, as PP-YRO, Oct 56. Then to Lóide Aéreo Nacional Sep 58 as PP-LEW, and to VASP Jan 62. Damaged at Santos Dumont Airport, Rio de Janeiro, 6 Nov 68. Broken up Sep 70.

CURTISS C-46 COMMANDO

4X-ACE C-46A-15-CU MSN: 26532/LN CU172
Delivered to USAAF 17 Jun 43, 41-12405. Assigned to India-China Wing, Air Transport Command (India-China Division from 1 Jul 44), 7 July 43. Returned to U.S.A. 15 Aug 44 at Brookley Field (Mobile, AL). To RFC at Ontario, CA, 30 Oct 45.

Acquired by Schwimmer Co. for "Service Airways" and then registered in Panama for Lineas Aéreas de Panama, S.A. ("LAPSA") as RX-137. Panamanian registration canceled 17 Sep 48. Israel Air Force serial no. 1707, May 48. Registered to El Al as 4X-ACE, 24 Jan 50. Registration canceled 1 Mar 55.

4X-ACF (4X-ALB) C-46A-55-CK MSN: 261/LN CK238
Delivered to USAAF 14 Feb 45, 43-47190. Assigned to Troop Carrier Command, Baer Field, and retianed in U.S. To RFC at Walnut Ridge, AZ, 6 Nov 45. Sold to Howard Korth Nov 45. To TACA, El Salvador, 15 Dec 45 and registered YS-01C 4 Sept 46. Then registered in U.S. to Intercontinental Airways as N75393.

Registered in Panama for LAPSA as RX-130 by Apr 48. Then registered in Cuba as CU-T-450. Registered in name of El Al as 4X-ACF, 24 Jan 50. Operated some El Al Jewish refugee airlift flights from other countries to Israel, and even some regular El Al flights to Europe and Eilat, under Cuban registration (CU-T-450). 4X-ACF registration canceled 17 Dec 50, and re-registered as 4X-ALB 14 May 52. Registration 4X-ALB canceled 18 Jul 55 and delivered to U.S. via U.K. 21 Jul 55.

Sold to AAXICO and registered as N75393, 24 Aug 55. Sold to TACA, El Salvador, and registered as YS-35, 19 Mar 56. Sold to Aeromar, Dominican Republic, and registered as HI-196, 1970. Sold to Argo for spares use 1978.

4X-ACG C-46A-50-CU MSN: 30575/LN CU1111
Delivered to USAAF 21 Sep 44, 42-101120. Assigned to Central African Wing (Air Transport Command-Central African Division, from 1 Jul 44). Returned to U.S. at Morrison, NJ, 24 Jul 45. To RFC at Ontario, CA, 14 Oct 45.

Registered to A. W. Schwimmer in U.S. as N67926, 1947. Registered in Panama in name of LAPSA, probably as RX-138, in early 1948. To Israeli Air Force, serial 1708, May 48. Registered in name of Al-Sam Ltd. (a fictitious name used by the Israeli Government) 10 Nov 48. Per Capt. Sam Lewis log book, flew under El Al name on 22 Jan 49, and was used on El Al special flight, 31 Jan–17 Feb 49, carrying Finance Minister Eliezer Kaplan on route Lydda—Rome—Corsica—Athens—Lydda. Crashed during 6-9 May 49 on take-off from Avraham, an improvised landing strip about 55km (35mi) north of Eilat, while engaged in *Operation Fact* (also known as *Operation Uvda*), an Israeli Air Force mission to supply Israeli troops who advanced to Eilat and occupied it on 10 Mar 49. All 13 persons on board the aircraft survived without serious injury.

4X-ACT (4X-ALC) C-46A-45-CU MSN: 30202/LN CU738
Delivered to USAAF 7 Jul 44, 42-96540, at St. Joseph and retained in U.S. To RFC at Walnut Ridge 6 Nov 45.

Registered in Panama in name of LAPSA in early 1948. Registered as 4X-ACT in name of Al-Sam Ltd., 11 Oct 49. Aircraft transferred to Arkia 11 Oct 49. Registered to El Al, 24 Jan 50. This aircraft, operated by El Al and with El Al markings and added passenger windows installed, initially comprised the entire Arkia fleet. Operated first official flight to Eilat 28 Feb 50. Re-registered as 4X-ALC, 14 Oct 52. Reverted to Arkia 27 Feb 55. Registration canceled 17 Feb 56 as sold to AAXICO and registered in U.S. as N5141B, 27 Jan 56.

Sold to LANICA, Nicaragua, and registered AN-AIR, 26 Mar 56. Sold to H. Davis 17 Sep 58 and registered N4198A, 12 Feb 59. Final fate unknown.

4X-AEF C-46A-35-CU MSN: 26805/LN CU445
Delivered to USAAF 3 Feb 44, 42-3672. Assigned to Central African Wing, Air Transport Command, 8 Mar 44. Returned to U.S. at Morrison, NJ, 21 Jul 45. To RFC at Ontario, CA, 6 Nov 45.

Acquired by Schwimmer Co. for "Service Airways" and then registered in Panama for LAPSA as RX-131 in 1948. To Israeli Air Force, serial 1702, May 48. Panamanian registration canceled 17 Sep 48. Registered as 4X-AEF in name of El Al 12 Mar 52. Registration canceled 8 May 53 as sold by El Al to Al Schwimmer May 53.

Registered in U.S. as N2714A, 8 May 53. Sold to John S. Russell Jr. 26 Jun 53. Sold to American Aviation Leasing

4X-ALB (same aircraft as 4X-ACF) at New York (Idlewild, now JFK). (J.M.G. Gradidge)

4X-ALC (same aircraft as 4X-ACT) at London (Heathrow), 31 August 1953. (Peter R. Keating)

4X-ALE at London (Heathrow), 15 August 1954. (Peter R. Keating)

4X-ALF at London (Heathrow), May 1954. (J.M.G. Gradidge)

4X-AEK at Tel Aviv. (BIAF-Israel Aviation & Space Magazine)

4X-AKA at Tel Aviv. (Yigal Levy collection)

4X-AKB at London (Heathrow), 17 August 1954. (Peter R. Keating)

4X-AKC at New York (Idlewild). (J.M.G. Gradidge)

4X-AKD (Peter R. Keating)

4X-AGA at London (Heathrow), 20 April 1960. (Peter R. Keating)

4X-AGB at the Farnborough Air Show, England, September 1957. (J.M.G. Gradidge)

18 Aug 53. Sold to 4th Street Corp., Miami, FL, 8 Oct 54. With Aerovias Sud Americana May 55. Believed leased as HP-228 to Aerovias Panama 1958/59 and later to COPA. To HK-791 Taxader, Colombia, prior to 1964. Sold about 1968 to Luis Bonilla and leased to Aeropesca. To Aeronorte 1971. To Lineas Aéreas Orientales Ltda., Mar 72. Blew tire on landing and crashed 30 Apr 73 at Leticia Airport, Colombia, and written off.

4X-ALA C-46A-36-CU MSN: 26809/LN CU449
Delivered to USAAF 10 Feb 44, 42-3676. Assigned to Central African Wing, Air Transport Command, 10 Mar 44. Returned to U.S. at Morrison, NJ, 2 Jul 45. To RFC at Ontario, CA, 24 Oct 45.

Acquired by Schwimmer Co. for "Service Airways" and then registered in Panama for LAPSA as RX-132. To Israeli Air Force, serial 1705, May 48. Registered as 4X-ALA in name of El Al, 4 Apr 52. Sold to Alaska Airlines 20 Feb 56 and Israeli registration canceled 4 Mar 56.

To AAXICO 2 Mar 56. Damaged in hard landing short of runway at Granite, AK, 20 Oct 56. Crashed, and two crew killed, following attempted landing with elevator control difficulties at Dyess AFB, Abilene, TX, 2 Sep 59.

4X-ALB see 4X-ACF above (same aircraft).

4X-ALC see 4X-ACT above (same aircraft).

4X-ALE see 4X-AQD below (same aircraft).

4X-ALF see 4X-AQE below (same aircraft).

4X-AQD (4X-ALE) C-46D-10-CU MSN: 33271/LN CU1807
Delivered to USAAF 12 Feb 45, 44-77875. Assigned to Troop Carrier Command, Baer Field and retained in U.S. To RFC at Walnut Ridge, AZ, 12 Mar 46.

Registered in Cuba as CU-T-449. To Israeli Air Force, serial 1703, May 48. Registered as 4X-AQD in name of El Al, 28 Jul 50. Operated some El Al Jewish refugee airlift flights from other countries to Israel, and even some regular passenger flights between Tel Aviv and Eilat, under Cuban registration CU-T-449. Registration 4X-AQD canceled, and re-registered as 4X-ALE, 14 Oct 52. Registration 4X-ALE canceled 21 Jul 55 and ferried to U.S. 21 Jul 55 via London (Heathrow) and Prestwick.

To Mexican Air Force as X-T-1. Sold in U.S. as N10012 with Cordova Airlines, AK. Then to Reeve Aleutian. Went through ice on landing at Nondalton, AK, 10 Feb 71, and written off.

4X-AQE (4X-ALF) C-46D-15-CU MSN: 33452/LN CU1988
Delivered to USAAF 21 Mar 45, 44-78056. Assigned to Troop Carrier Command, Baer Field and retained in U.S. To RFC at Bush Field 30 Jan 47

Acquired by Al Schwimmer for "Service Airways" then then registered in Panama for LAPSA as RX-139. To Israeli Air Force, serial 1709, May 48. Registered as 4X-AQE in name of El Al, 28 Jul 50, then registration canceled and re-registered as 4X-ALF, 4 May 52. Registration canceled 18 Jul 55 and sold in U.S. to AAXICO Aircraft Sales Inc., 21 Jul 55.

Ultimate fate unknown.

DOUGLAS DC-3

4X-ATA C-47-DL (DC3C) MSN: 6227
Delivered to USAAF 13 Jan 43, 42-5639. To RAF as FD773 (reported FD772 by Douglas). Registered to BOAC as G-AGGB, 19 Feb 43. To Airways Training Ltd., 1 Jun 47. To Automobile Aircraft Services 17 Jun 48.

To Westair Transport Ltd. (owned by Israeli interests) 12 Jul 48. To Universal Airways, South Africa, and registered ZS-DAJ, 12 Jul 48, but NTU. To Westair Ltd. and registered ZS-DDJ, 16 Sep 49. To Israeli Defense Forces as 4X-FAI, 12 Nov 50. To El Al as 4X-ATA, 22 Feb 51. Inaugurated service to Istanbul 1 Mar 51. Registration canceled 25 Jan 52 and returned to IDF. (Interestingly, 4X-ATA was later used as the registration for El Al's first Boeing 707 in 1961). To Arkia as 4X-AEO, 2 Apr 57 (see photo page 129). To Israel Aircraft Industries, 4 Sep 68. Withdrawn from use 30 Jul 71, and used for fire practice at Lod Airport.

DOUGLAS DC-3s Leased by El Al

Oct 49–Oct 50. DC-3s occasionally leased from Universal Airways of South Africa, usually with Universal crew, for charter flights.

AIRSPEED AS.65 CONSUL

4X-AEK MSN: 4324
CofA 5 Dec 46. Ex-RAF PK260. To British Aviation Services. Then to Malayan Airways as VR-SCD. Then registered as G-AIKY to W. S. Shackleton Aug 52 and subsequently to Aeroservices May 53. Sold to Israel Jul 53 and registered 4X-AEK 26 Aug 53. Utilized Jul 53–Feb 57 by El Al for crew training, to familiarize aircrew on the type before submitting to the DCA examination for instrument rating. The DCA used another Consul, 4X-AEN, which had a modified cockpit layout in order to test El Al aircrew for instrument ratings. Withdrawn from use 18 Feb 57.

LOCKHEED CONSTELLATION

Note: Lockheed subsequently referred to the Model 49 Constellation as the Model 049 to bring the designation in line with the three-digit system of the 649/749 series. However, this designation revision was not used by the U.S. Federal Aviation Agency (FAA) which maintained the Model 49 as such in its official certification paperwork, and this style is used here.

4X-AKA Model 49-46-10/C-69-1-LO MSN: 1965
Delivered to USAAF 25 Jan 45, 43-10313. Held at Burbank, CA, for storage from 20 Oct 45, and held by War Assets Administration 31 Mar 47 for disposal.

Purchased by Al Schwimmer (Schwimmer Aviation) late 1947 or Jan 48, and registered NC90827. Overhauled, and converted from a military C-69 to a civilian Model 49 Constellation at Burbank, winter 1947-48, for "Service Airways" (Al Schwimmer) and in turn for the clandestine Panamanian airline, Lineas Aéreas de Panama, S.A. (LAPSA), established by Jewish interests in preparation for the defense of Israel in its May 48 War of Independence. Registered in Panama under LAPSA name as RX-123, and flown by Capt. Sam Lewis, 10-11 Mar 48, Burbank—Millville, NJ. Aircraft impounded by FBI as an illegal export from the U.S. to Israel and stored at Millville. Panamanian registration canceled 17 Sep 48. Restored as N90827 to Service Airways Inc. (Al Schwimmer), and returned to Burbank. Purchased by El Al Oct 50 and registered as 4X-AKA 5 Oct 50. Converted to a Model 149 and referred to by El Al as a 249 (an unofficial designation). Arrived in Israel 25 Mar 51. Stored at Lod, 1961/62 and canceled from Israeli register, 8 Jan 62.

Purchased from El Al by Universal Sky Tours, U.K., and re-registered G-ARXE, 13 Feb 62 with CofA issued 10 May 62. Delivered to Luton, Apr 62, in Euravia livery. Repainted in Skyways colors Oct 62. Ownership transferred to Britannia Airways 2 Feb 65 and withdrawn from use prior to CofA expiration, May 65. Broken up at Luton, 28 Jan 66.

4X-AKB Model 49-46-10/C-69-1-LO MSN: 1967
Delivered to USAAF 19 Feb 45, 43-10315. To Burbank, CA, 26 Nov 45, and held by War Assets Administration 31 Mar 47 for disposal.

Purchased by Al Schwimmer (Schwimmer Aviation) late 1947 or Jan 48, and registered NC90828. Overhauled, and converted from a military C-69 to a civilian Model 49 Constellation at Burbank, winter 1947-48, for the above-mentioned Panamanian "airline", Lineas Aéreas de Panama, S.A. (LAPSA). Registered in Panama under LAPSA name as RX-124. Test flown by Capt. Sam Lewis at Burbank under RX-124 registration, 5 Apr 48. Aircraft remained in storage at Burbank. Transferred to The Jewish Agency Inc. and re-registered NC67930. Ferried by Capt. Lewis, Burbank—Millville, NJ, under registration N67930, 7 Jun 48. Panamanian registration canceled 17 Sep 48. Purchased by El Al 1950, registered as 4X-AKB, 5 Oct 50, and arrived in Israel 22 Dec 50. Converted to a Model 49D (a Lockheed designation indicating higher gross weights) and referred to by El Al as a 249. At one time named *Mazal Tov* (Hebrew for "Good Luck"). Stored at Tel Aviv by El Al from at least fall 1961. Registration canceled 8 Jan 62. Total flying time 23,001hr as of Feb 62. Sold by El Al to Universal Sky Tours and registered in U.K. as G-ARVP, 13 Feb 62.

Delivered Tel Aviv—Heathrow—Luton, 11-12 Apr 62

4X-AGB in Air Spain colors at London (Heathrow), March 1967. (B. N. Stainer via Peter R. Keating)

4X-AGC at London (Heathrow), September 1965. (John Wegg collection)

4X-AGD at London (Heathrow). (Peter R. Keating)

4X-AGE at London (Heathrow). (J.M.G. Gradidge)

G-ASFU (same aircraft as 4X-AGD) at London (Heathrow), March/April 1963. (B.N. Stainer via Gordon Reid)

4X-ATA in first livery at Tel Aviv. (El Al)

4X-ATB in first livery at London (Heathrow), July 1961. Note the seating for spectators near the taxiway! (Gordon Reid)

4X-ATC in third livery and bearing the emblem of the 25th anniversary of the State of Israel, 1973. (MAP)

4X-ATD in third livery landing at Amsterdam, June 1983. (Bob Neumeier)

4X-ATR in second livery at Tel Aviv, November 1966, with Flying Tiger Line colors visible on tail. (Israel Government Press Office)

in livery of Euravia. Ownership transferred to Britannia Airways 2 Feb 65 and withdrawn from use 2 Apr 65. Broken up at Luton.

4X-AKC Model 49-46-10/C-69-1-LO MSN: 1968
Delivered to USAAF 11 May 45, 43-10316. Retained at Burbank, CA, initially and apparently never left there. Aircraft hangared at Burbank in Oct 45 and parked there for disposal by 24 Feb 47. To U.S. War Assets Administration 31 Mar 47, and deleted by USAAF 28 May 47.

Sold to Al Schwimmer of Schwimmer Aviation late 47 or Jan 48 and registered NC90829. Converted at Burbank from a military C-69 to a civilian Model 49. Flown by Capt. Sam Lewis from Burbank to Millville, NJ, 26 Jan 48 and registered as RX-121 in the name of the clandestine Panamanian "airline", Lineas Aéreas de Panama, S.A. (LAPSA), established by Jewish interests in preparation for the defense of Israel in its May 48 War of Independence. Flown by Capt. Sam Lewis 13 Mar 48 Newark—Kingston, Jamaica,—Tocumen, Panama; and 19-21 Jun 48 Tocumen—Paramaribo—Dakar—Casablanca—Zatec, Czechoslovakia. In service for Israeli Air Force on airlift of arms from Czechoslovakia to Israel, Jun-Jul 48. Retained RX-121 registration during this period and never bore military serial. Suffered hydraulic failure and damaged in subsequent wheels-up landing at Zatec, 13 Jul 48, and had to be taken out of service. Panamanian registration RX-121 canceled, 17 Sep 48. Aircraft remained in Czechoslovakia for repairs. Per Capt. Sam Lewis' log book, test flights made on 30-31 May 49, after incomplete repairs at Zatec then ferried by Capt. Lewis on three engines from Zatec to Amsterdam, 17 Sep 49. Former U.S. registration restored as N90829. Ferried, with landing gear in fixed down position, to U.S. for overhaul, Amsterdam—Keflavik—Gander—Chicago—Burbank, starting 22 Oct 49. Overhauled at Al Schwimmer's Intercontinental Airways in Burbank. Purchased by El Al and delivered Apr 51. Registered as 4X-AKC 15 Jul 51. Converted to a Model 149 and referred to by El Al as a 249. Arrived in Israel, week of 8 Aug 51. While on a scheduled flight from London to Tel Aviv via Vienna, was shot down by Bulgarian MiG-15 fighters 27 Jul 55 over Bulgaria a few miles from the Greek-Bulgarian border, with all 7 crew and 51 passengers killed.

4X-AKD Model 49-46-10/C-69-5-LO MSN: 1980
Allocated USAAF serial 42-94559, but NTU and registered as NC90606. Converted to Model 49-51-26 for BOAC, and registered in U.K. as G-AHEN, 1 Jul 46. Named *Baltimore* by BOAC, converted to Model 49-46-26 and in service 31 Aug 46. Severely damaged after overshooting at Filton-Bristol, England, 8 Jan 51, on a training flight. Written off by BOAC but remains shipped by insurer as deck-cargo to New York Feb 51, and rebuilt by Lockheed Aircraft Service Co. at New York (Ildewild) with parts of MSN 1966, an ex-military C-69. Sold to Kirk Kerkorian (Los Angeles Air Service Inc.), late 1951, registered N74192, and leased to California Hawaiian Airlines, Apr 52.

Purchased by El Al Oct 53 and registered as 4X-AKD, 24 Dec 53. Damaged by fire at Lod, 2 Apr 58, but repaired. Canceled from Israeli register, 12 Mar 61. Stored at Lod, 1961/62 then sold to Universal Sky Tours, U.K., Feb 62.

Converted to a Model 49D (a Lockheed designation indicating increased gross weights) and re-registered as G-AHEN, 13 Feb 62. Painted in Euravia colors and delivered to Luton, Apr 62. Ownership transferred to Euravia (London) Ltd. 23 May 63 and to Britannia Airways 2 Feb 65. Withdrawn from use 21 Apr 65, and broken up at Luton, May 65.

4X-AKE Model 49-46-26 MSN: 2061.
Delivered 14 May 46 to Pan American as NC88861 (N88861 from 1949), named *Clipper Atlantic* and *Clipper Winged Arrow*. Transferred to Cubana Jun 53 as CU-T532.

Purchased by El Al Oct 55 and delivered Dec 55. Registered as 4X-AKE, 16 Dec 55. In service by Feb 56. Registration canceled 6 Feb 62, and transferred to Israel Aircraft Industries. Stored at Lod for possible Israeli Air Force use, but not taken up. Removed to location adjacent to Avia Hotel in Yehud for possible use as a restaurant, but broken up late 1960s.

Note: There have been different opinions in aviation enthusiast literature as to whether the famous Panamanian-registered "RX-121", the only Constellation that served in the 1948 Israeli War of Independence, later became El Al's 4X-AKA or the ill-fated 4X-AKC. The missing historical confirmation is supplied by the original log book of Capt. Sam Lewis, reviewed by the author, from which it is clear that U.S. registry NC90829 became RX-121 and that RX-121 was

later re-registered in the U.S. as N90829. Since (a) per Lockheed's records, MSN 1968 is the identity of NC90829, (b) per
Capt. Lewis' log book, NC90829 became RX-121 which
became N90829, and (c) per Lockheed's records, N90829
became 4X-AKC, it follows that MSN 1968, RX-121 and
4X-AKC were one and the same aircraft. Capt. Lewis' log
book is also consistent with 4X-AKA being the former RX-
123 and 4X-AKB being the former RX-124.

Leased Constellations

Oct 55   Constellation aircraft leased from South
            African Airways for Tel Aviv—Johannes-
            burg service.

1961-62   Model 1049 Super Constellations leased
            from KLM for Tel Aviv—Johannesburg ser-
            vice.

BRISTOL 175 BRITANNIA

4X-AGA Series 313 MSN: 13232
Registered as 4X-AGA, 18 Feb 57. First flown at Filton,
England, 28 Jul 57. Officially handed over to El Al 5 Sept
57. Delivered Filton—Tel Aviv 12 Sep 57. Damaged rear
fuselage during training flight at Tel Aviv and returned to
Filton for repair 10 Nov 57. Test flown after repair 29 Nov
57 and returned to El Al 1 Dec 57. Leased to British United
Airways (BUA) 17 Mar 63, canceled from Israeli register
and registered as G-ASFV 19 Mar 63, for operation by
BUA on behalf of El Al during El Al strike. Returned to El
Al as 4X-AGA 1 Apr 63. Sold to Globe-Air of Switzerland 3
Apr 64 and registered HB-ITB.
    Leased to International Air during 65 for Europe—
Johannesburg charters. Crashed at Nicosia, Cyprus 20 Apr
67.

4X-AGB Series 313 MSN: 13233
Registered as 4X-AGB, 18 Feb 57. First flown Filton,
England, 2 Sep 57. Displayed at the SBAC Show, Farn-
borough, Sep 57. Handed over to El Al at Filton 19 Oct 57.
Flown Heathrow—Tel Aviv 20 Oct 57. Operated first El Al
Britannia service Tel Aviv—London—New York, 22 Dec
57. Leased to British United Airways (via Bristol Aircraft),
registered as G-ARWZ and delivered Tel Aviv—Stansted
13 Feb 62, and canceled from Israeli registry 28 Feb 62.
Returned to El Al 26 Mar 65, and restored as 4X-AGB.
Registration canceled 8 May 67 (after being the last Britannia in service with El Al), as sold to Air Spain Feb 67 and registered EC-WFL.
    Delivered to Air Spain 3 Mar 67 and named Can-
tabrico, re-registered as EC-BFL 2 May 67. Withdrawn
from use at Palma de Mallorca, 1972. Sold to International
Aviation Services (IAS) for spares, Sep 73, and broken up
in winter 1974.

4X-AGC Series 313 MSN: 13234
Originally built as Series 250 and registered G-ANGK to
Bristol 23 Nov 53, but NTU and registration canceled 11
Mar 55. Registered as 4X-AGC, 18 Feb 57. First flown at
Filton 4 Oct 57. Handed over to El Al at Filton 28 Nov 57.
Flown Heathrow—Tel Aviv 29 Nov 57. On 18-19 Dec 57 set
new speed and distance records on a proving flight between
New York and Tel Aviv by flying the 9,270km (5,760mi)
nonstop in 14hr 46min at an average speed of 645km/h
(401mph). Leased to British United Airways (via Bristol
Aircraft), registered as G-ARXA 12 Mar 62 and delivered
Tel Aviv—Stansted 14 Mar 62, and canceled from Israeli
registry 4 Jul 62. Returned to El Al 27 Sep 64 and restored
as 4X-AGC, 13 Oct 64. Registration canceled 19 Apr 66, as
sold to British Eagle International Airlines (BEIA) and re-
registered as G-ARXA 22 Apr 66, and delivered to
Heathrow 1 May 66.
    Stored at Liverpool upon collapse of BEIA 6 Nov 68,
and U.K. registration canceled 8 Nov 68. Ferried to Luton
Nov 70 and broken up for spares by Monarch Airlines.

4X-AGD Series 313 MSN: 13431
Registered as 4X-AGD, 3 Feb 59. First flown Filton 21 Feb
59. Delivered to El Al at Filton 7 Mar 59 and flew Filton—
Heathrow—Tel Aviv. Canceled from Israeli registry 17 Mar
63, and registered G-ASFU to British United Airways
(BUA) 18 Mar 63, for operation by BUA on behalf of El Al
during El Al strike. Returned to El Al as 4X-AGD 8 Apr 63.
Registration canceled 8 Mar 65, as sold to Globe-Air,
Switzerland, and registered as HB-ITC 8 Mar 65.
    Leased to International Air/African Tourist Develop-
ment Co. in 1965. Abandoned at Luton by International Air
crew 17 Oct 67 when Globe-Air went bankrupt. Sold to

4X-ATR in Sun d'Or livery at Manchester, August 1981. (Paul Tomlin via John Wegg)

4X-ATS in third livery at Düsseldorf, March 1977. (Bernd-Olaf Hagedorn)

4X-ATT in third livery at Tel Aviv, upon return from inaugural flight to Mexico City, November 1976. (El Al)

4X-ATX in third livery at Munich, April 1973. (Klaus Mohr)

4X-ATY in second livery, and with later version star in the front, at New York (JFK). (via John Wegg)

4X-ATY in Sun d'Or livery at Amsterdam, August 1985 (note armored car protective vehicle). (Bob Neumeier)

PP-VJB at Tel Aviv, 1961. (El Al)

N373WA at Paris (Orly), July 1965. (Roger Caratini via Peter R. Keating)

N324F at Amsterdam, 1968. (J. W. Bossenbroek via John Wegg)

4X-BYM at Amsterdam, May 1977. (Bob Neumeier via John Wegg)

African Safari Airways Dec 67 and registered 5X-UVH, Jun 68. Re-registered as 5Y-ALT, Apr 70. Sold to African Cargo Airways as 5Y-ALT in 1973 and used until 31 Oct 73. To Aero-Checks, Nov 73. Withdrawn from use at Stansted 22 May 75. Severely burned in fire service training, 9 Oct 75.

4X-AGE Series 306 MSN: 12920
First flown at Belfast, Northern Ireland, as G-18-3, 1 June 57 (as Series 305). Intended for Northeast Airlines as N6595C, but order postponed Sep 57 and then canceled Jun 58. Registered 3 Jan 58 to Bristol Aircraft as G-ANCD and painted in Cubana colors for sales tour to Spain, Cuba and Brazil Jun 58.

Repainted in El Al colors 8 Jul 58, and registered as 4X-AGE, 10 Jul 58. Leased to El Al from Bristol Aircraft Company 17 Jul 58. Canceled from Israeli registry, and returned to Filton on termination of lease, 6 Mar 59.

Later leased to Air Charter as G-ANCD, and subsequently converted to Series 307 in Aug 59. Sold to Air Charter 23 Aug 61. Continued as G-ANCD, and registered to or operated by, successively, British United Airways (BUA), Silver City Airways, Lloyd International (17 Jan–17 Feb 69) (converted to Series 307F), Shackleton Air, Aivex Holdings Ltd. (Jul 73) and IAS Cargo Airlines (Sep 73). Stored at Luton Dec 74–13 May 75. Became 5Y-AYR 13 May 75 and served with, successively, African Cargo Airways, Westwings Aviation Services (Feb 77), Black Arrow Finance, Westwings Aviation Services, Trans Gulf Air Cargo, All Cargo Airways, and Gaylan Air Cargo (79). Withdrawn from use at Bournemouth-Hurn, 10 Dec 79. Scrapped Oct 82.

BOEING 707

4X-ATA 707-458 MSN: 18070/LN 205
Ordered 25 Mar 60. First flight 14 Apr 61. Registered as 4X-ATA, 28 Mar 61. Delivered to El Al 22 Apr 61. Hijacked by Arab terrorists to Algeria, 23 Jul 68, but returned without damage to El Al, 31 Aug 68. Withdrawn from use Mar 84. Registration canceled 3 Sep 84. Broken up at Ben-Gurion Airport Jul 84. Airframe saved and (with a different cockpit) used at Ben-Gurion as an El Al training and instruction center. Original cockpit saved and now on display aboard the aircraft carrier *U.S.S. Intrepid* museum, New York City.

4X-ATB 707-458 MSN: 18071/LN 216
Ordered 25 Mar 60. Registered as 4X-ATB in name of El Al, 28 Mar 61. First flight 3 Jun 61. Delivered to El Al 7 Jun 61. Survived a foiled attempted hijack by Arab terrorists, 6 Sep 70. Leased to Arkia 1 Apr 84–13 Jul 86. Last commercial service 6 Jul 86. Registered to Boeing as N32824, 2 Sep 86. Canceled from Israeli registry 20 Nov 86 and delivered to Lufthansa 20 Nov 86 for museum purposes, after being re-registered in Frankfurt as N130KR (U.S. registration) 9 Oct 86 for purposes of ferry flight to Berlin and repainted in old Lufthansa 707 colors. Delivered 22 Nov 86 to City of Berlin at Berlin's Tegel Airport for preservation at the airport. Aircraft now wears German registration "D-ABOC".

4X-ATC 707-458 MSN: 18357/LN 272
Ordered Feb 61. First flight 9 Feb 62. Delivered to El Al and registered as 4X-ATC, 13 Feb 62. Israeli registration canceled 29 Jan 80.

To Zaire Aero Service as 9Q-CPM, 14 Feb 80. Re-registered 9Q-CWR to Wolf Aviation, Nov 83, and to R. Waynns, 1985. Withdrawn from use following landing accident at Kinshasa, Jul 84.

4X-ATÐ 707-331B MSN: 18985/LN 496
First flight 20 Apr 66. Delivered to Trans World Airlines 21 May 66 as N18709. Purchased by El Al, and registered as 4X-ATD, 23 Apr 82. Delivered to El Al 26 Apr 82. Leased to Arkia 1 Apr 85. Returned to El Al and registration canceled 29 Jan 89, as sold to Hartford Power Systems, Inc., 26 Jan 89. Last service with El Al, 29 Jan 89, Tel Aviv—Rome. Re-registered N707HP, 8 Feb 89, and ferried to U.S. for USAF KC-135E parts.

4X-ATR 707-358B MSN: 19004/LN 459
Ordered Sep 64. Registered as 4X-ATR to El Al 30 Oct 65. First flight 10 Dec 65. Delivered to El Al 7 Jan 66. Leased to Flying Tiger Line 7 Jan 66 as N317F, and wet-leased (with crew) back to El Al. Reverted to El Al 3 Oct 66 as 4X-ATR. Damaged in terrorist attack at Athens, 26 Dec 68, and repaired. Leased Aug 81 to Sun d'Or. Reverted to El Al 1 May 82, still as 4X-ATR. Leased to Arkia 6 Jan 87.

Returned to El Al, and last service Madrid—Tel Aviv 14 Apr 88, as sold to Jet Aviation Components and Aircraft. Israeli registration canceled 15 Apr 88.

Re-registered N53302 and ferried Tel Aviv—Brussels, 9 May 88. Re-registered in Iceland as TF-AYG, withdrawn from use and stored at Brussels in 1988.

4X-ATS 707-358B MSN: 19502/LN 551
Ordered Jul 66. Registered as 4X-ATS to El Al 17 Jan 67. First flight 23 Jan 67. Delivered to El Al 2 Feb 67. Leased to Arkia 24 Apr 87. Returned to El Al 7 Oct 88. Registration canceled 20 Nov 88. Sold to Omega Air as N898WA but NTU. Re-registered as 4X-ATS to Israel Aircraft Industries 29 Jan 89. Registration canceled 23 May 89 and finally sold to Omega Air as N898WA.

To USAF for KC-135E program.

4X-ATT 707-358B MSN: 20097/LN 779
Ordered Oct 67. Registered as 4X-ATT to El Al 1 Aug 68. First flight 15 Jan 69. Delivered to El Al 22 Jan 69. Registered as 4X-ATT, 29 Jan 69. Leased to Arkia 11 Apr 88. Returned to El Al 31 May 88. Sold to Jet Aviation of America, and Israeli registration canceled, 9 Jun 88.

Withdrawn from use and stored at Brussels Jun 88. Re-registered in Iceland as TF-AYF. In USA Jan 90, possibly for KC-135E program.

4X-ATX 707-358C (convertible, passenger/cargo) MSN: 20122/LN 807
Ordered Oct 67. Registered as 4X-ATU to El Al 1 Aug 68, but NTU. Re-registered as 4X-ATX, 9 Jan 69. First flight 6 May 69. Delivered to El Al 15 May 69. Leased to Arkia 12 Oct 86–5 Jan 87. Returned to El Al and used as freighter, 5 Jan–20 Apr 87. Leased to Arkia 20 Apr 87. Returned to El Al, and hush-kitted in U.S., 4 Jan–12 Feb 88. Leased back to Arkia 14 Feb 88. Current.

4X-ATY 707-358C (H) (convertible, passenger/cargo) MSN: 20301/LN 835
Ordered Oct 68. First flight 20 Jan 70. Delivered to El Al, and registered as 4X-ATY, 28 Jan 70. First 707 built with Boeing Carousel III inertial navigation system. Leased 1 May 82 to Sun d'Or. Returned to El Al 7 Jul 86 and used as freighter through 25 Dec 87. Leased to Arkia 9 Mar 88.

Leased Boeing 707s

PP-VJB 707-441 MSN: 17906/LN 129
First flight 2 Jun 60. Delivered to VARIG (Brazil) 15 Jun 60. Leased to El Al Dec 60–May 61. Operated first pure-jet service by El Al, 8 Jan 61.

N373WA 707-373C MSN: 18582/LN 344
First flight 26 Jun 63. Delivered to World Airways 16 Jul 63. Leased to El Al, May 65–Nov 65. Filled in while El Al awaited delivery of its fourth 707, 4X-ATR.

N324F 707-349C MSN: 19354/LN 503
First flight 9 Jun 66. Delivered to Flying Tiger Line 21 Jun 66. Wet-leased (with crew) to El Al, 1 Apr 68–Aug 68.

N325F 707-349C MSN: 19355/LN 553
First flight 2 Feb 67. Delivered to Flying Tiger Line 6 Feb 67. Wet-leased (with crew) to El Al, Aug 68–Dec 68. Originally leased to fill in for the El Al 707 (4X-ATA) hijacked to Algeria.

G-AYBJ 707-321 MSN: 17597/LN 68
First flight 18 Sep 59. Delivered to Pan American as N719PA, 2 Oct 59. Leased by El Al from British Midland Airways, in partial El Al colors, Aug 72–9 Sep 72 (see photo page 85).

4X-BYM 707-329 MSN: 18460/LN 328
First flight 9 Jan 63. Delivered to SABENA as OO-SJG, 19 Jan 63. Leased by El Al from Israel Aircraft Industries, 1977.

N792FA 707-138B MSN: 17701/LN 60
First flight 21 Aug 59. Delivered to QANTAS 4 Sep 59. Leased by El Al from F. B. Ayer & Associates via Israel Aircraft Industries, 13 Mar 78 -1 Nov 78.

4X-ATE 707-328B MSN: 18456/LN 325
First flight 3 Dec 62. Delivered to Air France 15 Dec 62 as F-BHSV *Château de Vincennes*. Sold to TRATCO Apr 83. Leased to El Al as 4X-ATE, 15 Jul 83. Israeli registration canceled 6 Nov 83 as returned to TRATCO and stored at

N792FA at Copenhagen, August 1978. (Tommy Lakmaker via John Wegg)

4X-ATE at Paris (Orly), September 1983. (Jacques Guillem)

4X-ATG at Tel Aviv. (Noam Hartoch)

4X-ABA at Paris (Orly), July 1962. (Gordon Reid)

4X-ABB at Bucharest (Otopeni), 1970s. (El Al)

EI-ALA at London (Heathrow), January 1969. (B. N. Stainer via Peter R. Keating)

4X-AXA at London (Heathrow), 1973, with Official Carrier stickers for Israel's 25th anniversary. (Peter R. Keating)

4X-AXB at Amsterdam, 9 August 1984. (J. W. Bossenbroek)

4X-AXC at Johannesburg, September 1973. (Peter R. Keating)

4X-AXD. March 1977, with small "CAL" titles on forward fuselage. (Bernd-Olaf Hagedorn via John Wegg)

Luxembourg. Sold to AirXport Oct 84 for Trans European Airways and broken up for spares at Brussels Nov 89.

4X-ATG 707-323B MSN: 20174/LN 808
First flight 13 May 69. Delivered to American Airlines as N8435, 23 May 69. Leased to South Pacific Island Airways 20 Mar 81 then purchased by SPIA and re-registered N145SP 1 Nov 83. Sold to Jetran Inc. Mar 88 and leased to Arkia 14 Dec 89. Subleased at times from Arkia to El Al.

BOEING 720

4X-ABA 720-058B MSN: 18424/LN 281
Ordered May 61. First flight 16 Mar 62. Registered as 4X-ABA to El Al, 19 Oct 61. Delivered to El Al 23 Mar 62. Sold to Jet Power Inc., 21 Nov 80, and registered in U.S. as N8498S. Canceled from Israeli registry 24 Oct 80 and converted to 720-058B (F) Nov 80.

To James A. Molans Feb 83, Melvin Kessler Jan 84, Boeing Military Airplane Company 27 Aug 84, USAF 27 Aug 84. Stored at Kirkland AFB, NM, then ferried to Davis-Monthan AFB, AZ, for spares use for the KC-135E program.

4X-ABB 720-058B MSN: 18425/LN 290
Ordered May 61. Registered as 4X-ABB to El Al, 19 Oct 61. First flight 23 Apr 62. Delivered to El Al 30 Apr 62. Damaged in terrorist attack at Zürich, 18 Feb 69, and repaired. Sold to Jet Power Inc. 12 Dec 80, and registered in U.S. as N8498T. Canceled from Israeli registry 24 Oct 80.

Then to Central Airlines as N8498T, Dec 80. Re-registered N4228G to Jet Power Inc. Apr 81. Then to Global International Airways 20 Apr 83 and Boeing Military Airplane Company 20 Jul 83. Withdrawn from use and stored at Davis-Monthan AFB, AZ, Jul 83.

Leased Boeing 720s

EI-ALA 720-048 MSN: 18041/LN 172
First flight 14 Oct 60. Delivered to Aer Lingus, 25 Oct 60. Leased to El Al, 1 Nov 68–27 Apr 69.

OO-TEB 720-048 MSN: 18043/LN 188
First flight 22 Mar 61. Delivered to Aer Lingus, 6 Apr 61. Leased by El Al from Trans European Airways, 1 Mar—Aug 77 and 30 Sep–Oct 78.

BOEING 747

Note: The Series -200C is a convertible version of the basic -200B version with an upward opening nose cargo door and redesigned interior permitting all-passenger, all-cargo, or mixed (Combi) passenger/cargo configurations. A side cargo door is optional and is not installed on El Al's -200Cs. The Series -200F is a pure-cargo aircraft with an upward opening nose cargo door. A side cargo door is also optional and is fitted to El Al's -200F. The -100 (F) is an all-cargo conversion of a -100 passenger 747 and features a side cargo door but no nose cargo door.

4X-AXA 747-258B MSN: 20135/LN 140
First flight 15 May 71. Delivered to El Al, and registered as 4X-AXA, 26 May 71. Current.

4X-AXB 747-258B MSN: 20274/LN 164
First flight 29 Oct 71. Delivered to El Al, and registered as 4X-AXB, 22 Nov 71. Current.

4X-AXC 747-258B MSN: 20704/LN 212
First flight 5 Apr 73 with test registration N1799B (this was first -200B with JT9D-7A engines and a MGTOW of 356,070kg/785,000lb). Delivered to El Al and registered as 4X-AXC, 18 Apr 73. This was the 200th 747 to be delivered by Boeing (although the 212th built). Current.

4X-AXD 747-258C MSN: 21190/LN 272
First flight 22 Oct 75. Delivered to El Al 31 Dec 75. Registered as 4X-AXD, 11 Apr 76. Current.

4X-AXF 747-258C MSN: 21594/LN 327
First flight 7 Jun 78. Delivered to El Al 16 Jun 78. Registered as 4X-AXF 17 Jun 78, and first arrived Tel Aviv 17 Jun 78. At times appears in C.A.L. (Cargo Air Lines) livery. Current.

4X-AXG 747-258F MSN: 21737/LN 362
First flight 7 Mar 79. Delivered to El Al 19 Mar 79. First

arrived Tel Aviv 20 Mar 79. Current.

4X-AXH 747-258B MSN: 22254/LN 418
First flight 6 Dec 79. Delivered to El Al 21 Dec 79. Current.

4X-AXQ 747-238B MSN 20841/LN 233
First flight 28 Feb 74. Delivered to QANTAS 22 Mar 74 as VH-EBG *City of Hobart*.
    Purchased by El Al, registered 4X-AXQ 7 May 88, and delivered 8 May 88. Leased to QANTAS, and re-registered as VH-EBG, 5 Sep 88. Re-registered as 4X-AXQ, 23 May 89. Returned by QANTAS to El Al 2 Jun 89. Current.

4X-AXZ 747-124 (F) MSN: 19735/LN 64
Delivered to Continental Airlines 12 Aug 70 as a Series-124, N26863. Sold to Boeing 30 Oct 75 and converted to freighter (-124 (F)). To Imperial Iranian Air Force 30 Oct 75 with serial 5-291, later 5-8112. To Boeing as N8289V, 11 Apr 77.
    Purchased by El Al, 21 Jun 77, and registered as 4X-AXZ. Leased to AVIANCA, and registered in Colombia as HK-2400, 21 Jul 81. Reverted to El Al, and re-registered as 4X-AXZ, Jul 82. Operated by El Al in AVIANCA colors for some time before being repainted in El Al livery. Current.

Leased Boeing 747s (in chronological order)

N748WA 747-273C MSN: 20652/LN 211
Delivered to World Airways 25 May 73, as N748WA. Leased to El Al Jan 13–Mar 77.

N801FT 747-123 (F) MSN: 20101/LN 57
Delivered to American Airlines 16 Jul 70, as N9662. Sold to Flying Tiger Line and registered N801FT, 24 Sep 74, after trade-in by American Airlines to Boeing, and conversion to freighter. Leased to El Al, 15 Aug 77–1 Jul 78.

N93117 747-131 MSN: 20322/LN 113
Delivered to Trans World Airlines 24 May 71, as N93117. Sold to GATX Leasing 1 Jun 86. Leased to El Al 8 Mar—24 Apr 88.

BOEING 737-200

4X-ABN 737-258 (Advanced) MSN: 22856/LN 910
First flight 2 Sep 82. Registered to El Al as 4X-ABN, 13 Jan 83. Delivered to El Al 18 Jan 83. Leased to GPA/LAN Chile as CC-CJK, 10 Mar 88. Returned to El Al as 4X-ABN, 23 Dec 88. Leased to Arkia 4 Jan 89. Current.

4X-ABO 737-258 (Advanced) MSN: 22857/LN 919
First flight 11 Oct 82. Delivered to El Al 18 Jan 83. Stationed at Montreal 3 Jul–11 Sep 87. Leased to GPA/LAN Chile as CC-CJM, 10 Mar 88. Returned to El Al as 4X-ABO, 15 Dec 88. Leased to Arkia 3 Jan 89. Current.

Leased Boeing 737s

4X-ABL 737-2M8 (Advanced) MSN: 21736/LN 557
First flight 16 Feb 79. Delivered 1 Mar 79 to Trans European Airways as OO-TEL *Ilana*. Leased to El Al, 1 Oct 80 and registered as 4X-ABL, 3 Oct 80. Returned to TEA as OO-TEL, and Israeli registration canceled, 30 Jun 82.

4X-ABM 737-2M8 (Advanced) MSN: 22090/LN 664
First flight 2 May 80. Delivered 19 May 80 to Trans European Airways as OO-TEO *Jonathan*. Leased to El Al, 1 Oct 80 and registered as 4X-ABM, 3 Oct 80. Last commercial flight with El Al 13 Sep 82. Returned to TEA and Israeli registration canceled 30 Sep 82.

BOEING 767

4X-EAA 767-258 MSN: 22972/LN 62
First flight, as N6066Z, 23 Jun 83. Registered to Government of Israel 12 Jul 83. Delivered to El Al 18 Jul 83. First arrived in Tel Aviv 18 Jul 83. Current.

4X-EAB 767-258 MSN: 22973/LN 68
First flight, as N6018N, 30 Aug 83. Registered to Government of Israel 12 Jul 83. Delivered to El Al 13 Sep 83. Current.

4X-AXZ at Los Angeles, February 1985. (John Wegg)

4X-AXF at Amsterdam, November 1978 with State of Israel 30th Anniversary markings. (Bob Neumeier)

4X-AXG at Amsterdam, June 1979. (Bob Neumeier via John Wegg)

4X-AXH at Paris (Orly), August 1980. (Jacques Guillem)

4X-AXQ at Paris (Orly), August 1988. (Jacques Guillem)

VH-EBG (4X-AXQ) at Sydney. (Rob Finlayson)

4X-AXZ in AVIANCA colors at Amsterdam, August 1982.
(Bob Neumeier)

N801FT at London (Heathrow), 1978. (Peter Jary via John Wegg)

N93117 at Paris (Orly), April 1988. (Jacques Guillem)

4X-ABL in TEA colors. (BIAF—Israel Aviation & Space Magazine)

4X-ABM at Paris (Orly), January 1981, in TEA colors. (Jacques Guillem)

4X-EAC 767-258 (ER) MSN: 22974/LN 86
First flight, as N6018N, 6 Mar 84. Registered to Government of Israel 26 Mar 84. Delivered to El Al 26 Mar 84. Current.

4X-EAD 767-258 (ER) MSN: 22975/LN 89
First flight, as N6046P, 10 Apr 84. Registered to Government of Israel 1 Jun 84. Delivered to El Al 1 Jun 84. Current.

BOEING 757

4X-EBL 757-258 MSN: 23917/LN 152 First flight 6 Nov 87. Registered to, and delivered to El Al, 25 Nov 87, Fleet Number 501. Current.

4X-EBM 757-258 MSN: 23918/LN 156
First flight 4 Dec 87. Registered to, and delivered to El Al, 17 Dec 87, Fleet Number 502. Current.

4X-EBR 757-258 MSN: 24254/LN 185
First flight 6 Jul 88. Registered to El Al 17 Jul 88, and delivered to El Al 19 Jul 88, Fleet Number 503. Current.

Leased Boeing 757-200s

G-BPEA 757-236 MSN: 24370/LN 218
Leased from North American Airlines for New York—Los Angeles services 22 Jan 90–Mar 90.

N757NA 757-23A MSN: 24567/LN 257
Leased from North American Airlines for U.S. and Canada connector services from 1 Mar 90. Named *Lisa Caroline.*

Other Aircraft Types Leased by El Al

Douglas DC-6

Oct 55	Aircraft leased from Alitalia for Tel Aviv—Rome—Paris—London route.
Dec 55–early 58	Aircraft leased at various times, probably from SABENA, for routes to Brussels, Amsterdam, and certain other European destinations.
Dec 55–Feb 56	Aircraft leased from Union Aeromaritime de Transports (UAT) of France for weekly Tel Aviv—Johannesburg route via North Africa.
Mar 56–1960	Aircraft leased from SABENA for weekly Tel Aviv—Johannesburg route via North Africa. In 1958, OO-AWW (MSN 43149) was leased from SABENA. Later replaced by DC-7Cs leased from SABENA.

Douglas DC-7C

1960–62	Aircraft leased from SABENA for weekly Tel Aviv—Johannesburg route via North Africa, replacing DC-6Bs.

Handley Page H.P.R. 7 Dart-Herald

1967	Wet-leased from Arkia for Tel Aviv—Nicosia service.

Convair 990A (Convair Model 30A-6)

HB-ICH MSN: 30-10-17
Leased by El Al early 1968.

McDonnell Douglas DC-9-81 (MD-81)

HB-INB MSN: 49101/LN 1051 Leased from Balair 13–23 Sep 82.

McDonnell Douglas DC-8

N6163A DC-8-63F (CF) MSN: 46062/LN 486
Leased from Airlift International 17 Jan–Mar 79.

HB-IDZ DC-8-63F (PF) MSN: 46074/LN 468
Leased from Balair 7–30 Oct 82.

McDonnell Douglas DC-10-30

PH-MBN DC-10-30F (CF) MSN: 46924/LN 218 Leased
from Martinair Holland 17–30 Sep 82.

HB-IHK DC-10-30 MSN: 46998/LN 267
Leased from Balair 8–29 Apr 84 and 4–21 Apr 85.

Boeing 727-100

1989- Wet-leased from Bradley Air Services/First Air,
Carp/Ottawa, Ontario, for Miami and Montreal
service from New York.

4X-ABN at Tel Aviv, January 1988. The aircraft displays the logo of the 40th anniversary of the State of Israel. (Marvin Goldman)

4X-ABO at Paris (Orly), May 1984. (John Wegg)

4X-EAA at Amsterdam. (El Al)

4X-EAB at Paris (Orly), April 1988, with State of Israel 40th anniversary sticker. (Jacques Guillem)

4X-EAD at Zürich. (Rob Finlayson)

4X-EAC at Los Angeles, 1989, with El Al 40th anniversary sticker. (Michael J. Chew)

4X-EBL on a pre-delivery test flight. (Boeing)

4X-EBM at Tel Aviv. (Noam Hartoch)

4X-EBR at Zürich, 6 February 1989, with El Al 40th anniversary sticker. (Lukas Lusser)

N90441 (4X-ACB) at London (Heathrow), 6 April 1950. (via John Havers)

4X-AQE (via John Havers)

4X-AKE at London (Heathrow), March 1956. (C. Holland via John Havers)

G-BPEA of North American Airlines (leased from Caledonian Airways), at Los Angeles, January 18, 1990. (Jukka Kauppinen)

ARKIA ISRAELI AIRLINES LTD. FLEET LIST

CURTISS C-46 COMMANDO

4X-ACT (4X-ALC) MSN: 30202 (see El Al section for further details)
To Arkia 11 Oct 49. Made first official flight to Eilat, in El Al markings, 28 Feb 50. Back to El Al as 4X-ALC, 17 Dec 50. Reverted to Arkia 27 Feb 55 as 4X-ALC. Registration canceled 17 Feb 56.

DE HAVILLAND D.H.89 DRAGON RAPIDE

4X-ACN MSN: 6399.
Ex-G-AFEN. Registered 21 Sep 39 as VQ-PAC. Impressed by RAF as Z7188, 1 Aug 40. Then to HK864, 17 Feb 42; TJ-AAI, 1946; G-AFEN, 21 Apr 47. To Israel Defense Forces as 1307 by Jun 49. Registered 4X-ACN to Arkia 4 Jul 49. Broken up at Lod, and registration canceled, 10 Jan 50.

4X-ACU MSN: 6806
Ex-RAF NR718. Registered as VQ-PAR to Aviron Dec 47. To Israel Defense Forces May 48. Registered as 4X-ACU in name of Aviron 13 Nov 49. Operated by Arkia upon its formation in 1950. Registered in name of Arkia as 4X-ACU, 9 Mar 53. Broken up between Aug–Dec 57, and registration canceled 18 Dec 57.

4X-AEH MSN: 6496
Ex-RAF X7323; G-AJFM; VP-KEE; Israel Defense Forces 1310. Registered to Arkia as 4X-AEH, 27 Nov 53. Written off following take-off accident at Lod, 1954. Registration canceled 2 Jul 54.

4X-AEI MSN: 6895
Ex-RAF NR831; PH-RAD; VP-KED; Israel Defense Forces 1306, 1948–Nov 53. Registered as 4X-AEI to Arkia, 27 Nov 53. Sold to Aeroservice Ltd. 11 Aug 55. Israeli registration canceled 19 Aug 55. Registered as G-ADYL, 22 Aug 55. Broken up at Luton, 1964.

BEECH 18 (TC-45G)

4X-ADQ C-45G-BH MSN: AF-126
Ex-USAF 51-11569. In Arkia service Apr 58–1963. Registered to El Al 3 Dec 57–13 Apr 58. Sold as N7208C, 17 Nov 63.

4X-ADS C-45G-BH MSN: AF-61
Ex-USAF 51-11504. In Arkia service Oct 58–1963. Registered to El Al 3 Dec 57–28 Jul 58. Sold as N7199C, 17 Nov 63.

Note: A photograph of a Beech 18 exists showing both 111504 and 4X-ADQ registrations; another photograph shows both 111504 and 4X-ADS registrations on the same aircraft.

DOUGLAS DC-3

4X-ACW C-47B-5-DK MSN: 14609/26054
Ex-USAAF 43-48793; HB-IRD (Swissair); Israel Defense Forces 1408/4X-FAH. Registered 4X-ACW to Arkia 9 Oct 55. Withdrawn from use, and registration canceled, 26 Jun 66. To Lod Airport for fire practice.

4X-ADA C-47B-15-DK MSN: 15347/26792
Ex-USAAF 43-49531; NC63186; Israel Defense Forces 1407. Registered 4X-ADA to Arkia 9 Oct 55. Withdrawn from use, and registration canceled, 20 Jan 65.

4X-AEO C-47-DL MSN: 6227
Ex-USAAF 42-5639; RAF FD773; BOAC G-AGGB. Following intermediate owners, to Israel Defense Forces as 4X-FAI, 12 Nov 50. To El Al as 4X-ATA, 22 Feb 51. Probably then to Israel Defense Forces. To Arkia as 4X-AEO, 2 Apr 57. To Israel Aircraft Industries, and registration canceled, 4 Sep 68. To Lod Airport for fire practice, Jul 71.

4X-AES C-47A-1-DK MSN: 11923
Ex-USAAF 42-92154; RAF FL562; HB-ATO; NC74136; OO-AFB. Then to Israel Defense Forces. Registered to Arkia as 4X-AES, 2 Apr 57. Withdrawn from use, and registration canceled, 26 Jun 66.

4X-AEZ C-47-DL MSN: 6224
Ex-USAAF 42-5636; RAF FD770; G-AGFY; ZS-DAH. Then to Israel Defense Forces as 1402/4X-FAH. Leased by Arkia as 4X-AEZ, 26 Jan 61. Registration canceled 4 Dec 61. To Israel Aircraft Industries as 4X-AOE, 14 Dec 61. To Israel Defense Forces as 4X-FAH, 25 Jan 62.

4X-ASR C-47A-50-DL MSN: 10146
Ex-USAAF 42-24284; ZS-AVM. Then to Israel Defense Forces. Registered as 4X-ASR to Arkia 9 Jun 61. Registration canceled, and to Israel Aircraft Industries, 4 Sep 68. To Lod Airport for fire practice Jul 71.

G-AMGD C-47A-30-DL MSN: 9628
Ex-USAAF 42-23766; RAF FD906; SAAF 6802; ZS-DDV; G-AJXL. Leased by Arkia from British European Airways, summer 1960.

G-ANAF C-47B-35-DK MSN: 16688/33436
Ex-USAAF 44-77104, RAF KP220. Leased by Arkia from BKS Air Transport, 1956.

HANDLEY PAGE H.P.R. 7 DART-HERALD

4X-AHN Series 209 MSN: 197
Registered 21 Jul 68. First flight 13 Aug 68. Delivered to Arkia 16 Aug 68. Delivered to Field Aircraft, 6 Apr 78 as G-BFRK. Israeli registration canceled 9 Apr 78. Then to Express Air Freight; Express Air Services; Jersey European Airways; Soc. Columbia as I-ZERD, Dec 84; Aligiulia Mar 86; Channel Express as G-GNSY, 3 Jun 87.

4X-AHO Series 209 MSN: 195
Registered 4 Apr 68. First flight 5 Apr 68. Delivered to Arkia 10 Apr 68. Delivered to Field Aircraft 30 Mar 78 as G-BFRJ. Registration canceled 2 Apr 78. Then to Express Air Freight; Express Air Services; Air Ecosse; Express Air Services; Jersey European Airways; Soc. Columbia as I-ZERC Mar 84; Aligiulia Mar 86; Channel Express as G-CEXP, 29 Oct 87.

4X-AHR Series 209 MSN: 183
Registered 6 Jan 64. First flight 26 Mar 64. Delivered to Arkia 17 Apr 64. Registration canceled 30 May 73. Delivered to British Island Airways, Jun 73, as G-BAZJ. To Air UK 15 May 80.

4X-AHS Series 209 MSN: 174
Registered 6 Jan 64. First flight 18 Apr 64. Delivered to Arkia 18 May 64. Then to Field Aviation 28 Jul 77 as G-BEZB. Israeli registration canceled 1 Aug 77. Then to Intra Airways and operated in Express Air Freight livery (later Jersey European Airways). Withdrawn from use at Hurn, Dec 87.

4X-AHT Series 209 MSN: 189
First flight 12 May 65. Delivered to Arkia 28 Jul 65. Registered 30 Jul 65. Then to Field Aviation as G-ATDS, 28 Jul 77. Israeli registration canceled 1 Aug 77. Then to Intra Airways 1 Aug 77, and operated in Express Air Freight livery (later Jersey European Airways).

D-BEBE Series 213 MSN: 179
Leased from Bavaria Fluggesellschaft 16 Nov 67–16 Apr 68 and 24 Nov 68–13 Nov 70.

VICKERS VISCOUNT

4X-AVA Series 814D MSN: 370
Ex-D-ANAC; G-AYOX. Registered as 4X-AVA, 7 Apr 71. In Arkia service 8 Apr 71–29 Mar 78. Registration canceled 2 Apr 78.

4X-AVB Series 833 MSN: 424
Ex-G-APTB. Registered as 4X-AVB, 19 Dec 69. Purchased by Arkia from British United Airways 20 Dec 69. Sold by Arkia to Go Group, 25 May 82. Broken up and major parts flown to England, Apr 89.

4X-AVC Series 833 MSN: 425
Ex-G-APTC. Registered as 4X-AVC, 15 Oct 69. In Arkia service 16–26 Oct 69. Landing gear collapsed while taxiing at Lod, and written off; registration canceled, 26 Oct 69.

4X-AVD Series 833 MSN: 426
Ex-G-APTD; JY-ADC; G-APTD. Registered as 4X-AVD, 21 Feb 70. Purchased by Arkia from British Midland Airways 24 Feb 70. Sold by Arkia to Go Group, 6 Apr 83.

4X-AVE Series 831 MSN: 403
Ex-G-APNE; JY-ADA; G-APNE. Registered as 4X-AVE, 19 Sep 72. Purchased by Arkia from British Midland Airways 21 Sep 72. Sold by Arkia to Go Group, 17 May 82.

4X-AVF Series 831 MSN: 402
Ex-G-16-20; G-APND; JY-ADB; G-APND. Registered as 4X-AVF, 5 Dec 73. Purchased by Arkia from British Midland Airways 21 Dec 73. Sold by Arkia to Go Group, 25 May 82. Broken up at Ben-Gurion Airport, early Apr 89, and cockpit and other major parts flown to England.

4X-AVG Series 831 MSN: 419
Ex-ST-AAN; G-ASED; EC-WZK; EC-AZK; G-ASED. Registered as 4X-AVG, 6 Mar 74. Purchased by Arkia from Alidair 7 Mar 74. Sold by Arkia to Go Group, 17 May 82.

4X-AVH Series 814D MSN: 344
Ex-D-ANIZ; G-BAPG. Leased by Arkia from Intra Airways, 20 Sep 79. Transferred by Arkia to Jersey European Airways 18 Dec 79.

BAC ONE-ELEVEN

4X-BAR Series 520FN MSN: 230
Ex-PP-SDR; G-BEKA; G-16-22. Registered as 4X-BAR, 27 Jul 77. Purchased by Arkia from British Aircraft Corp. 16 Aug 77. Sold by Arkia to Dan-Air as G-BEKA, 12 Sep 79.

4X-BAS Series 523FJ MSN: 199
Ex-G-AXLM; PP-SDV; G-AXLM; G-16-23. Registered as 4X-BAS, 5 Apr 78. Leased by Arkia from British Aircraft Corp. 20 May 78–Sep 79. Purchased by Philippine Airlines as RP-C1194, 7 Jul 80.

BOEING 707
(See El Al Boeing 707 fleet histories for further details).

4X-ATB Leased from El Al, 1 Apr 84–13 Jul 86.

4X-ATD Leased from El Al, 1 Apr 85–1988.

4X-ATG Leased from Jetran Inc., 14 Dec 89.

4X-ATR Leased from El Al, 6 Jan 87–early 1988.

4X-ATS Leased from El Al, 24 Apr 87–7 Oct 88.

4X-ATT Leased from El Al, 11 Apr 88–31 May 88.

4X-ATX Leased from El Al, 12 Oct 86–5 Jan 87; 20 Apr 87–Dec 87. Returned to El Al. Leased back to Arkia 14 Feb 88.

4X-ATY Leased from El Al, 9 Mar 88–current.

EI-ASO 707-349C MSN: 19354/LN 503
Leased from Aer Lingus in full Arkia colors, 15 Dec 84–24 Feb 85.

BOEING 727

4X-BAE Series 727-95 MSN: 19249/LN 304
Delivered to Northeast Airlines as N1633, 15 Aug 66. Then G-BFGM and HK-2960X. Leased by Arkia from Aeron Aviation Corp., New York, 7 May 84. Named *City of Jerusalem*. Returned as N727ZV, 14 Jun 85.

BOEING 737

4X-BAA 737-210 (Advanced) MSN: 21820/LN 578
Ex-N491WC Wien Air Alaska. Acquired by Arkia from Wien 8 May 81 and immediately leased to Air Berlin as N491WC. Returned to Arkia as N491WC 1 Dec 81. Registered to Arkia as 4X-BAA, 1 Apr 82. Sold to Dan-Air as G-BKNH, 30 Mar 83.

4X-BAB 737-2E7 (Advanced) MSN: 22875/LN 917 First flight 1 Oct 82 as N45708. Delivered by Boeing to Arkia 2 Mar 83. Sold to Dan-Air 22 Mar 84 and registered G-BMDF.

4X-BAC 737-2E7 (Advanced) MSN: 22876/LN 922 First flight 22 Oct 82 as N4571A. Delivered by Boeing to Arkia 15 Mar 83. Sold to Dan-Air as G-BLDE, 22 Dec 83. Leased by Arkia as 4X-BAC, 26 Mar 84. Returned to Dan-Air 22 Apr 84.

4X-AVB (via Marvin G. Goldman)

4X-BAA (via Marvin G. Goldman)

Note: In addition to the above, Arkia has operated several types of small aircraft, including SA226/227 Metro II/III; Piper PA-31-350 Navajo Chieftain; BN-2A Islander; Cessna 337; Piper PA-28/-32 Cherokee/Cherokee Six; Grand Commander 680FL; and DHC-6-300 Twin Otter (4X-AHZ). Arkia also leased a Fokker F27-500 (MSN 10687, 9Q-CBD), 27 Mar—11 Sep 87.

DE HAVILLAND CANADA DHC-7 (Dash 7)

4X-AHA Series 102 MSN: 60
First flight 1 Sep 81 as C-GEWQ. Delivered to Arkia as 4X-AHA 10 Oct 81.

4X-AHB Series 102 MSN: 64
First flight 23 Oct 81 as C-GFCF. Delivered to Arkia as 4X-AHB 6 Nov 81. Sold to City Express as C-GGXS, 6 Jul 84.

4X-AHC Series 102 MSN: 82
First flight 29 Apr 82 as C-GFUM. Delivered to Arkia as 4X-AHC 14 May 82.

4X-AHD Series 102 MSN: 55
Delivered to Maersk Air as OY-MBD; then N8102N. Delivered to Arkia as N8102N, 17 Jun 89. Registered as 4X-AHD, while still in Maersk Air colors, 23 Jun 89.

4X-AHI Series 103 MSN: 8
Ex-Canadian Air Forces Model CC-132 132001, then C-GJSZ. Delivered to Arkia as 4X-AHI, 15 Aug 87.

HELICOPTERS

(operated by Arkia/Aliza, a joint company in which Arkia and French aero-engine manufacturer Turboméca each had a 50% interest).

4X-BAA Sud Aviation SE 3130 Alouette II MSN: 1223
In Arkia/Aliza service 5 Jun 59–17 May 61.

4X-BAB Sud Aviation SE 3130 Alouette II MSN: 1222
In Arkia/Aliza service 13 May 59–17 May 61.

4X-BAC Sud Aviation SE 3130 Alouette II MSN: 1224
In Arkia/Aliza service 13 May 59–17 May 61.

BRITISH MANDATE PALESTINE CIVIL REGISTER (July 1937—May 1948)

PALESTINE AIRWAYS, LTD.

VQ-PAA Short S.16 Scion MSN: PA.1001
(5-seat, 2 x 90hp Pobjoy Niagara engines) Registered 16 Jul 37. Impressed by RAF as Z7189, 1 Aug 40. Crashed on take-off with excessive cargo, and broken up, 15 Apr 41.

VQ-PAB Short S.16 Scion MSN: PA.1002
Registered 16 Jul 37. Impressed by RAF as Z7190, 1 Aug 40. Crashed after starboard propeller disintegrated and hit fuselage, and broken up, at Ein-Shemer, 24 Dec 42.

VQ-PAC De Havilland D.H.89A Dragon Rapide MSN: 6399
Ex-G-AFEN. Registered as VQ-PAC 21 Sep 39. Impressed by RAF as Z7188, 1 Aug 40. Then to HK864, 17 Feb 42; TJ-AAI, 1946 (NTU); G-AFEN, 21 Apr 47; to Israeli Defense Forces, serial 1307 by Jun 49. Registered 4X-ACN to Arkia 4 Jul 49. Broken up at Lod, and registration canceled, 10 Jan 50.

VQ-PAD Short S.22 Scion Senior MSN: S.810
(9-seats)
Ex-G-AECU. Registered as VQ-PAD 16 Dec 39. Impressed by RAF as Z7187, 1 Aug 40. Registration canceled 7 Sep 42. Later re-serialled as HK868.

AVIRON

VQ-PAE RWD 15 MSN: 177
(Polish 5-seat high-wing monoplane)
Ex-SP-BFX. Registered as VQ-PAE to Aviron 14 Dec 39. Burnt by Arab terrorists at Lydda Airport, and written off, 13 Apr 48.

VQ-PAG RWD 8 MSN: 179
(Polish 2-seat parasol monoplane)
Ex-SP-BCE. Arrived in Israel Jun 37. Registered 10 Jan 40. Damaged in landing accident, 1946. Rebuilt with parts from RWD 8 SP-BLL in 1946/47. Withdrawn from use 1948.

VQ-PAH Taylorcraft A MSN: 627
(U.S. 2-seat, 55 hp Lycoming, high wing monoplane)
Registered to Palestine Flying Service Apr 39. Sold to Aviron about Aug 39. Withdrawn from use 1940.

VQ-PAI Taylorcraft BL MSN: 1156
Ex-NC22218. Registered to Palestine Flying Service 8 Apr 39. Sold to Aviron about Aug 39. To Israeli Defense Forces May 48. Withdrawn from use 1949/50.

VQ-PAJ Taylorcraft BL MSN: 1155
Ex-NC22217. Registered to Palestine Flying Service 8 Apr 39. Sold to Aviron about Aug 39. To Israeli Defense Forces May 48. Withdrawn from use 1949/50.

VQ-PAK RWD 8 MSN: 178
Ex-SP-BLK. Registered VQ-PAK to Aviron 10 Jun 39. To Israeli Defense Forces May 48. Withdrawn from use 1950/51.

VQ-PAL RWD 13 MSN: 165
(Polish 3-seat high-wing monoplane)
Ex-SP-BFR. Registered VQ-PAL to Aviron 10 Jun 39. To Israeli Defense Forces May 48. Withdrawn from use 1950/51.

VQ-PAM RWD 13 MSN: 166
Ex-SP-BFM. Registered VQ-PAM to Aviron 20 Feb 40. To Israeli Defense Forces May 48. Destroyed at Sde Dov by an Egyptian Spitfire attack on the airfield, 15 May 48.

VQ-PAN De Havilland D.H.82A Tiger Moth MSN: 3314
Purchased in England by representatives of Jewish agencies in Palestine and registered in name of Yitzhak Chizik as G-ACYN, late 1934. Operated by Aviron as G-ACYN starting 17 Mar 38. VQ-PAN registration allocated, but NTU as aircraft crashed near Afiqim, May 39. Aircraft then broken up.

VQ-PAO Miles M.3A Falcon Major MSN: 181
Ex-G-ADHH. Registered VQ-PAO to Aviron Mar 40. Sold in Egypt as SU-ADA. Crashed at Marsa-Aalem, and written off, 12 Feb 48.

VQ-PAP Zlin XII-II MSN: 258
(Czech 2-seat low-wing monoplane)
Ex-SU-AAZ. Registered VQ-PAP in name of Benjamin Kahane on behalf of the Etzel Organization, 1941. Operated by *Sherut Ha'avir* from 30 Oct 47. Damaged on landing and written off, Bnei Brak, 5 May 48.

VQ-PAQ Benes-Mraz Be.550 Bibi MSN: 9
(Czech 2-seat low-wing monoplane)
Ex-SU-ACD. Registered VQ-PAQ to Aviron Jun 42. Crashed and written off, Beit Yitzchak, 29 Nov 47.

VQ-PAR D.H.89A Dragon Rapide/Dominie MSN: 6806
Ex-RAF NR718. Registered VQ-PAR to Aviron Dec 47. To Israel Defense Forces May 48. Registered 4X-ACU to Aviron 13 Nov 49. Operated by Arkia upon its formation in 1950. Registered to Arkia as 4X-ACU, 9 Mar 53. Withdrawn from use 1954, and parts used to rebuild 4X-AEI of Arkia. Registration canceled 18 Dec 57.

VQ-PAS Auster J/1 Autocrat MSN: 2024
Ex-G-AHHV. Registered VQ-PAS to Aviron 11 May 46. Operated by *Sherut Ha'avir*, Nov 47–May 48. To Israel Defense Forces May 48, as no. 32; 0115 from Nov 48. Left military service in 1951-52.

VQ-PAT De Havilland Canada DH.82C Tiger Moth MSN: 1747
Ex-RCAF 8945, CF-CJA. Registered VQ-PAT to Aviron Aug 47. To *Sherut Ha'avir*, 10 Nov 47. Hit by anti-aircraft fire and crashed near Maale Hachamisha, 28 Mar 48.

VQ-PAU De Havilland Canada DH.82C Tiger Moth MSN: 1653
Ex-RCAF 8851, CF-CTB. Registered VQ-PAU to Aviron Aug 47. To *Sherut Ha'avir*, 10 Nov 47. Hit by anti-aircraft fire and crashed near Ramat Rachel, May 48.

VQ-PAV Republic RC-3 Seabee MSN: 1018
Ex-NC6731K. Registered Mar 48 to J. Sczupak. To Israel Defense Forces 14 Apr 48. Damaged, Sde Dov, 15 May 48. VQ-P registration NTU. Destroyed at Sde Dov by an Egyptian Spitfire attack on the airfield, 15 May 48.

Other Commercial Aviation

VQ-PAF Fokker F.XVIII MSN: 5310
Ex-PH-AIQ; OK-AIQ. Registered 8 Jan 39 to Hevra Avirit Miskharit which transported fresh fish from the Red Sea on the route Aqaba, Transjordan, to Lydda. Damaged on landing at Lydda Jan 39, but repaired and resumed flights. Damaged again on landing at Lydda later in 1939, and written off.

APPENDIX IV: El Al Insignia Through the Years

Three symbols stand out among El Al's insignia—(1) the flying six-pointed Star of David (*magen david*); (2) the El Al block with the slanted left side of the the "A"; and (3) the linear El Al logo in English and Hebrew usually followed by the Israeli flag.

Flying Six-pointed Star of David

The six-pointed Star of David with the flying wings was adopted by El Al as part of the livery of its first purchased aircraft, the DC-4s 4X-ACC and ACD, in March 1949. The symbol looks like the following, and often appears with the airline name in English and Hebrew on either side.

The flying star continued in use by El Al into the 1960s and was phased out by 1970.

El Al Designer Block

In 1962 Otto Treuman, a Dutch designer, in conjunction with George Him, an El Al design consultant at the time, conceived the El Al block in which the left side in the "A" is slanted and the right side is vertical. It appears as follows:

This design won several awards, including recognition as one of the "significant typographical contributions of the 20th century" at the Typomundus 20 exhibition of the International Centre for the Typographic Arts. The El Al block was introduced by November 1962 when in appeared on souvenir postal material issued in connection with the Israeli stamp honoring El Al's 13th anniversary, or bar-mitzvah year.

The El Al block is sometimes still used today, although it has been largely supplanted in advertising by the linear arrangement of the El Al letters in Hebrew and English (the third major symbol described below). The slanted "A" designed by Treuman lives on as part of the still current livery of El Al aircraft and as a design element of the third major symbol below.

The Linear El Al Symbol With Flag

By early 1971 El Al introduced on the livery (color scheme) of its aircraft a new linear arrangement of its name, with the lettering in English and Hebrew: Since Hebrew reads from right to left, the two Hebrew letters on the right say "El" and the two on the left "Al". The new logo was conceived and designed by Israeli artist Danny Reisinger, who has been a design consultant to El Al for over 20 years. By summer 1978, El Al advertising material added the Israeli flag to the right of the logo, and the use of the flag became official El Al policy for all its advertising starting 1 January 1980. The flag was not added to the El Al name on the aircraft livery, however, probably because the flag already appeared as a matter of course on the aircraft tail. At the beginning of 1988 El Al moved its linear El Al logo onto a vertical slant on a field of two shades of blue, also designed by artist Danny Reisinger.

Liveries (Color Schemes) of El Al Aircraft

El Al utilized a variety of aircraft liveries until its current one was designed in 1971. The following guide (together with the other portions of this Appendix) can serve as a useful aid for dating photographs and other El Al memorabilia.

1. "El-Al Ltd." was used starting September 1948, even before El Al's official incorporation on 15 November of that year. The C-54 (DC-4) aircraft with that livery made the special Weizmann Geneva flight on 29-30 September 1948, the first flight to Paris in October 1948 and possibly some other early special flights as well.

2. In March 1949 El Al introduced the six-pointed flying Star of David on its newly purchased DC-4s, 4X-ACC and ACD. At first, the livery also featured the name "El Al Israel Aviation Company".

3. With the acquisition by El Al of two DC-4s from United Air Lines in May 1950, El Al kept the blue and silver United livery where the blue rose in tiered steps from the window line towards the front.

4. C-46s of El Al in the early 50s had a variety of simple liveries. Some, usually those in cargo configuration, were unpainted except for the El Al name in English and Hebrew. Others were painted white with a pair of simple colored stripes at the window line. By 1955 most non-cargo C-46s had a dark blue and white livery similar to the Constellations.

5. El Al's Constellations, introduced in December 1950, featured a royal blue and white livery. The El Al name on the aircraft originally featured an "A" with a pointed top. A year or two later an "A" with a flat top started to be used.

6. The Britannia featured one basic livery, again blue and white, during its period of service 1957-67. A late version livery in 1965, however, features slightly different El Al lettering, including a return to a pointed "A" and a redesign of the tail decoration to move the Israeli flag up to the top of the tail (as in the 707s) and to remove the separate flying Star of David from the tail.

7. 707s and 720Bs featured three basic liveries.

   The first, starting in 1961, featured "El Al" with a pointed "A".

   The second, introduced not later than 1966, featured "El Al" with the designer "A" slanted on the left side.

   The third, starting March 1971, featured a major change to the livery and has continued in use through the start of the 1990s—a white base with two-tone El Al lettering in black and gold and a wider window line with two shades of blue, the darker blue rising upwards into the tail. This livery was simultaneously introduced with El Al's 747s which started joining the fleet in June 1971.

8. El Al's later aircraft—its 747s, 737s, 767s and 757s—have all used the same livery as the third 707 livery described above.

   In certain years El Al's aircraft and promotional materials have featured anniversary logos. These include:

   25th anniversary of the State of Israel (1973-74):

   30th anniversary of the State of Israel (1978-79):

   40th anniversary of the State of Israel (1988-89):

   40th anniversary of El Al (1988-89):

El Al Uniforms and Wings

The uniforms and their insignia (also called "wings") worn by El Al pilots and flight attendants also fall into distinctive time periods, as follows.

1. *1948*
   A "Flying Camel" insignia was utilized for the very first flights prior to scheduled service, starting with the Weizmann flight of 29-30 September 1948 (even before El Al's incorporation) through about March 1949 (see pages 24-25).

2. *Early 1949*
   A metal wing with the flying Star of David was the first uniform insignia introduced by El Al after its incorporation in November 1948. The hat badge was round, in light blue and white, and the coat badge was enameled, usually in white with gold trim. Some personnel used them through about 1950 (see pages 30 & 36).

3. *Mid-1949–1969*
   a. Uniforms. Constellation-era uniforms (1950-57) were, at first, bluish-grey (see page 47), and later a dark grey with silver stripes. With the introduction of the Britannias in December 1957, El Al crew uniforms were changed to a beautiful navy blue with gold stripes (see photo 58).
   b. Wings. Cloth hat and coat insignia were introduced. Hat insignia included a Star of David in the center with six branches, three on each side, one rising vertically, one at an angle, and one horizontal on each side, and the words El Al in Hebrew and English at the top. At least three varieties exist. Coat insignia included a full flying wing with Star of David in center and also two varieties of a half flying wing with the Star of David on the side. All the foregoing known to the author have gold thread (see, e.g., pages 32, 25, 45, 49, 61).

4. *October 1969–Fall 1984*
   a. Uniforms. El Al introduced totally new uniforms on 12 October 1969. Air hostesses winter uniforms were of grey wool material with the top coat, hat and blouse in orange and accessories in black leather. The uniforms were meant to fit in with the jet age. The distinctive hat of the hostesses was said to be "reminiscent of this space-conquering era". Mini-skirts were also in fashion (see page 89). Ground hostess uniforms were in olive green and sky blue colors, which for some years had already been identified with El Al's award-winning ground transport color schemes. Male uniforms were a conservative dark gray color scheme.
   b. Wings. New cloth hat and coat insignia were introduced. Hat insignia included the El Al block in English centered within a Star of David, surrounded by a braided wreath on either side, and El Al in Hebrew on top. Colors were black, blue and orange, with the orange being worn by stewardesses. Coat insignia were of matching cloth and colors, some being double-winged and some single winged. All have silver thread. Towards the later part of this period, flight attendants also wore several types of metal wings, usually of gold color with one flying wing and the Star of David on the left.

5. *Fall 1984–to date*
   a. Uniforms. New uniforms were introduced in fall 1984. Hostess uniforms are in navy blue and white, complemented by bourdeaux vests and colorful scarves. Male crew uniforms are also in navy blue.
   b. Wings. Flight attendant wings are usually gold metal. While some are still in the form of a flying wing, others are a simple rectangular shape bearing the individual's name. At first, pilots continued with similar insignia to those in use immediately prior to the 1984 uniform change. However, they presently wear redesigned dark blue cloth insignia with gold thread.

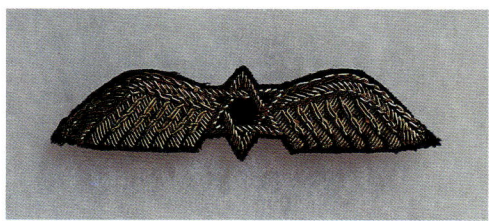

El Al wing selection, from top: pilot's metal wing badge, 1949-50 (Joram Kagan collection); pilot's gold braid wing, 1949-69 (Marvin Goldman collection); pilot's cap badge, 1969-84 (Marvin Goldman collection); stewardess wing, 1969-84 (Marvin Goldman collection); pilot's gold cap badge, 1984-present (Joram Kagan collection).

BIBLIOGRAPHY

References Applicable to Multiple Chapters

1. *Airliners Monthly News*. Published by World Transport Press, Inc., P.O. Box 521238, Miami, FL 33152-1238. (monthly fleet and airline news of all airlines including El Al).
2. Angelucci, Enzo. *World Encyclopedia of Civil Aircraft*. Crown Publishers, Inc., New York (1982).
3. *BIAF—Israel Aviation & Space Magazine* (in Hebrew), P.O. Box 3144, Rishon Le-Zion, Israel. Publisher and Editor, Yehuda Borovik (articles on El Al and other Israeli civil aviation in every issue).
4. Davies, R.E.G. *A History of the World's Airlines*. Oxford University Press (1967, reprinted 1983).
5. El Al Israel Airlines.
   a. Annual Reports (1955 to date).
   b. El Al Advertising Department. *Ad Idea Exchange Vols. I-II* (compiled by Joram Kagan) (1979).
   c. *El Al at a Glance* (Nov. 1974, and 1989).
   d. *EL-AL Bulletin* "15 Years", no. 11 (Sept. 1964) (English and Hebrew).
   e. *El Al Cargo* (Dec. 1989).
   f. *El Alon* (employee magazine) early editions in English and Hebrew; current editions in Hebrew (Sept. 1965 to date. (See, *e.g.*, 20th anniversary issue, 1968).
   g. Flight Schedules (numerous issues, 1951 to date).
   h. *Israelal* in-flight magazine (quarterly) (Winter 1981-on). (See, *e.g.*, special edition for El Al's 40th anniversary, no. 24, Fall 1988).
   i. Marketing Digest (quarterly) (Summer 1982 to date).
   j. Sales Digest (periodical) (early 1960s to late 1970s).
6. Gunston, Bill (ed.).
   a. *The Illustrated Encyclopedia of Commercial Aircraft*. Exeter Books, New York (1980).
   b. *The Illustrated Encyclopedia of Propeller Airliners*. Exeter Books, New York (1980).
7. Hartoch, Noam. "Ben-Gurion Airport: History and Development" (in Hebrew). *BIAF -Israel Aviation & Space Magazine*, no. 38, pp. 16-22 (March 1981).
8. *Jerusalem Post* Archives. Compilation of articles on El Al from newspaper editions of the *Jerusalem Post*.
9. Roach, J.R. & Eastwood, A.B. *Jet Airliner Production List: 1949-1989*. The Aviation Hobby Shop, West Drayton, Middlesex, England (1989).
10. Sachar, Howard M. *A History of Israel: From the Rise of Zionism to Our Time*.
11. Shalit, Ury. *Catalogue of Israel Philatelic Items*. (catalogs El Al and Arkia flight covers). Tel Aviv (1976).
12. Sherman, Arnold.
    a. *El Al: Challenging the Skies* (revised edition of "To the Skies"). Zmora, Bitan, Modan publishers, Tel Aviv (1981).
    b. *El Al: Odyssey in the Skies*. Bitan publishers, Tel Aviv (1972) (Hebrew version of "To The Skies" with slight differences).
    c. *To The Skies: The El Al Story*. Bantam Books (1972).

Chapter 1. 1917-48 (early aviation in the Holy Land and Israel's War of Independence).

1. Bercuson, David J. *The Secret Army*. Lester & Orpen Dennys Limited, Toronto. (1983).
2. *BIAF—Israel Aviation and Space Magazine* (in Hebrew). Several articles on early aviation in the Holy Land, including *e.g.*, the de Havilland D.H.82A/C (no. 56, pp. 24-27); the RWD 8 (no. 8, p.33); the Palestine Flying Service and the Etzel movement (no. 34, pp.13-16); and Palestine Airways (in Hebrew, Land of Israel Airways) (no. 69, pp. 22-24, winter 1989-90).
3. Gunston, Bill. *An Illustrated Guide to the Israeli Air Force*. Salamander Books Ltd. (1982).
4. Hartoch, Noam. "Defunct Registers: 2-Palestine". *Air-Britain Digest*, Nov.-Dec. 1976, pp. 128-30.
5. Heckelman, A. Joseph. *American Volunteers and Israel's War of Independence (1947-1949)*. Ktav, New York (1974).
6. Israel Defense Forces. Air Force Historical Branch. *Roots of the Israeli Air Force; 1912-48* (in Hebrew), by Ado Ambar, Eli Eyal and Avi Cohen (1988).
7. Jackson, Robert. *The Sky Their Frontier: The Story of the World's Pioneer Airlines and Routes 1920-1940*. Arco Publishing, Inc., New York (1984).
8. Mardor, Munya M. *Haganah*. The New American Library, Inc., New York (English version, 1964) (originally published in Hebrew in 1957).
9. Rubinstein, Murray & Goldman, Richard. *The Israel Air Force Story*. Steimatzky, Tel Aviv (1979).

10. Slater, Leonard. *The Pledge*. Simon and Schuster, New York. (1970).
11. Van Zandt, J. Parker. "Aviation in the Holy Land". U.S. Air Services, Dec. 1938, pp. 13-15.

Chapter 2. 1948-50 (DC-4s; C-46s).

1. Air-Britain. *The Douglas DC-4* (1967).
2. Barer, Shlomo. *The Magic Carpet*. Harper & Row (1952).
3. Davis, John M. & Martin, Harold G. *The Curtiss C-46 Commando*. Air-Britain (Historians) Ltd. (1978).
4. Hartoch, Noam & Borovik, Yehuda.
   a. "Douglas C-54 Skymaster" (in Hebrew). *BIAF—Israel Aviation & Space Magazine*, no. 46, pp. 41-45 (1983).
   b. "Curtiss C-46 Commando" (in Hebrew). *BIAF*, no. 45, pp. 41-46 (1983).
5. Levett, Gordon.
   a. "Early Days at El Al". *Air Enthusiast*, no. 35, pp. 78-80 (Jan.-April 1988).
   b. "Relief of the Negev". 51 *Air Pictorial* 179-82 (May 1989).
6. Satterfield, Archie. *The Alaska Airlines Story*, chapter 12, "Operation Magic Carpet". Alaska Northwest Publishing Company. (1981).

Chapter 3. 1951-57 (Constellations).

1. Aviner, A. "Israel's Place in World Aviation". 7 *Interavia* 325-29 (No. 6, 1952).
2. Cain, Charles W.
   a. "Civil Aviation in Israel". 17 *Air Pictorial* 148-50 (May 1955).
   b. "Israel's International Air Line". 88 *The Aeroplane* 279-81 (4 March 1955).
3. "Israeli Report on Tragedy over Bulgaria: El Al Plane Shot Down Without Warning". 63 *Aviation Week* 51-54 (26 Dec. 1955).
4. Hartoch, Noam & Borovik, Yehuda. "Lockheed C-69 Constellation" (in Hebrew). *BIAF—Israel Aviation & Space Magazine*, no. 47, pp. 41-46 (1983).
5. Marson, Peter J. *The Lockheed Constellation*. Air-Britain (1982).
6. Powell, Dennis M. "El Al to Euravia". *Air-Britain Digest*, Jan. 1963.
7. State of Israel, Ministry of Communications. *Report of Commission of Inquiry on the Shooting Down of El Al Aircraft 4X-AKC on 27 July 1955*. Government Printer, Jerusalem (1955).
8. Wixey, Kenneth E. *Lockheed Constellation*. Ian Allen Ltd., England (1987).
9. *World Airline Record* 1952, section on El Al, pp. 62-63; and *World Airline Record* 1955, section on El Al, pp. 67-68.

Chapter 4. 1957-1960 (Britannias).

1. Bristol Aircraft Limited, Sales Engineering. "Bristol Britannia: Record in Airline Service". (S.E.B.131, May 1958; S.E.B.185, Sept. 1958; S.E.B.228, March 1959).
2. Hartoch, Noam. "Bristol Britannia in the Service of El Al" (in Hebrew). *BIAF—Israel Aviation & Space Magazine*, no. 69, pp. 26-29 (winter 1989-80).
3. "Record Breaking Britannias: El Al's Small Yet Very Efficient Britannia Operation". 30 *Propliner* 10-15 (Spring 1987).

Chapter 5. 1961-1971 (707s).

1. Brownlow, Cecil.
   a. "El Al Tests Group Fares as Traffic Builder". 75 *Aviation Week & Space Technology* 38-40 (18 Dec. 1961).
   b. "Present El Al Jet Fleet May Be Expanded". 80 *Aviation Week and Space Technology* 30-32 (8 June 1964).
2. "El Al, 'Short-Year' Airline, Is 365-Day Success". *Airlift World Air Transportation*, August 1961.
3. Fink, Donald E. "El Al Returning to Schedule After Arab Attack at Zurich". 90 *Aviation Week & Space Technology* 29-30 (24 Feb. 1969).
4. Gollan, David. "El Al Takes Leap Into 'Major Leagues'". *Travel Agent*, 28 June 1965.
5. Hankin, Raymond. "Airline of the Month: El Al". *Aeroplane*, 26 July 1967, pp. 4-7.
6. Kolcum, Edward H. "El Al Growth Surges Despite Arab Threats". 92 *Aviation Week & Space Technology* 34-35 (15 June 1970).
7. May, Daryl. "Airline Profile: El Al Israel Airlines". *Flight International* (5 Jan. 1967).
8. Murphy, Joseph S. "A New Era Dawns At El Al". *Air Transport World* (Nov. 1966).
9. Parrish, Wayne. "How a Small-Country Airline Looks At Fares, Costs and SST", and "How El Al Became a Major Operator in the International Market". *American Aviation*, July 1964.

10. Peltz, Stephen. "Israel Airlines and Industry". 23 *Flying Review International* 13-16 (Jan. 1968).
11. Wetmore, Warren C. "Israeli Airlines Mobilized for Mideast War". 87 *Aviation Week & Space Technology* 26-28 (31 July 1967).

Chapter 6. 1971-1982 (747s).

1. Brown, David A. "El Al Changing Management Approach". 108 *Aviation Week & Space Technology* 36-38 (26 June 1978).
2. Coleman, Herbert J. "El Al Spurs New Fares To Increase Productivity". 102 *Aviation Week & Space Technology* 21-22 (10 March 1975).
3. "El Al in the Jumbo Age". *Israel Economist*, Special Supplement (7 pp.) (Oct. 1972).
4. El Al Israel Airlines. In-flight brochures for 1977, 1979 (30th Anniversary), and 1981.

Chapter 7. 1982-1989 (737s; 767s; 757s).

1. Brown, David A. "El Al Starts 767 Transatlantic Service in Attempt to Rebuild Image". 122 *Aviation Week & Space Technology* 41-43 (25 March 1985).
2. Duckworth, Leslie. "El Al: Six Days and Three Directions to Profits". *Airline Executive*, February 1989, pp. 22-24.
3. "El Al: The Six-Day Airline". *Flight International*, 27 September 1986, pp. 25-28.
4. Funke, Phyllis Ellen. "Why Is This Flight Different From All Other Flights?". *Hadassah Magazine*, January 1989, pp. 18-21.
5. "Will El Al Go Private?". *Airfinance Journal*, No. 106 (Sept. 1989).

Appendix I. Arkia Israeli Airlines Ltd.

1. Arkia Israeli Airlines.
   a. *Arkia—Forty Years From Take-Off* (1988).
   b. *The Story of an Airline* (1968).
2. Cowell, G. *Handley Page Herald*. Jane's, London (1980).
3. Gradidge, J.M.G. (in collaboration with J. M. Davis and J. A. Whittle). *The Douglas DC-3 and its Predecessors*. Air-Britain (1984).
4. Hartoch, Noam. "Arkia Israel Inland Airlines". *Air-Britain Digest*, Jan.-Feb. 1979, pp. 3-6.
5. Hartoch, Noam & Borovik, Yehuda. "Douglas C-47 Dakota" (in Hebrew). *BIAF—Israel Aviation & Space Magazine*, no. 50, pp. 41-46 (1984).
6. Sherman, Arnold. *Blue Skies, Red Sea: The Story of the Town of Eilat and Arkia, Israel's Inland Airline*. Edan Books, Jerusalem (1977).

INDEX

EL AL על אל

EA